Merchandising Mathematics for Retailing

Third Edition

Cynthia R. Easterling
The University of Southern Mississippi

Ellen L. Flottman
University of North Texas

Marian H. Jernigan
Texas Woman's University

Suzanne G. Marshall
California State University, Long Beach

Prentice
Hall

Upper Saddle River, NJ

Library of Congress Cataloging-in-Publication Data

Merchandising mathematics for retailing/Cynthia R. Easterling . . . [et al.].--3rd ed.
    p. cm.
    Rev. ed. of: Merchandising mathematics for retailing/Cynthia R. Easterling, Ellen L.
Flottman, Marian H. Jernigan. c1992.
    Includes bibliographical references and index.
    ISBN 0–13–048421–0
    1. Retail trade--Mathematics. 2. Merchandising. I. Easterling, Cynthia R. II.
    Easterling, Cynthia R. Merchandising mathematics for retailing.

HF5429 .E18 2003
381.′01′513--dc21   2002066252

Editor-in-Chief: Stephen Helba
Executive Editor: Vernon R. Anthony
Assistant Editor: Marion Gottlieb
Managing Editor: Mary Carnis
Marketing Manager: Ryan DeGrote
Production Liaison: Adele M. Kupchik
Production Management: UG / GGS Information Services, Inc.
Interior Design: UG / GGS Information Services, Inc.
Director of Manufacturing and Production: Bruce Johnson
Editorial Assistant: Ann Brunner
Manufacturing Buyer: Cathleen Petersen
Creative Director: Cheryl Asherman
Senior Cover Design Coordinator: Miguel Ortiz
Formatting: UG / GGS Information Services, Inc.
Electronic Art Creation: UG / GGS Information Services, Inc.
Copy Editor: UG / GGS Information Services, Inc.
Proofreader: UG / GGS Information Services, Inc.
Printer/Binder: Banta Harrisonburg
Cover Design: Marianne Frasco
Cover Illustration: Ghislain and Marie David de Lossy/Imagebank
Cover Printer: Phoenix Color Corp.

Pearson Education LTD.
Pearson Education Australia PTY, Limited
Pearson Education Singapore, Pte. Ltd.
Pearson Education North Asia Ltd
Pearson Education Canada, Ltd
Pearson Educación de Mexico, S.A. de C.V.
Pearson Education—Japan
Pearson Education Malaysia, Pte. Ltd

10 9 8 7 6 5
ISBN 0-13-048421-0

Contents

Chapter 5   **Markup as a Merchandising Tool**   **125**

Chapter 6   Retail Pricing for Profit   175

Chapter 7   Inventory Valuation   203

PREFACE

This book is designed to be used as a text in a merchandising mathematics course taken by students majoring in retail management or merchandising. Such courses are also appropriate for students majoring in apparel design or manufacturing, interior design, and marketing. The textbook was developed to familiarize students with principles and terminology important to understanding profitable merchandising. This knowledge is important in preparing students for entry-level positions in retailing and for eventual careers as buyers, merchandise managers, and upper-level executives. It is also of value to students seeking careers in the apparel and home furnishings industries and in interior design.

In addition to being used as a textbook in the college classroom, this book can be used in retail executive training programs and as a reference for the practicing buyer or small store owner. The fundamental principles and techniques of merchandising mathematics provided can be applied when solving specific retail merchandising problems.

Many students fear mathematics and have inadequate knowledge of basic arithmetic. A special feature of this book is a review of the fundamentals of arithmetic, including percents, fractions, and decimals. Because many students have not worked with basic arithmetic since junior high school, an additional review of arithmetic fundamentals is provided in the appendix.

Basic practical problems, which occur in everyday merchandising situations, are presented with explicit formulas and solutions. Each topic is introduced and explained, followed by example problems. Solutions for the examples are provided to demonstrate the mathematical principles. Practice problems with work space are provided to help the student develop skill in learning the principles presented.

Answers for the practice problems are provided at the back of the book to enable students to check their own progress. At the end of each chapter there is a summary exercise to reinforce learning of the entire chapter. Word problems demonstrating practical situations are used. Answers to the summary exercises are provided in the instructor's manual. In addition, there is a Companion Website to accompany this text, available at www.prenhall.com/easterling. This website includes chapter summary information, a glossary of terms for each chapter, and review questions with immediate feedback for each chapter. The use of this website is free of charge.

The relationship of understanding profit factors is stressed throughout the book. The material is presented in ten chapters:

Chapter 1, "Introduction," defines retail merchandising and briefly discusses store organization, emphasizing the relationship of the merchandising division to other divisions within the store.

Chapter 2, "Basic Merchandising Mathematics," provides a review of decimals and percents.

Chapter 3, "Profitability," presents the major factors involved in a skeletal profit and loss statement and emphasizes the importance of controlling expenses to maximize profit.

Chapter 4, "Cost of Merchandise Sold," describes discounts, dating, anticipation, loading, and transportation costs.

Chapter 5, "Markup as a Merchandising Tool," emphasizes the importance of markup to profitable merchandising, explaining the calculation of initial, maintained, and cumulative markup.

Chapter 6, "Retail Pricing for Profit," presents the factors that influence the determination of retail prices and discusses price changes, including markdowns, additional markup and markup cancellations, and discounts to employees and special customers.

Chapter 7, "Inventory Valuation," covers the calculation of book inventory, shortage, retail method of inventory, and gross margin.

Chapter 8, "The Dollar Merchandise Plan," explains stock turnover and the steps involved in completing the six-month merchandise plan.

Chapter 9, "Dollar Open-to-Buy," presents calculation of dollar and unit open-to-buy as a control device to see that purchasing is done according to the merchandise plan.

Chapter 10, "Performance Measures," presents concepts that calculate productivity or efficiency measures, such as sales per square foot, sales per full-time employee equivalent, gross margin return on inventory (GMROI), and sales curves.

Each chapter begins with objectives and key points to assist the student in reading the chapter. At the end of the chapters are definitions of key terms. The appendices at the back of the book include a review of fractions, selected formulas, and answers to the practice problems in each chapter.

ACKNOWLEDGMENTS

The authors are grateful to the many businesspeople and educators who assisted in developing the book. We wish to thank the retailers and apparel manufacturers who provided various forms and materials. Appreciation is also extended to the students in our classes throughout the years who contributed to the development of this book.

A particular note of appreciation is extended to Dr. Tim Christiansen, College of Business, Montana State University and Dr. Leslie Stoel, The Ohio State University for their time and efforts in reviewing the manuscript. We would also like to thank our families for their support.

Cynthia R. Easterling
Ellen L. Flottman
Marian H. Jernigan
Suzanne G. Marshall

CHAPTER 1

Introduction

OBJECTIVES

- To define retail merchandising.
- To describe retail store organization.
- To understand merchandising from a corporate level and a store level.
- To recognize the importance of mathematics as a merchandising tool in the achievement of profit.

KEY POINTS

- Merchandising includes all the activities necessary to buy and sell merchandise at a profit. Merchandising takes place at both retail and wholesale levels.
- A successful merchant is one who can effectively and profitably blend the five rights of merchandising: providing the right merchandise, at the right place, at the right time, in the right quantities, and at the right price.
- The organization of a retail store varies according to the store's size and type. Most stores' organizational plans have evolved from the Mazur Plan.
- Currently most buying, along with other specialized retail functions, is centralized at corporate headquarters.
- Buyers are judged by management according to objective measurements that include sales, inventory, margin results, and ultimately, profitability.
- Achievement of profit requires knowledge of the mathematical techniques or merchandising tools that assist the merchandiser in operating a store or department.

This textbook deals with the mathematical concepts used in merchandising fashion goods. This chapter lays the foundation for understanding the retail arm of the fashion industry by defining some key terms and giving a brief overview of the organization of retail stores.

RETAIL MERCHANDISING DEFINED

Retailing includes all the functions involved in obtaining goods from manufacturers and selling these goods to the ultimate consumer. Retail functions include store operations, personnel, financial control, sales promotion, information systems, and merchandising. Although merchandising is only one of these functions, it is the "heart" of retailing. The other functions exist to support the profitable buying and selling of goods and services.

Merchandising has been defined a number of different ways. It may be defined as the management of the buying and selling of merchandise or as the planning involved in estimating customers' requirements and procuring the merchandise. The American Marketing Association defines merchandising as "the planning and supervision involved in marketing particular merchandise at places, times, prices, and in quantities that will best serve to realize the marketing objectives of a business."*

Broadly defined, merchandising includes all the activities necessary to buy and sell merchandise at a profit. These activities include (1) estimating customers' needs and wants, (2) planning purchases, (3) buying goods and making them available when and where the customer wants them, and (4) motivating customers to buy the goods made available to them.

Five Rights of Merchandising

Simply put, to be successful a merchandiser should follow a long-held marketing axiom: **the five "rights" of merchandising**. It is necessary to provide the right merchandise, at the right place, at the right time, in the right quantities, and at the right price. The successful merchandiser understands the five rights of merchandising and knows how to use the tools of merchandising to determine and satisfy consumers' needs and wants.

Retail and Wholesale Merchandising

Merchandising takes place at both retail and wholesale levels. Both retailers and manufacturers are concerned with sales and inventory. Manufacturers produce inventory that retailers purchase and then sell to individual consumers. The primary goal for both manufacturers and retailers is selling. Both need to identify the ultimate consumer's wants and needs in order to make a profit. Although this workbook is focused mainly toward the retail level of the distribution chain, many of the same mathematical concepts also apply to merchandising at the wholesale level.

RETAIL STORE ORGANIZATION

The organization of a retail store varies according to the store's size and type. Most retailers' organizational plans evolved from the **Mazur Plan**. In 1927 Paul M. Mazur developed his four-function plan for store organization. This plan established merchandising as one of four divisions, along with financial control, store operations/management, and sales promotion. As stores expanded in size, other divisions such as human resources, technology, real estate, and maintenance and construction have been added to the organizational structure, as shown in Figure 1-1.

Stores vary considerably in their organizational structures; however, all stores, both large and small, must perform the same functions. A smaller store combines

---

*American Marketing Association. (2000). (http.//www.ama.org).

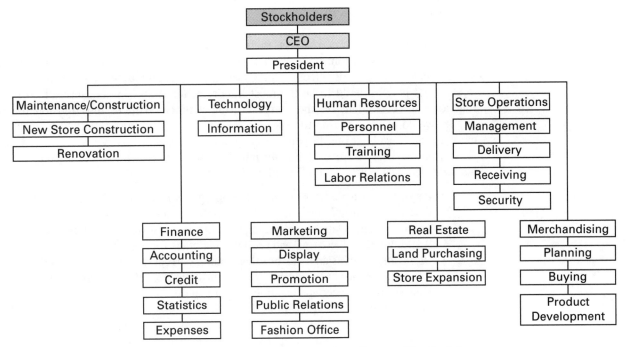

Figure 1-1. Organizational chart for a retail store corporation. *Source:* Wet Seal, Inc.

several areas together under one division, whereas a larger store operates with a greater number of divisions, each of which is more specialized.

The Merchandising Function

Recent changes in store ownership have resulted in changes in retail store organization and, thus, the buying function. Prior to the 1980s, retail stores were largely independently owned specialty stores and local department store chains. Buyers were usually headquarted in the **flagship store**—the original store location—of a department store chain. Buyers could visit the departments for which they bought merchandise and talk with sales personnel as well as customers. They could even visit store branches, which frequently were located in the suburbs of a single metropolitan city.

The 1980s, however, ushered in an age of department store consolidation that altered the retail landscape. Store ownership groups such as the Federated Department Stores, May Department Stores Company, and Dayton Hudson Corporation (now called Target Corporation) expanded by purchasing independent retail stores and other ownership groups. For example, Federated Department Stores now operates more than 450 department stores in 34 states, Guam and Puerto Rico. Among the names of Federated stores are Bloomingdale's, Macy's, The Bon Marché, Burdines, Goldsmith's, Lazarus, and Rich's. Today the majority of department stores are part of a large ownership group or chain.

As a result, buying has changed. Today buyers typically have offices in a central headquarters location—far removed from the store and its selling floor. For example, the J. C. Penney Company's central headquarters is in Plano, Texas. The buyers procure the merchandise for all J. C. Penney stores from this location. This is referred to as **centralized buying**. Many of the other retail functions such as strategic planning, advertising, sales and inventory planning also are carried out at central headquarters.

Centralized buyers often purchase inventory for hundreds of stores, whereas **decentralized buyers** purchase for only one or a few stores. Consolidation of buying efforts is one way to reduce expenses and therefore increase profits.

Centralized Merchandising

In centralized buying organizations, merchandising functions are performed for all stores at a central location, typically the corporate headquarters. The merchandising division is responsible for selecting, purchasing, pricing, and allocating merchandise to stores. It is considered to be the most important retail division because all other functions are dependent on the merchandising activity. Without this division the retailer would have no reason to exist. As a result of the growth of retail chains from mergers and consolidations, buying has become more specialized.

Many retailers have split buying into four separate functions: (1) buying, (2) planning, (3) distribution, and (4) product development.

- **Buying** responsibilities include developing buying plans, selecting merchandise, establishing retail prices, placing orders and reorders, maintaining proper vendor relations, managing merchandise assortments, pricing, and working with advertising and promotional plans for the stores.
- **Planning** involves analysis of sales history, current market trends, and the retailer's performance objectives in order to project sales and inventories.
- **Distribution** concerns allocation of merchandise to individual stores based on the store's planned inventory levels.
- **Product development** identifies product ideas for internal development. Responsibilities include establishing design specifications, sourcing the fabrics and trims, and negotiating with contractors to produce the goods. These goods come into the store bearing the store's **private label**, such as Macy's INC label or Nordstrom's Classique. They are goods for which there is no direct price comparison because they are exclusive to the store that developed them; thus the buyer has more leeway with markup.

Organization of the Merchandising Division

The organizational hierarchies for planning and distribution typically parallel organizational hierarchies for buying. Figure 1-2 shows the merchandising division of a retail corporation with its three main divisions: merchandising, planning, and product development. Key executive positions found within a typical merchandising division include general merchandise manager, divisional merchandise manager, buyer, and fashion director. Other positions in this division are associate buyer, assistant buyer, and clerical assistant.

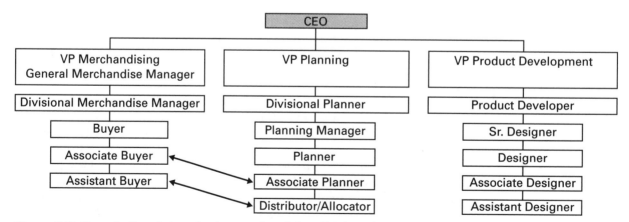

Figure 1-2. Organizational chart for the merchandising division of a retail corporation. *Source:* Wet Seal, Inc.

General Merchandise Manager

At the head of a merchandising division is a **general merchandise manager (GMM)**, who often carries the additional title of vice president. The GMM reports directly to the president of the company. As a member of top management, a GMM takes an active part in the formulation of the retailer's policies. These policies develop the image of the store as perceived by its customers. In addition these policies guide in the selection of merchandise by defining merchandise classifications, price zones or ranges, brand names, and fashion orientation of the retailer. A GMM has several other responsibilities. The GMM not only helps create merchandising policies, but he/she must establish and interpret these policies. The two main functions of a GMM are planning and control.

Divisional Merchandise Manager

As the number of departments and buyers increases, it becomes impossible for one merchandise manager to supervise all buyers and merchandising activities. Related departments are grouped into divisions, headed by **divisional merchandise managers (DMMs)**. DMMs report directly to the general merchandise manager and are responsible for merchandising a related group of selling departments or a division. Each divisional merchandise manager supervises a group of buyers. The DMM monitors sales, inventories, and promotional activities of departments to ensure consistency and maintain profit goals.

The Buyer

The buyer reports directly to the DMM. The buyer is responsible for implementing company merchandising policies, plans, and procedures within the department. Under the supervision of a DMM, the buyer is responsible for planning purchases and buying merchandise for the department. The specific functions of the buyer vary greatly. In a one-store firm or small store the buyer also may be the department manager directly responsible for supervision of salespeople and for arrangement of merchandise in the department. In many retail stores the buyer no longer performs the duties of a department manager but still is responsible for planning purchases and sales.

Another type of buyer is the owner/manager of a "mom-and-pop" operation. This person—or, as is often the case, husband and wife—may be responsible for the total operation of the store as well as the buying and merchandising of the goods.

The successful operation of a small store or an individual department depends on the buyer. Responsibilities of the buyer include developing plans, selecting merchandise, establishing retail prices, placing orders and reorders, maintaining proper vendor relations, managing merchandise assortments, and coordinating advertising and promotion plans for the store or department.

Assistants

In large corporations there are many levels of assistants. For example, the senior planner might be aided by a junior assistant planner. Reporting to and assisting the buyer may be the associate buyer, assistant buyer, and/or clerical assistant. All assistants serve as understudies for the next level position. For example, buying assistants are often given the responsibility of buying one or more classifications within a department. They are "buyers in training."

Merchandising Staff Bureau

Large corporations may also have staff bureaus that provide specialized information of importance to the buying and merchandising of goods. Examples of these bureaus include comparison shopping, fashion office, standards and testing (quality control), merchandise research, unit control, and resident buying office. For example, the fashion director would establish the fashion direction for the store and would provide the merchandising staff information on colors, trends, and styles for apparel, accessories, and home furnishings and establish the fashion direction for the stores.

Decentralized Merchandising Organization

In decentralized buying, the buyer typically works out of the store rather than a centralized headquarters. The specific functions of the buyer in a noncorporate setting vary more than the very specialized duties of a buyer in a corporate setting. In a sole proprietorship or "mom-and-pop" operation, the buyer is often the owner and may be responsible for the total operation of the store as well as the buying and merchandising of the goods. In a one-store firm or small store chain, the owner/buyer must perform all planning, buying, pricing, advertising, and inventory control. In addition, the owner/buyer may be responsible for the supervision of salespeople and for the arrangement of merchandise in a department. The owner/buyer also may be the department manager; therefore, salespeople and stockers are directly responsible to this person. Larger stores or departments may have a head of stock who supervises the merchandise in the reserve stockroom and the transfers of merchandise between stores. The head of stock works closely with the buyer and assistant buyer to maintain the proper flow of merchandise to the stores.

Retail Merchandising by Manufacturers

There is a trend among fashion manufacturers (wholesalers), particularly those bearing a popular national brand or designer label, to start their own retail divisions. For example, Liz Claiborne, St. John, Levi Strauss, DKNY, Calvin Klein, and Guess all have retail stores. For these manufacturer-owned stores, the buyers are "buying" merchandise only from their company's inventory. For example, St. John boutiques, located nationwide, are stocked exclusively with St. John apparel and accessories. The St. John buyer, located at the company's corporate headquarters in Irvine, California, allocates an assortment of St. John goods for each boutique. St. John benefits by the high visibility given to St. John products. In addition, St. John store division experiences an increase in profits from purchasing goods internally. Figure 1-3 illustrates the organization of a typical fashion manufacturing company with a retail division.

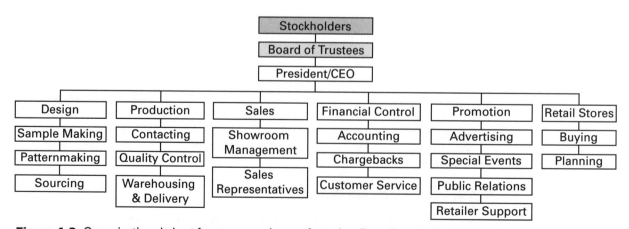

Figure 1-3. Organizational chart for an apparel manufacturing firm. *Source:* St. John Knits.

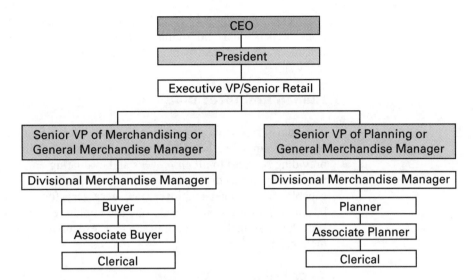

Figure 1-4. Organizational chart for the retail division of an apparel manufacturing firm. *Source:* St. John Knits.

Figure 1-4 shows how one apparel manufacturing company has divided responsibilities between buying and planning tracks.

RELATIONSHIP OF MERCHANDISING TO OTHER DIVISIONS

The central function of retailing is carried out by the merchandising division whether the buyer is located at the store or at corporate headquarters. The merchandising division drives the other functions of the retail organization. Stated differently, the other divisions support the merchandising division. If the merchandising division is to achieve its sales goals, close cooperation with other divisions must be maintained. In larger corporations, some of these functions are performed at central headquarters and others are performed at the stores. A discussion of these additional divisions follows.

Financial Control Division

The financial control division supervises the budget. This division maintains accounting records, supervises the credit department, and keeps merchandising statistics. As head of the division, the **controller** or financial manager is concerned with controlling the spending activities of all divisions and managing cash flow.

The financial control division works with the merchandising division in maintaining all merchandising plans and expense budgets. The controller is responsible for preparation of statistical reports that are used to guide the buying and selling activities of the merchandising division and sees that budgets are maintained.

Operations Division

This division is responsible for a wide variety of activities including store maintenance and housekeeping, delivery, receiving and marking, warehousing, workrooms, and customer services. The major purpose of the management division is to provide a pleasant and safe environment in which customers may shop.

Under the original Mazur Plan the operations division also supervised the functions of personnel and training. However, as stores grew in size and operations became more complex, personnel (human resources) became a separate division in many stores.

Human Resources Division

The human resources division is responsible for hiring and training new employees, managing employee benefits, and handling labor relations. It is also concerned with providing services to all employees and evaluating employees' job performance. The relationship of this division to every division, including merchandising, is obvious, as capable, well-trained employees are necessary for the profitable operation of any business. This division is headed by the human resources director who is aided by a staff that may include a training director, executive recruiter, and executive development head.

Sales Promotion Division

The sales promotion division, headed by the promotion director or marketing director, is concerned with advertising, visual merchandising, and public relations. This division is responsible for all forms of advertising including newspaper, television, radio, magazines, and direct mail. It handles window and interior displays, architectural and interior design of new stores, store remodeling, and merchandise presentation. Visual merchandising develops signage, displays, promotional materials, floor plans, fixtures, and merchandise presentation standards.

The sales promotion division also oversees the store's public relations program, which plans publicity events such as fashion shows, parades, and store special events. The primary purposes of sales promotion are (1) to communicate information about the store and its merchandise to both present and potential customers and (2) to bring customers into the store with a desire to buy.

All areas of sales promotion are important in assisting with the development of store image as perceived by the customer. Sales promotion works closely with the merchandising division to promote the merchandise selected by the store's buyers. Because the buyer is the one who best knows the customers' preferences, he/she is responsible for selecting merchandise to be promoted and for communicating the important facts about the merchandise to the advertising department. The buyer is usually responsible for checking advertising proofs and ensuring that advertisements are truthful and accurate.

IMPORTANCE OF MATHEMATICS TO BUYING AND MERCHANDISING

Merchandising is a very competitive business, especially when fashion goods are involved. Fashion merchandise is found throughout the department store. Fashion influences not only the clothing we wear but every aspect of our lives. Fashion affects how we decorate our homes, the way in which we entertain, and how we spend our leisure time. Fashion has brought color and design to bed and bath linens as well as to home furnishings, housewares, and home electronics. In fact, many well-known designers have introduced home furnishings lines in their product offerings. For example, the Ralph Lauren name appears on linens, home accessories, furniture, and even paint! Currently, most products are available in an assortment of styles and colors. Fashion has greatly increased the variety of goods available and, in effect, made the merchandiser's job more complicated.

Competition in retailing has become keen as many retailers vie for the consumer's business. Because of retailing's competitiveness, merchandisers must compete effectively to realize profit goals. An understanding of buying practices and techniques is necessary in order to secure the maximum return on investment.

Sales volume is influenced by cost of merchandise, expenses of doing business, competition, and profit goals. The merchandiser needs to understand the interrelationships of all factors that influence the buying and selling of merchandise. The buyer needs to be able to plan adequately in order to achieve established sales and profit goals.

Measuring the Buyer's Efficiency

It is important that buyers are efficient in performing stated duties. If not, the company could suffer losses in profits and in customers. Therefore, it is essential that management use objective measurements in evaluating a buyer's efficiency. These objective measurements are broken into three categories: sales, inventory, and margin results.

1. **Sales**: A buyer is constantly being compared to established goals and last year's figures. For example:

   - Sales goals are set for the current year, and the buyer is expected to achieve these figures or surpass them. Sales can be measured readily in units and/or dollars.
   - Sales per square foot of selling space are also considered in evaluating effectiveness.
   - The percentage increase or decrease in sales can be calculated based on the previous year's figures.
   - Sales figures can be compared to the figures for similar departments in other stores. Government agencies and trade associations such as the National Retail Federation provide comparative data. Also, many stores are owned by large ownership groups such as May Department Stores Company, Federated Department Stores, or Saks Inc.; thus figures may be compared to other stores owned by the same group.

2. **Inventory**: Inventory results provide the second measure of the buyer's efficiency. This includes stock turnover, proportion of old stock in inventory, and percentage of stock shortage to sales.

3. **Margin**: The third measurement of the buyer's efficiency is margin results, which include initial markup, maintained markup, gross margin, operating profit, and gross margin return on inventory. Buyers need to understand the meaning of each of these figures and should be able to evaluate their own performance at any given time.

Importance of Profit

Ultimately, the most important part of a buyer's job is to make a profit for the retailer. The buyer's job is highly accountable, and the buyer needs to understand the mathematics of managing a department in order to achieve a profit. Buying in retail stores is quite quantitative. Computers make available much data that may be used in managing the business and planning purchases.

Successful buying and merchandising involve an understanding of profitability. Achievement of a profit requires knowledge of mathematical techniques or merchandising tools that assist in operating a department. The mathematics of merchandising involves simple arithmetic. It is not necessary to be a mathematician to understand the principles of merchandising. You do not need to know algebra or trigonometry. The common operations of addition, subtraction, division, and multiplication with an understanding of percents, fractions, and decimals are the basis for merchandise mathematics.

DEFINITIONS

Centralized Buyer   Buyer who is located at and purchases inventory from a centralized location such as central headquarters or a regional office.

Centralized Buying   The concentration of the responsibility for merchandise selection and purchase for a chain or group of stores in the hands of the headquarters staff rather than in the individual store units.

Controller   Executive who is responsible for preparation of statistical reports that are used to guide the buying and selling activities of the merchandising division and also sees that budgets are maintained.

Decentralized Buyer   Buyer who is located in a retail store and purchases inventory for that store and its branches from this location.

Divisional Merchandise Manager (DMM)   Retail executive who supervises a group of buyers and is responsible for the merchandising activities of a related group of selling departments or divisions.

Five Rights of Merchandising   Refers to having the right merchandise, at the right place, at the right time, in the right quantities, and at the right price.

Flagship Store   The main store of a large retailing firm having a number of units. Traditionally the flagship store was the original downtown store.

General Merchandise Manager (GMM)   Retail executive who is responsible for supervising a group of divisional merchandising managers and interpreting and executing store policies.

Mazur Plan   Four-function plan for store organization: merchandising, financial control, store operation/management, and sales promotion.

Merchandising   The planning and supervision involved in marketing particular merchandise at places, times, prices, and in quantities that will best serve to realize the marketing objectives of a business.

Product Development   Process of originating a product idea, sourcing the fabrics and trims, and negotiating for a contractor to produce the goods.

Private Label   Goods developed by a retailer to be sold exclusively in that particular company's stores and that bear the retailer's label.

Retailing   All the functions involved in obtaining goods and selling these goods to the ultimate consumer.

Chapter 1 • Discussion Questions

1. What are the primary functions of retailing?
2. Merchandising includes all the activities necessary to buy and sell merchandise at a profit. What are these activities?
3. What are the five rights of merchandising?
4. What is the primary goal of both manufacturing and retailing?
5. What were the original divisions in the Mazur Plan for store organization?
6. As stores have expanded in number and size, what divisions have been added to the organizational structure?
7. How do small stores and large stores differ in organizational structure?
8. What is the title of the executive who heads the merchandising division in a department store?
9. Describe the organizational structure of the merchandising division of a retail store corporation and the retail division of an apparel manufacturing company.
10. Name the major responsibilities of each of the following department store personnel: GMM, DMM, and buyer.
11. What merchandising staff bureaus might be found in large department stores?
12. What are the primary activities of a store's merchandising division?
13. What is the relationship of each store division to the merchandising division?
14. What objective measurements are used by management to evaluate store buyers?
15. Why is mathematical ability important in merchandising?
16. Explain the differences between centralized and decentralized buying.

CHAPTER 2

Basic Merchandising Mathematics

OBJECTIVES

- To understand basic mathematical calculations frequently used in making decisions related to merchandising and management activities.
- To sharpen skills and improve speed and accuracy in using mathematics.
- To review the use of decimals and percents.
- To develop competency in applying basic mathematical formulas to solve merchandising problems.
- To understand and use unit measures.

KEY POINTS

- A basic knowledge of mathematics is essential to conduct successful merchandising activities and operations. The understanding of fractions, decimals, and percents is essential to conduct the daily functions of business.
- Every merchant in every store, no matter how large or small, should be familiar with basic mathematics.
- It is important to master basic merchandising mathematics in order to make effective merchandising decisions.

Merchandisers constantly make decisions that require a thorough understanding of retail mathematics. To be a successful merchandiser you must both understand this math and be proficient at it. Performing calculations with speed and accuracy is essential to operating a successful retail, wholesale, or manufacturing business. To operate a profitable business you must be able to work effectively with numbers and to visualize numbers quickly.

Although calculators and computers will help you to do your work, they are only tools and must be told what to do by people. Some believe that an understanding of mathematics is not important in the computer age; however, the reverse is true. To understand what the computer is doing, you must first understand basic mathematics. The computer is only a tool to help people do their work. Although computers provide you with information, you need to know what this information means and what to do with it. You also need to be able to figure mathematical calculations when you do not have a calculator or computer available to do this for you.

The mathematics of merchandising involves simple arithmetic, such as addition, subtraction, multiplication, and division. Although you may be familiar with these concepts, a good review of basic arithmetic is important to help sharpen your skills and to improve the handling of calculations with speed and accuracy.

The understanding and use of fractions, decimals, and percents are also essential to achieve success in merchandising. It is important to understand these basic mathematical concepts and to be able to apply mathematical formulas when solving all types of merchandising problems. This chapter will help you improve basic mathematical skills that will provide input for making effective merchandising decisions. It is essential that you build confidence and work with accuracy in order to avoid simple mistakes, which can be very costly to a business.

The following pretest can serve as a guide to identify your strengths and weaknesses in basic merchandising mathematics. Work as rapidly as you can, but do not work so fast that you make unnecessary mistakes. Let the pretest guide you in determining where you need review. If you find that review is needed, see Appendix A for additional explanations and practice problems.

Observe these three rules as you complete the Basic Arithmetic Pretest:

1. **When figures are given in dollar and cent amounts, use a dollar sign ($) with your final answer.**
2. **Round your final answer to the nearest hundredth (cent). Do not round until you have the final answer.**
3. **Use a comma to divide thousands.**

Answers to the Pretest may be found in Appendix D.

Basic Arithmetic Pretest

1. Add:

(a) 570
    225

(b) $102.59
      3.49
    10.99

(c) $ 499.99
   1,489.50
      23.03
    405.99

(d) $19.99
   29.99
   49.99

2. A customer bought the following items:

    2 towels at $14.99 each

    4 washcloths at $3.89 each

    6 washcloths at $2.25 each

    2 beach towels at $28.49 each

What was the total amount purchased?

3. Subtract:

(a) $11.99
  − 0.19

(b) $349.55
  −219.99

(c) $5,450.00
  −325.05

4. A buyer for the men's department purchased 34 dress shirts costing $29.50 each. If 8 of the shirts were damaged and returned to the vendor, what was the total bill for the shirts kept by the buyer?

5. Multiply:

(a) $425.50
  × .325

(b) $4,444.49
  ×   10.50

6. Divide:

   (a) $145.48 \div 1.2$ (b) $299.50 \div 0.50$

7. What was the total cost for a customer who purchased 4 blouses at $28.98 each, with a sales tax of 5%?

8. Last week a salesperson worked 28 hours and had total sales of $2,170. Find the average sales per hour.

9. Solve the following problems:

   (a) 25% of $200 = _____

   (b) 50 = _____% of 5,500

   (c) $12.50 = 50% of _____

   (d) $15\frac{1}{2}\%$ of $45 = _____

10. A customer selected a dress marked $89.99 and received a 15% discount. What was the price of the dress after the discount?

11. Calculate the average monthly sales for a salesperson in the children's department who made the following sales:

June	$4,350.50
July	$2,200.00
August	$3,509.99

12. A woman purchased $8\frac{1}{4}$ yards of lace at $5.49 a yard. What was the total that she paid with a 6% sales tax?

13. A hosiery department had a sale on pantyhose at three pairs for $12. How much would four pairs cost?

14. What is the total cost of the following order?

     45 plates at $10.50 each

   130 glasses at $21 a dozen

    32 cups at $30 a dozen

DECIMALS

Decimals are used to indicate fractions of tenths, hundredths, thousandths, or some multiple of 10. For example, 1.3 indicates one and three tenths; the number 1.35 means one and thirty-five one hundredths. Decimals are used in statements of dollars and cents. The amount $4.25 indicates four dollars plus twenty-five one hundredths of a dollar.

When working with decimals, always remember that any number of zeros may be added to the right of the decimal point without changing the value of the number. For example, $4 is the same as $4.00; and $4.25 is the same as $4.2500.

When using a calculator, you only need to enter decimals correctly. The calculator will do the rest. Be certain your calculator displays at least three numbers to the right of the decimal.

Adding and Subtracting Decimals

Adding and subtracting numbers with decimal points is very similar to working with whole numbers; however, all the decimal points must be aligned in the same column. When a whole number is written without a decimal point, it is understood that the decimal point is located to the right of the whole number. For example, 125 is the same as 125.0.

When adding and subtracting decimals, any number of zeros may be added to the right of the decimal point to line up the numbers correctly.

EXAMPLE 2-1

255.25	255.250		
125	125.000	630	630.000
+ 75.321	or + 75.321	− 25.255	or − 25.255
455.571	455.571	604.745	604.745

Multiplying Decimals

The rules for multiplying decimal numbers are the same as for multiplying whole numbers, except for determining the location of the decimal point in the answer. (The answer is known as the product.) To locate the position of the decimal point in the answer, add the number of decimal places in the numbers to be multiplied. This sum will give you the number of places to count off in the answer. Begin at the right and count off the number of decimal places.

EXAMPLE 2-2

$$\begin{array}{r} 2.35 \\ \times\ \ 2.1 \\ \hline 235 \\ 470 \\ \hline 4.935 \end{array}$$

There are two decimal places in 2.35 and one decimal place in 2.1; therefore, three decimal places (2 + 1) should be counted off in the answer.

Dividing Decimals

When dividing decimal numbers with a calculator, the decimal will be positioned automatically in the answer. To divide with a calculator, enter the dividend first, then the divisor.

EXAMPLE 2-3

$$48.24 \div 12$$

This problem can be expressed verbally in two different ways: 48.24 divided by 12 or 12 divided into 48.24. The two expressions mean the same thing.
Without a calculator the problem would be set up:

$$12\overline{)48.24}$$

The decimal point in the answer (known as the quotient) would be directly above the decimal point in the dividend.

$$\begin{array}{r} 4.02 \rightarrow \text{quotient} \\ 12\overline{)48.24} \end{array}$$
$$\text{divisor} \leftarrow \qquad \rightarrow \text{dividend}$$

It is important to understand the basic principles of dividing decimal numbers and to be able to divide without using a calculator; one may not always be available. When the divisor is a whole number, proceed as with regular division. The decimal point in the quotient (the answer) is always directly above the decimal point in the dividend.

If the divisor is a decimal number, it must first be changed to a whole number. This procedure is done by moving the decimal point to the right; the decimal in the dividend must also be moved to the right the same number of places. This actually multiplies the divisor and the dividend by the same number, which does not affect the relative value of the numbers. For each position the decimal point is moved to the right, the value is multiplied by 10. Perform division as usual, making sure to position the decimal point in the quotient directly above the one in the dividend.

EXAMPLE 2-4

$$48.486 \div 0.12$$

Because the divisor contains two decimal places, move the decimal point in the divisor and in the dividend two places to the right.

$$0.12\overline{)48.486} = 12.\overline{)4,848.6} = 12\overline{)4848.60}^{\,404.05}$$

If the dividend is a whole number, add zeros where necessary when moving the decimal.

EXAMPLE 2-5

$$300 \div 0.5$$

$$0.5\overline{)300.0} = 5\overline{)3,000} = 5\overline{)3,000.}^{\,600.}$$

Rounding Decimals

Rules for rounding decimals may differ depending on the degree of accuracy desired and the particular purpose of the figures. For example, if men's pants were priced at two pairs for $45.95 and a customer wanted only one pair, you would charge $22.98. The amount would be rounded up to the nearest cent, which is the nearest hundredth. In some situations the accountant must be more accurate with figures and may need to round off to the nearest thousandth, ten thousandth, and so forth. Retail stores usually round numbers off to the nearest hundredth.

> *Rule:* **When working problems in this workbook, round all final answers to the nearest hundredth (two decimal places) unless instructed otherwise.**

That is, carry out figures three positions to the right of the decimal point and round to two decimal places. When rounding off a number, check the number in the third position to the right of the decimal point, then round to two places. If the number in the third place is 5 or more, drop this number and add one to the number to its left. If the number in the third place is less than 5, drop this number and leave the others as they are.

EXAMPLE 2-6

45.678 is rounded to 45.68

45.674 is rounded to 45.67

45.675 is rounded to 45.68

78.998 is rounded to 79.00

119.965 is rounded to 119.97

119.998 is rounded to 120.00

1. Add the following numbers:

(a) 5.21, 77.6, 50 =

(b) 25, 3.333, 7.67, 0.8, 135.1 =

(c) 455.67, 330.995, 0.55, 0.3, 88 =

(d) $550.05, $63.75, $89 =

2. Subtract the following numbers:

(a) 550 – 25.733 =

(b) 0.88 – 0.13495 =

(c) 55.721 – 0.3 =

(d) $87 – $1.35 =

3. Multiply the following numbers (without using a calculator):

(a) $14.25
   $\times$ 4

(b) $50.25
   $\times$ 3.5

(c) $16.35
   $\times$ 0.3

(d)   0.653
   $\times$ 1.2

4. Multiply the following numbers:

(a) $625.35 $\times$ 3.1 =

(b) $4,560.21 $\times$ 21.7 =

(c) 2,868.79 $\times$ 68.300 =

(d) 6,777.75 $\times$ 0.12 =

5. Divide (without using a calculator): (round answer to the nearest hundredth)

(a) $5\overline{)35.5}$

(b) $5.5\overline{)75.555}$

(c) $2.164\overline{)1,350.2}$

(d) $10.64\overline{)283}$

6. Divide: (round answer to the nearest hundredth)

(a) $35,000.69 ÷ 9 = _____

(b) 5,635.02 ÷ 5.5 = _____

(c) $2,351.12 ÷ 0.125 = _____

(d) $1,520 ÷ 0.26 = _____

7. Round the following numbers so they are correct to two decimal places:

(a) 405.333 = _____   (f) 49.995 = _____

(b) 21.357 = _____   (g) 0.996 = _____

(c) $21,544.897 = _____   (h) 597.895 = _____

(d) 42,896.563 = _____   (i) 10.366 = _____

(e) .095 = _____   (j) 534.009 = _____

THE UNIT MEASURE

A unit measure is used in buying certain merchandise categories such as toiletries, cosmetics, underwear, and glassware. These items are often sold in dozens or fractions of a dozen. Furthermore, in the apparel industry, unit measures are used in purchasing the findings and trimmings used to complete a garment. Findings include such small functional items as buttons, hooks, snaps, zippers, and shoulder pads. Trimmings include decorative items such as ribbon, braid, and lace.

Common unit measures are:

- 2 units = 1 pair
- 12 units = 1 dozen
- 144 units = 12 dozen = 1 gross

It is important to understand fractional parts of a dozen because many items are ordered by the dozen or fractional parts of a dozen, such as $\frac{2}{3}$ dozen, $1\frac{3}{4}$ dozen, or $3\frac{5}{6}$ dozen. To find a fractional part of a dozen, such as $\frac{1}{3}$ dozen, multiply by 12 (number in a dozen).

EXAMPLE 2-7

$$\frac{2}{3} \times 12 = \frac{2}{3} \times \frac{12}{1} = \frac{24}{3} = 8$$

$$3\frac{5}{6} \times 12 = \frac{23}{6} \times \frac{12}{1} = \frac{276}{6} = 46$$

$$1\frac{3}{4} \times 12 = \frac{7}{4} \times \frac{12}{1} = \frac{84}{4} = 21$$

When working with fractional parts of a dozen, it is critical to use the quantity as a whole number. For example, $3\frac{5}{6}$ dozen is 46 units; it cannot be used as 45.96 ($3.83 \times 12 = 45.96$). **The number must be rounded to a whole number.** An order of $3\frac{5}{6}$ dozen blouses is for 46 units, and the cost and retail value of this merchandise must be calculated using 46 rather than 45.96.

The following equivalents are frequently used in retail merchandising:

- 1 dozen = 12
- $\frac{1}{3}$ dozen = $\frac{1}{3} \times \frac{12}{1} = \frac{12}{3} = 4$
- $\frac{2}{3}$ dozen = $\frac{2}{3} \times \frac{12}{1} = \frac{24}{3} = 8$
- $\frac{1}{4}$ dozen = $\frac{1}{4} \times \frac{12}{1} = \frac{12}{4} = 3$
- $\frac{3}{4}$ dozen = $\frac{3}{4} \times \frac{12}{1} = \frac{36}{4} = 9$
- $\frac{1}{6}$ dozen = $\frac{1}{6} \times \frac{12}{1} = \frac{12}{6} = 2$

Practice Problems • Exercise 2.2

1. A buyer for children's wear received an order of designer jeans. He decided to keep $14\frac{1}{4}$ dozen pairs of jeans at the main store and send $4\frac{1}{2}$ dozen pairs to the branch store. How many individual pairs of jeans (units) were purchased?

2. The buyer in men's furnishings ordered the following quantities of ties: $8\frac{2}{3}$ dozen, $15\frac{1}{6}$ dozen, $9\frac{3}{4}$ dozen, and $3\frac{1}{2}$ dozen. How many ties were ordered? (Give your answer in units.)

3. How many pairs of shoulder pads are there in 5 dozen? 12 dozen?

4. Express $2\frac{1}{2}$ gross buttons in terms of dozens. In units.

5. How many dozen machine needles are there in a package of 156?

6. If there are on hand 25 dozen buttons, how many garments can be completed if each garment requires 9 buttons?

7. Convert these dozen quantities into their unit equivalents:

(a) $5\frac{1}{4}$ dozen = _____   (f) $1\frac{3}{4}$ dozen = _____

(b) $2\frac{1}{3}$ dozen = _____   (g) $7\frac{1}{2}$ dozen = _____

(c) $10\frac{1}{6}$ dozen = _____   (h) $11\frac{2}{3}$ dozen = _____

(d) $21\frac{5}{6}$ dozen = _____   (i) $18\frac{1}{4}$ dozen = _____

(e) $3\frac{2}{3}$ dozen = _____   (j) $22\frac{3}{4}$ dozen = _____

PERCENTS

Percents are one of the most commonly used mathematical concepts in merchandising. Many merchandising calculations are expressed in both percent and dollar amounts. Percents are often more meaningful than dollar amounts because they can be compared. Using percents, a division or department can compare itself to similar divisions or departments in its own company and to other companies, or can compare itself to a previous season or year. Throughout this workbook you will find that you will need to figure a percent. Percents are used to answer some of the following questions:

- What is the markup percent on merchandise?
- What is the markdown percent on merchandise?
- What is the percent gain or loss in sales over last year?
- What is the percent of an individual unit to a total company's sales?
- What percent profit did a department or a firm achieve?
- What percent of sales was spent on advertising and promotion?
- What is a company's share of the market?

Percents are also used in figuring discounts, taxes, and commissions. The percent of a number can be easily determined using the % key on a calculator; however, it is important that you understand the meaning of percents and know how to figure a percent when a calculator is not available.

A percent is a part of a whole, expressed in hundredths. Therefore, 90% equals ninety/hundredths, or 90/100, and 20% equals twenty/hundredths or 20/100. A percent may be expressed as a fraction or a decimal.

EXAMPLE 2-8

$47\% = 47/100 = 0.47$
$50\% = 50/100 = \frac{1}{2} = 0.50$

Figuring a percent is easy when you are working with units of 100. It is just as easy with other numbers if you realize that a percent is merely the relationship of one number to the whole.

EXAMPLE 2-9

If you received a shipment of 80 blouses and sold 60 at full price, the relationship would be 60 to 80. The percent of blouses sold at full price would be determined by dividing the total into the number sold.

$60/80 = 0.75 = 75\%$

EXAMPLE 2-10

If a buyer ordered 40 dresses with 5 in size 14, the percent of size 14 dresses would be determined by dividing 5 by 40.

$5/40 = 0.125 = 12.5\%$

When working problems without a calculator, a percent must be converted to a fraction or a decimal. The following examples show percents written in various forms:

EXAMPLE 2-11

$$50\% = \frac{1}{2} = 0.50 \quad \text{or} \quad 20\% = \frac{1}{5} = 0.20$$

BASIC PERCENT CALCULATIONS

Review the following calculations. You should be comfortable with converting a percent to a decimal to a fraction in any order.

1. **Percent to a Fraction—to convert a percent to a fraction, drop the percent sign and divide by 100. Reduce if possible.**

EXAMPLE 2-12

$$20\% = 20/100 = 1/5$$

2. **Percent to a Decimal—to convert a percent to a decimal, move the decimal point two places to the left (dividing by 100) and drop the percent sign. Zeros may be added to complete the procedure of moving the decimal.**

EXAMPLE 2-13

$$5\% = 0.05$$
$$35\% = 0.35$$

When working with a fractional percent, first convert the fraction into its decimal form and then proceed using the rule above. Add zeros when needed.

EXAMPLE 2-14

$$4\frac{1}{2}\% = 4.5\% = 0.045$$
$$12\frac{3}{4}\% = 12.75\% = 0.1275$$

3. **Decimal to a Percent—to convert a decimal to a percent, move the decimal point two places to the right (multiply by 100) and add a percent sign.**

EXAMPLE 2–15

$$0.75 = 75\%$$

4. Fraction to a Percent—to convert a fraction to a percent, change the fraction to a decimal, that is, divide the denominator into the numerator, and then convert to a percent.

EXAMPLE 2-16

$$\frac{1}{4} = 1 \div 4 = 0.25 = 25\%$$

Practice Problems • Exercise 2.3

1. Change the following percents to fractions and reduce to lowest terms:

   (a) 25% _____

   (b) $\frac{1}{4}$% _____

   (c) 0.2% _____

   (d) $45\frac{1}{2}$% _____

   (e) 0.5% _____

   (f) $35\frac{3}{4}$% _____

   (g) 0.8% _____

   (h) 85% _____

   (i) 95% _____

   (j) 168.75% _____

2. Convert the following percents to decimals:

   (a) $12\frac{1}{2}$% _____

   (b) 200% _____

   (c) 60% _____

   (d) $88\frac{1}{4}$% _____

   (e) 154.8% _____

   (f) 8% _____

   (g) 145% _____

   (h) 100% _____

   (i) 5% _____

   (j) 0.58% _____

3. Change the following decimals to percents:

   (a) 0.02 _____

   (b) 0.125 _____

   (c) 0.5 _____

   (d) 1.5 _____

   (e) 10.86 _____

   (f) 1.25 _____

   (g) 0.335 _____

   (h) 2.65 _____

   (i) 0.04 _____

   (j) 1.7965 _____

4. Change the following fractions to percents:

   (a) $\frac{1}{4}$ _____

   (b) $1\frac{1}{5}$ _____

   (c) $\frac{2}{5}$ _____

   (d) $2\frac{5}{8}$ _____

   (e) $\frac{3}{4}$ _____

   (f) $\frac{2}{3}$ _____

   (g) $\frac{5}{8}$ _____

   (h) $\frac{1}{10}$ _____

USING PERCENTS

Any problem involving a percent has three major components: percentage amount, rate, and base. The percentage amount is the fractional amount, the rate is the percent, and the base is the total amount. The following example illustrates the three major parts of a percentage problem.

EXAMPLE 2-17

As a salesperson in the children's department, Jane will receive a 10% commission on all sales that she makes. During August, she sold $1,500.00 worth of goods. Her commission for that month was $150.00. Listed below are the three parts of this percentage problem:

Base   = $1,500
Rate   = 10% or .10 in a decimal form
Percentage amount = $150 (commission made)

Finding Percentage Amount

To find the percentage amount, change the percent (rate) to a decimal and multiply by the base.

Percentage Amount = Rate × Base

EXAMPLE 2-18

Find 12% of $400.

12% = 0.12
Percentage Amount = Rate × Base
             = 0.12 × $400
             = $48

EXAMPLE 2-19

A buyer for women's sportswear purchased 150 skirts from a Texas manufacturer. Of this group, 20% were wraparound styles. How many were wraparounds?

20% = .20

Percentage Amount = Rate × Base
             = .20 × 150
             = 30

When using a calculator with a percent key, it is not necessary to convert the percent (rate) to its decimal form, as shown in the previous example. The percent key automatically makes the conversion. Most calculators are programmed so the base number must be entered first rather than the rate. Check your calculator to see whether the base number must be entered first.

Practice Problems • Exercise 2.4

1. (a) $\frac{1}{2}$% of $716 = _____

   (b) 107% of $385 = _____

   (c) 3% of 1,205 = _____

   (d) $41\frac{1}{2}$% of $11.98 = _____

   (e) $25\frac{1}{4}$% of 20 = _____

2. A buyer purchased 460 pairs of men's jeans. If 5% had straight legs, how many pairs of straight-leg jeans were in the order?

3. A salesperson in the furniture department receives an $11\frac{1}{4}$% commission on sales. If he sold $2,200 worth in May and $1,200 in June, what was his total commission for the two months?

4. A salesperson in the children's department waited on 50 customers in one day. If 42% were grandmothers, how many grandmothers were served?

5. A large corporation owns 20 retail stores across the United States. If 20% sell shoes, how many stores sell shoes?

6. Taxes reduce your weekly salary by 22%. How much is deducted if you make $280 a week?

Finding the Rate

To find what percent (rate) one number is of another, divide the base into the percentage amount. In most problems involving percents, the base amount is larger than the percentage amount, causing the quotient to be a decimal number. Thus, to find the rate (percent), move the decimal point two places to the right and add a percent sign.

$$\text{Rate} = \text{Percentage Amount} \div \text{Base}$$

EXAMPLE 2-20

20 is what percent of 40?

Rate = Percentage Amount ÷ Base
= 20 ÷ 40
= 0.50
= 50%

EXAMPLE 2-21

A suit retails for $240. If reduced by $60, what is the percent of reduction?

Rate = Percentage Amount ÷ Base
= $60 ÷ $240
= 0.25
= 25%

EXAMPLE 2-22

In the shoe department there are 3 women and 5 men sales associates. What percent are women?

Rate = Percentage Amount ÷ Base
= 3 ÷ 8 (total number)
= 0.375
= 37.5%

EXAMPLE 2-23

The store received 21 dozen Christmas tree ornaments. The buyer sent $6\frac{1}{2}$ dozen to one branch store and $8\frac{1}{3}$ dozen to another branch store. The remaining ornaments were kept at the main store. What percent of the ornaments were left at the main store?

Total ornaments received in units   = 21 dozen × 12 per dozen   = 252 units

Ornaments sent to branches in units = 6.5 dozen × 12 per dozen   =   78 units
                                  + $8\frac{1}{3}$ dozen × 12 per dozen = 100 units
                                  _____
                                                                            178 units

Ornaments left at the main store (percentage amount) = (252 − 178) = 74

Rate = Percentage Amount ÷ Base
     = 74 ÷ 252
     = 0.29365
     = 29.37%

Practice Problems • Exercise 2.5

1. (a) $2.42 = \underline{\hspace{2cm}}\%$ of $44

   (b) $123.75 = \underline{\hspace{2cm}}\%$ of $225

   (c) $277.55 = \underline{\hspace{2cm}}\%$ of 1,220

   (d) $55.2 = \underline{\hspace{2cm}}\%$ of 100

   (e) $7.38 = \underline{\hspace{2cm}}\%$ of $36.90

2. Sales for one week in the shoe department were $20,480. If John's sales were $1,280, what was his percent of sales?

3. The buyer in the gift department had 125 baskets in the stockroom. If 85 of the baskets were water-damaged because of a leaky roof, what percent were damaged?

4. A store received a shipment of 840 porcelain figurines. The buyer sent 230 to one branch store and 106 to another branch store. The remaining figurines were kept at the main store. What percent were left at the main store?

5. A firm's staff includes 161 males and 89 females. What percent of the staff is female?

6. The visual merchandising staff borrowed 410 sterling silver tree ornaments from the gift department to use for Christmas decorations throughout the store. This left only 200 silver ornaments in the department. What percent of the ornaments were used as store decorations?

7. The sportswear buyer ordered 18 dozen cotton sweaters and $21\frac{1}{2}$ dozen wool sweaters. What percent were cotton?

8. The china department received 32 dozen glasses. If 11 glasses were broken, what percent were broken?

Finding the Base

To find the base, divide the rate into the percentage amount. As you learned earlier in the chapter, if you are doing this without a calculator, the rate (percent) must be changed to its decimal form by moving the decimal point two places to the left. (This is the same as dividing by 100.)

Base = Percentage Amount ÷ Rate

EXAMPLE 2-24

48 is 12% of what amount?

Base = Percentage Amount ÷ Rate
= 48 ÷ 12%
= 400

Check your answer; find 12% of 400 = 48.

EXAMPLE 2-25

During a back-to-school sale, a salesperson in the shoe department sold $888 worth of children's shoes. This represented 8% of total sales. Calculate total department sales.

Reword the given information:

8% of _____ = $888

or

$888 is 8% of _____

Base = Percentage Amount ÷ Rate
= $888 ÷ 8%
= $11,100

Check: $11,100 × 8% = $888

EXAMPLE 2-26

The men's furnishings department received a shipment of ties. The department manager put 65% of the new ties in stock and the remainder in the stockroom. If the ties put in the stockroom had a value of $700, what was the value of the merchandise put on the floor?

Hint–Calculate the total value of the merchandise and then the value of merchandise on the floor.

$$\text{Total Merchandise or Base} = \text{Percentage Amount} \div \text{Rate}$$
$$= \$700 \div (100\% - 65\%)$$
$$= \$700 \div 35\%$$
$$= \$2,000$$

$$\text{Merchandise on the floor} = \$2,000 \times 65\%$$
$$= \$1,300$$

EXAMPLE 2-27

Sales last week totaled $12,638. This was an 8.6% increase over the previous week's sales. What were sales for the previous week?

Sales for the previous week represent the base amount	100.0%
Percent increase	+ 8.6%
	108.6%

Last week's sales were 108.6% of the previous week's sales.

$$\text{Base} = \text{Percentage Amount} \div \text{Rate}$$
$$= \$12,638 \div 108.6\%$$
$$= \$11,637 \text{ (rounded to nearest dollar)}$$

Check: $11,637 + ($11,637 \times 8.6\%) = $12,638

1. (a) $\$36.50 = 12\frac{1}{2}\%$ of _____

   (b) 25% of _____ = $144

   (c) $0.95 = 1\%$ of _____

   (d) $2\frac{1}{2}\%$ of _____ = 37.56

   (e) $3.198 = 20\%$ of _____

2. In a shipment of dishes, merchandise valued at $750 was damaged. The damaged goods amounted to 6% of the total order. What was the total value of the merchandise ordered?

3. Jane's sales for one week were $1,250, which was 2% of the department's weekly sales. What were the department's sales?

4. A salesperson made $842 in commissions during the month. If his commissions averaged $12\frac{1}{2}\%$ of total sales, what were the total sales for the month?

5. During a special Easter sale, two salespeople sold a total of $850, which was $12\frac{1}{2}\%$ of the total sales for the department. What were the department's sales?

6. The men's department received a new shipment of fleece robes. During the first day on the floor, 60 robes, or 30% of the group, sold. How many robes were in the shipment?

7. Forty-five percent of the handbags ordered for the spring–summer season were leather. If the leather handbags had a total value of $22,500, what was the value of the nonleather handbags?

8. Thirty-two sales associates were assigned to departments located on the second floor; this represented 16% of the total sales associates. How many sales associates were assigned to departments on other floors?

Calculating Percent Increase or Decrease

Retailers are constantly evaluating sales performance and comparing this year's figures to last year's. This is done both year-to-date and monthly. Retailers need to know how they are doing financially. Is the store having a gain or loss? Which departments or store units are increasing sales and which are having decreasing sales? Which merchandise classifications are reflecting a gain in sales and which are showing a loss? Store units, salespeople, managers, and buyers are evaluated in this manner. Percent change is determined because these figures can be compared more easily than dollar amounts.

To find the percent of increase or decrease, determine the difference between the two numbers and divide by the base number. The base number is always the previous number, as in last year, last month, or last week, depending on the time frame being used. The answer will be a decimal; therefore, convert it to a percent by moving the decimal point two places to the right and adding a percent sign. Use the following formula to find a percent increase or decrease:

$$\% \text{ Increase or Decrease} = \frac{\text{Difference Between Two Figures}}{\text{Previous Figure}}$$

EXAMPLE 2-28

The sales volume for the fashion jewelry department last year during the month of September was $20,000. This year September's volume was $22,000. Determine the percent increase in sales.

$$\% \text{ Increase} = (\text{This Year} - \text{Last Year}) \div \text{Last Year}$$
$$= \frac{\$22,000 - 20,000}{\$20,000}$$
$$= 0.10$$
$$= 10\% \text{ increase}$$

EXAMPLE 2-29

A man's suit was reduced from $500 to $400. Determine the percent decrease in price.

$$\% \text{ Reduction} = (\text{Current Price} - \text{Previous Price}) \div \text{Previous Price}$$
$$= (\$400 - \$500) \div \$500$$
$$= 0.20$$
$$= 20\% \text{ decrease}$$

EXAMPLE 2-30

Last year the men's clothing department had sales of $248,936. This year the sales were $256,782. What was the percent increase in sales?

% Increase = (This Year – Last Year) ÷ Last Year
= ($256,782 – $248,936) ÷ $248,936
= 0.031518
= 3.15% increase

EXAMPLE 2-31

The junior dress department had planned sales of $38,600 for the month. Actual sales for the month were only $33,846. What was the percent decrease from plan?

% Decrease = (Planned Sales – Actual Sales) ÷ Planned Sales
= ($38,600 – $33,846) ÷ $38,600
= 0.12316
= 12.32% decrease

Practice Problems • Exercise 2.7

1. The Loure-Decky factory in Switzerland produced 5,050 figurines this year. Last year 12,150 figurines were made. What was the percent reduction?

2. Last year the buyer for the children's department ordered 125 red velvet dresses for Christmas. This year the buyer ordered 205 velvet dresses. What was the percent increase?

3. A wool blazer was reduced from $225 to $175. What was the percent reduction?

4. During this year's midnight sale, the bedding department sold 195 bedspreads. Last year only 180 were sold. What was the percent increase?

5. Last year $226 was taken from Frank's monthly salary for taxes. This year the monthly taxes were $304.50. What was the percent increase?

6. As manager of the fabric department, next year you plan to sell $38,000 in notions. This year only $21,000 of notions were sold. What is the percent increase planned for next year's sales?

7. Sales for the month of October had been planned at $26,000; however, actual sales were $28,286. By what percent did sales exceed plan?

8. This year Peg's Boutique had sales of $86,916 during the month of March. Last year's sales for March were $82,374. Calculate the percent increase.

9. If sales for a period were planned at $2,600 and actual sales for the period were $1,800, what was the percent loss?

10. Determine the percent increase if last year's sales were $6,600 and this year's sales were $7,000.

DEFINITIONS

Findings Sewing or trade term for small functional items and trimmings used to complete a garment, such as buttons, snaps, zippers, hooks, shoulder pads, and seam tape.

Gross Twelve dozen items or 144 units.

Percent or Percentage A part of a whole, expressed in hundredths. Problems concerning percents involve three major elements:

Base The total amount, which is 100% (percentage amount ÷ rate)

Rate The percent one number is of another number (percentage amount ÷ base)

Percentage Amount The fractional amount of the result of multiplying the rate by the base (rate × base)

Chapter 2 • Summary Problems

1. Fill in the blanks for each of these problems:

   (a) $400 = \underline{20}$ % of 2,000

   $$\frac{400}{2,000} =$$

   (b) $60 = 12\%$ of $\underline{500}$

   $60 \div .12 =$

   (c) $\$66 = \underline{15}$ % of 440

   $66 \div 440 =$

   (d) 55% of $\$2,540 = \underline{\$1,397}$

   $.55 \times 2,540 =$

   (e) 4% of $244 = \underline{9.76}$

   $.04 \times 244 =$

   (f) $21\frac{1}{2}\%$ of $\$575.45 = \underline{\$123.72}$

   $.215 \times 575.45$

   (g) $\$552.50 = 6\frac{1}{2}\%$ of $\underline{\$8,500}$

   $552.50 \div .065 =$

   (h) $12 = \underline{75}$ % of 16

   $12 \div 16 =$

   (i) $49.5 = 55\%$ of $\underline{90}$

   $49.5 \div .55 =$

   (j) $232.17 = 35\frac{1}{2}\%$ of $\underline{654}$

   $232.17 \div .355 =$

   (k) $\$20.25 = \underline{1.50}$ % of $\$1,350$

   $20.25 \div 1,350 =$

   (l) $67\frac{3}{4}\%$ of $950.3 = \underline{643.83}$

   $.6775 \times 950.3 =$

   (m) $\$2,161.25 = 33\frac{1}{4}\%$ of $\underline{\$6,500.^{00}}$

   $\$2,161.25 \div .3325 =$

   (n) $\frac{1}{2}\%$ of $475.5 = \underline{2.38}$

   $.005 \times 475.5 =$

   (o) $\$24.98 = \underline{20}$ % of $\$124.90$

   $\$24.98 \div 124.^{90} =$

   (p) 12% of $8.65 = \underline{1.04}$

   $.12 \times 8.65 =$

   (q) $24.5 = 2\frac{1}{2}\%$ of $\underline{980}$

   $24.5 \div .025 =$

   (r) 105% of $2,500 = \underline{2,425}$

   $1.05 \times 2,500 =$

   (s) $54 = \underline{.5}$ % of $10,800$

   $54 \div 10,800 =$

   (t) $11\frac{1}{4}\%$ of $850 = \underline{95.63}$

   $.1125 \times 850 =$

   (u) $300 = 100\%$ of $\underline{300}$

   $300 \div 1 =$

   (v) $421 = \underline{5.00}$ % of $8,420$

   $421 \div 8,420 =$

2. John's sales for the week totaled $9,271.43. This was a 6.5% increase over his sales the previous week. What were his previous week's sales? $\$9,271.43 = 106.5\% \times x$
   $= 9,271.43 \div 1.065$
   $= \$8,705.57$

3. Hair combs were selling at a special price of 2 for $3.50. How many combs could you purchase for $12.25? $\$3.^{50} \div 2 = \$1^{75}$
   $\$12.^{25} \div 1.75 = 7$

55

4. Ann's sales for one hour consisted of the following transactions: $10.87, $4.21, $16.33, $7.99, $4.03, $11.12, and $1.25. Tom's sales for the same hour were: $15.43, $9.66, $28.03, and $8.43. Determine the average sale for each person.

Ann = $55.80 ÷ 7 = $7.97
Tom = $61.55 ÷ 4 = $15.39

5. What is the dollar savings when a customer receives a $14\frac{3}{4}$% discount on a $959 dining table?

$141.45

6. Find the cost of 125 men's suits at $310.15 each and 14 dozen ties at $4.25 each.

38,768.75 + 714 = $39,482.75

7. A total of 150 ties were placed on a markdown rack at $5.99 each. If $\frac{2}{3}$ of them were sold in one day, how many ties were left on the rack?

50

8. Washcloths were selling for $1.88 each. If $14\frac{1}{4}$ dozen cloths were sold, what was the retail value of total sales?

$1.88 × 171 = $321.48

9. A buyer in the men's department ordered ties from three different companies in the following quantities: $16\frac{1}{2}$ dozen, $21\frac{1}{3}$ dozen, and $9\frac{1}{4}$ dozen. What was the total number of ties ordered? (Give your answer in units.)

198 + 256 + 111 = 565

10. A salesperson had the following sales: $15.50, $18.98, $16.98, $14, $18.50, and $22. What was the average sale?

$17.66

11. A store gave a customer an allowance of $10.50 on a dress that originally sold for $285.99. How much did the customer pay for the dress if the sales tax was $6\frac{1}{2}$%?

$$\$293.40$$

12. A large retail store hired 27 new members for the executive training program. Of this group, $\frac{2}{3}$ had retail work experience. How many had previous retail work experience?

$$18$$

13. A customer bought the following items for her children during a back-to-school sale:

    2 dresses at $31.50 each $63.00

    1 purse at $10.98   10.98

    5 pairs of socks at 2 pairs for $3   7.50

    3 shirts at $8.99 each   26.97

    1 skirt at $12.95   12.95

What was the total purchase amount? $121.40

14. The manager for a clothing store planned to give free turkeys to salespersons selling over $10,000 during the fall harvest sale. Of the 110 salespersons, only 8 sold over this amount. What percent of the salespersons received turkeys?   7.27%

15. A buyer discovered that 5% of the merchandise was damaged during shipping. The manufacturer agreed to replace the blouses. How many blouses were replaced if 300 blouses were shipped?

$$15$$

16. Last week Linda's commission check was $84. If she earns a 12.5% commission on sales, what were her total sales? 12.5% of $x = \$84.00$

$$\$672.00$$

17. The volume in the infants' department last year was $150,000. The manager for that department is planning an increase of 13% for this year. What is this year's projected volume?

$169,500.00

18. What was the cost of $4\frac{3}{4}$ yards of fabric at $12.29 a yard?

$58.38

19. A manufacturer decided to reduce the monthly production of children's shoes from 3,200 to 2,400 pairs. What was the percent of reduction?

25%

20. During last year's anniversary sale, the rug department sold 425 wool area rugs. This year's sales declined 20%. How many rugs were sold this year?

340

21. A salesperson in the furniture department receives 8% commission on special orders and only 5% commission on goods on hand. How much would he receive in commissions if he sold $30,500 of special-order furniture and $20,552 of furniture on hand?

$2,440.00 + 1,027.60 = $3,467.60

22. A buyer for the men's department purchased $18\frac{1}{4}$ dozen leather belts that cost $96 a dozen. What was the total cost?

$1,752

23. Last year the china department sold $250,000 in crystal stemware. This year the manager plans sales of $375,000. What is the planned percent increase for this year's sales?

50%

24. In the lingerie department, the manager instructed you to keep 15% of the total inventory in the stockroom and the rest displayed on the floor. After meeting these instructions, you placed $30,000 worth of goods in the stockroom. What would be the dollar amount of inventory on the floor?

$$15\% \text{ of } x = \$30,000$$
$$x = \$30,000 \div .15$$
$$= \$200,000$$
$$\$200,000 \times .85 = \$170,000$$

25. On July 3 the buyer for the women's sportswear department at the main store decided to transfer the following items to a branch store:

20 blouses at $22 each $440
32 skirts at $14 each   448
10 pants at $18 each   180
9 blazers at $41 each   369
             1,437

If the department had $32,000 of inventory on July 2, what percent of the inventory was transferred?

4.49%

26. To cut costs and improve profits, a retailer announced the closing of 75 unprofitable stores and the release of 4,900 employees, 2% of its workforce. How many employees remained after these 4,900 left the company?

$$4900 = 2\% \text{ of } x$$
$$245,000 - 4,900 =$$
$$240,100$$

27. A firm announced its plan to release 2,300, or 10%, of its management people. How many management people were employed before the 2,300 reduction?

$$2,300 \div .10 = 23,000$$

28. Monthly *Women's Wear Daily* publishes a list of current, last month's, and year-ago fiber prices. Prices listed reflect the cost of one pound of fiber. Determine the percent increase or decrease for each of the following fibers:

Fiber	Price This Year on 12/27	Price Last Year on 12/27	% Increase/ Decrease
Cotton	88.23 cents	75.44 cents	+ 16.95%
Wool	$2.06	$2.07	− 0.48%
Polyester staple	89 cents	85 cents	+ 4.71%
Spandex	$14	$14	no change 0.00%
Rayon staple	$1.11	$1.05	+ 5.71%

CHAPTER 3

Profitability

OBJECTIVES

- To define the elements in a skeletal profit and loss statement.
- To complete a skeletal profit and loss statement.
- To understand the importance of controlling expenses in order to maximize profits.
- To express gross margin, expenses, and profit as a percent of net sales.

KEY POINTS

- Operating profit is the result of relationships among sales, cost of merchandise sold, and expenses.
- A loss occurs if expenses exceed gross margin. The use of percents on an operating statement facilitates analysis of individual factors.
- Department and specialty stores evaluate profitability on margin results such as gross margin, contribution, and profit.
- Controlling expenses is increasingly important, as escalating costs have created a "profit squeeze."

The purpose of retailing is to sell goods to satisfied customers at a profit. Profits are necessary to a business because they (1) allow for replacement of inventory and equipment, (2) allow for expansion of the business, and (3) provide a return for those who have invested in the business.

Many people have a misconception of typical operating profits of retail stores. Profits vary greatly according to the type of store and the skill of management. The **National Retail Federation** (NRF) annually publishes merchandising, financial, and operating results of participating department and specialty stores. The annual publication is *FOR/MOR, The Combined Financial, Merchandising, and Operating Results of Retail Stores.*

FOR and MOR figures report **median** performance levels. **A median figure is the midpoint in an array of figures arranged in order according to value.**

RELATIONSHIP OF BASIC FACTORS

Operating profit is the result of the relationships among the following:

1. Sales volume
2. Cost of merchandise sold
3. Expenses

The relationships of these three fundamental factors can be shown in a skeletal profit and loss statement. (This is referred to as a **skeletal statement** because it contains only the major components without showing in detail how these factors are computed.)

The skeletal statement shows five factors: the three basic merchandising factors of net sales, cost of merchandise sold, and expenses, plus gross margin and profit. Gross margin and profit are **margins** or "results"; they are left after the interactions of two or more of the basic factors.

EXAMPLE 3-1:

		$	%
	Net sales	100,000	100.00
(minus)	Cost of merchandise sold	– 60,000	– 60.00
	Gross margin	40,000	40.00
(minus)	Operating expenses	– 36,500	– 36.50
	Operating profit	3,500	3.50

Gross margin is the difference between net sales and cost of merchandise sold. Gross margin is sometimes referred to as **gross profit**, which can be misleading because expenses must be subtracted to determine profit. Gross margin is the amount available to cover expenses and provide profit. According to *FOR/MOR*, in 1997 the median gross margin of department stores was 35.9% and 41.5% for specialty stores.

Gross Margin = Net Sales – Cost of Merchandise Sold

Gross margin is an important figure because it shows the margin on merchandise alone. Sales and cost of merchandise sold are figures over which the buyer has a great deal of control. By looking at gross margin figures, buyers and merchandise managers can see at a glance whether sales and/or cost of merchandise sold figures need improvement. (Chapter 7 will explain how cost of merchandise sold is calculated.)

Gross Margin = Profit + Expenses

Gross margin can also be calculated by adding profit and expenses. (Remember that this is not the way it is shown on the skeletal statement.) The *FOR/MOR* reported that the median operating expenses in 1997 were 30.5% for department stores and 39.1% for specialty stores. The median pretax earnings for all participating department stores were 5.5% of net sales. This was an increase for three years in a row for department stores.

EXAMPLE 3-2

	$	%
Operating expenses	36,500	36.50
Operating profit	+ 3,500	+ 3.50
Gross margin	40,000	40.00

A company may have other sources of income, such as rent or interest, that provide another type of income and, consequently, contributes to profit.

EXAMPLE 3-3

		$	%
	Net sales	200,000	100.00
(minus)	Cost of merchandise sold	− 126,000	− 63.00
	Gross margin	74,000	37.00
(minus)	Operating expenses	− 60,000	− 30.00
	Operating profit	14,000	7.00
(plus)	Other income	+ 2,000	+ 1.00
	Net profit before federal income tax	16,000	8.00

When working with figures in a skeletal statement, the columns—both dollars and percents—can be checked by adding up from the bottom. If gross margin were eliminated, the dollars and percents would total net sales, 100%.

EXAMPLE 3-4

		$	%
	Cost of merchandise sold	126,000	63.00
(plus)	Expenses	+ 60,000	+ 30.00
(plus)	Operating profit	+ 14,000	+ 7.00
	Net sales	200,000	100.00

Operating profit occurs when gross margin exceeds expenses. If expenses are larger than gross margin, a **loss** occurs. A loss should be enclosed in parentheses to indicate that it is a loss rather than profit.

Profit/(Loss) = Gross Margin – Expenses

EXAMPLE 3-5

	$	%
Net sales	68,000	100.00
Cost of merchandise sold	– 39,500	– 58.09
Gross margin	28,500	41.91
Expenses	– 29,800	– 43.82
Operating loss	(1,300)	(1.91)

To find the percent of any one factor—gross margin, expenses, or profit—divide the dollar amount of that factor by net sales.

Expense % = $ Expenses ÷ $ Net Sales

Gross Margin % = $ Gross Margin ÷ $ Net Sales

Profit % = $ Profit ÷ $ Net Sales

EXAMPLE 3-6

If net sales are $100,000 and expenses total $40,000, find the expense percent.

Solution:

$$
\begin{aligned}
\text{Expense \%} &= \text{\$ Expenses} \div \text{\$ Net Sales} \\
&= \$40,000 \div \$100,000 \\
&= 0.40 \\
&= 40\%
\end{aligned}
$$

In other words, expenses totaled 40% of net sales.

The profit and loss statement (also known as an **operating statement** or **income statement**) summarizes the income, cost of merchandise sold, and expenses for a specific period of time, which may be a month, season, or year. The operating statement may be prepared for specific departments, an entire store, and/or several stores that make up a division within a corporation. **To be complete, the skeletal statement must show the percents corresponding to the dollar figures.**

The figures on a profit and loss statement may be utilized in many ways. For example, if profit is unsatisfactory, the relationships among all the contributing factors must be analyzed and compared with previous statements and industry-wide figures in order to determine the best opportunities for profit improvement. The only meaningful way to compare current performance with a previous season's performance or with industry statistics is to express each factor as a percent of net sales. Even though sales volume differs from season to season (hopefully increasing), the percents allow easy comparison.

EXAMPLE 3-7

	Last Year		This Year	
	$	%	$	%
Net sales	36,000	100.00	30,000	100.00
Cost of merchandise sold	– 16,920	– 47.00	– 14,000	– 46.67
Gross margin	19,080	53.00	16,000	53.33
Expenses	– 18,360	– 51.00	– 15,250	– 50.83
Profit	720	2.00	750	2.50

In the previous example, profit dollars increased slightly even though sales decreased. This improved performance was the result of decreases in both cost of merchandise sold and expenses.

Because cost of merchandise sold, gross margin, expenses, and profit all are expressed as percents of net sales, it is easy to calculate net sales when the dollar and percent figures are given for any one factor. (Remember the formula from Chapter 2: Base = Percentage Amount ÷ Rate)

$ Net Sales = $ Profit ÷ Profit %

EXAMPLE 3-8

Last season the operating profit was $5,000, which represented 2% of net sales. Find net sales.

Solution: $5,000 is 2% of what number?

$ Net Sales = $5,000 ÷ 2%
             = $250,000

Check your answer: $250,000 × 2% = $5,000

EXAMPLE 3-9

Set up a skeletal statement, given:

Gross margin $130,000
Expenses $125,000
Profit   2.0%

Solution: Set up relationships among factors:

	$	%
Net sales	(b)	100.00%
Cost of merchandise sold	− (c)	− (d)
Gross Margin	$130,000	(e)
Expenses	− $125,000	− (f)
Profit	(a)	2.00%

(a) Profit   = $130,000 − $125,000
　　　　　　 = $5,000

(b) Net sales = $5,000 ÷ 2%
　　　　　　 = $250,000

(c) Cost of merchandise sold = $250,000 − $130,000
　　　　　　　　　　　　　　 = $120,000

(d) Cost of merchandise sold % = $120,000 ÷ $250,000
　　　　　　　　　　　　　　　 = 48.00%

(e) Gross margin % = $130,000 ÷ $250,000
　　　　　　　　　 = 52.00%

(f) Expense % = $125,000 ÷ $250,000
　　　　　　　 = 50.00%

Problems 1–8: Set up skeletal statements.

1. Net sales $14,000
   Cost of merchandise sold $ 7,200
   Expenses $ 5,900

2. Net sales $187,000
   Cost of merchandise sold $109,000
   Expenses   38.5%

3. Net sales $242,000
   Cost of merchandise sold $134,600
   Expenses   38%

4. Net sales $687,520
   Cost of merchandise sold   56.12%
   Profit   4.08%

5. Net sales $79,800
   Gross margin   44.6%
   Expenses   45.0%

6. The designer department had net sales of $300,000. There was 1% loss; gross margin was 49%.

7.   Gross margin $47,800
         Expenses $49,150
         Loss   (0.8%)

[handwritten notes:]
NS   168,750   100.00%
COMS   120,950
GM   47,800
OE   49,150
LOSS   (1,350)   (0.8%)

8.   Gross margin $68,900
         Expenses $69,500
         Loss   (0.4%)

9. Determine the percent of gross margin necessary to achieve a net profit of 4%. Estimated net sales are $100,000; estimated operating expenses are $44,000.

10. Analysis of last year's figures showed gross margin and expenses of 42% and 39%, respectively. It is anticipated that this year expenses will increase 1.5%. A profit goal of 4.5% has been set. What cost of merchandise percent will be necessary?

BASIC PROFIT FACTORS

The store's operating income is received from customers in exchange for merchandise and services. In retailing, the terms **operating income, sales volume,** and **sales productivity** all refer to net sales.

Net Sales

To arrive at net sales as shown on the skeletal statement, customer returns and allowances are subtracted from gross sales.

Gross sales refers to the total of prices charged customers (both cash and credit sales) for all merchandise and services before any deductions for customer returns and allowances.

> Gross Sales = Net Sales + Customer Returns and Allowances

Net sales are the sales a store has left after deducting customer returns and allowances from gross sales.

> Net Sales = Gross Sales – Customer Returns and Allowances

Customer allowances are reductions in price generally given after the sale has been completed. Adjustments in price are sometimes given to customers when they discover merchandise is slightly damaged. For example, a customer might be given an allowance to have a soiled dress cleaned or to replace buttons when one is missing. The customer return and allowance percent is calculated by dividing the dollar sum of customer returns and allowances by gross sales. (**This is the *only* time when a percent is based on gross sales.**)

> Customer Return and Allowance % = $ Returns and Allowances ÷ $ Gross Sales

The following formula will also be helpful when working some problems.

> $ Gross Sales = $ Net Sales ÷ Gross Sales % Complement

EXAMPLE 3-10

Calculate the percent of customer returns and allowances for a week with the following figures: gross sales of $7,500. Monday a $55.00 coat was returned. Tuesday an allowance of $5.00 was given to have a coat cleaned. Wednesday the department gave a refund of $98.00. Friday refunds totaled $158.00 and a $7.50 allowance was given on a coat with missing buttons.

Solution: Returns and allowances:

Monday	$ 55.00
Tuesday	5.00
Wednesday	98.00
Friday	165.50
Total	$323.50

Return and Allowance % = $ Returns and Allowances ÷ Gross Sales
= $323.50 ÷ $7,500
= 4.31%

EXAMPLE 3-11

Net sales for a department were $128,644; customer returns and allowances amounted to $6,846. What was the percent of returns and allowances? (Remember: To express customer returns and allowances as a percent, the percent is based on gross sales.)

Solution: $ Gross Sales = $ Net Sales + $ Returns and Allowances
= $128,644 + 6,846
= $135,490

Return and Allowance % = $ Returns and Allowances ÷ $ Gross Sales
= $6,846 ÷ $135,490
= 5.05%

EXAMPLE 3-12

Net sales of handbags were $187,680. Customer returns and allowances were 8.5%. Find gross sales. (*Note: In this situation, gross sales = 100%.)

Solution:

Gross sales	100.00%*
Customer returns and allowances	− 8.50%
Gross sales complement	91.5%

$ Gross Sales = $ Net Sales ÷ Gross Sales % Complement
= $187,680 ÷ 91.5%
= $205,114.75

EXAMPLE 3-13

Set up a skeletal statement, given:

Gross sales	$583,260
Customer returns	8.65%
Cost of merchandise sold	48.35%
Expenses	$251,870

Solution:

	$	%
Net sales	(a)	100.00%
Cost of merchandise sold	– (c)	– (b)
Gross margin	(d)	51.65%
Expenses	– $251,870	– (f)
Profit	(e)	(g)

(a) Net Sales = $ Gross Sales – $ Customer Returns and Allowances
$$= \$583,260 - (\$583,260 \times 8.65\%)$$
$$= \$583,260 - \$50,452$$
$$= \$532,808$$

(b) Cost of Merchandise Sold % = Net Sales % – Gross Margin %
$$= 100.00\% - 51.65\%$$
$$= 48.35\%$$

(c) Cost of Merchandise Sold = Net Sales × Cost of Merchandise Sold %
$$= \$532,808 \times 48.35\%$$
$$= \$257,613$$

(d) Gross Margin = $ Net Sales – Cost of Merchandise Sold
$$= \$532,808 - \$257,613$$
$$= \$275,195$$

(e) Profit = Gross Margin – Expenses
$$= \$275,195 - \$251,870$$
$$= \$23,325$$

Corresponding Percent:

(f) Expense % = $ Expenses ÷ $ Net Sales   (g) Profit % = $ Profit ÷ $ Net Sales
    = $251,870 ÷ $532,808   = $23,325 ÷ $532,808
    = 47.27%   = 4.38%

Note: Working with customer returns is the only instance when gross sales represent 100%. Normally, percents are calculated with net sales as 100%, the base amount.

Practice Problems • Exercise 3.2

1. Determine net sales if gross sales were $98,656 and customer returns and allowances were 4.8%.

$$\$98,656 \times (1 - .048) =$$

2. Net sales amounted to $126,810; customer returns and allowances totaled $6,080. Calculate customer return and allowance percent.

3. Gross sales were $236,438; net sales amounted to $224,176. Determine customer return and allowance percent.

4. Last week Ms. Smith had gross sales of $986.35; her customer returns and allowances totaled $112. Calculate the percent of sales returned.

5. The ladies' shoe department has four salespeople. Calculate the sales return percent (a) for each salesperson and (b) for the department as a whole.

Salesperson	Gross Sales	Customer Returns
Alice	$1,441	$109
Brandon	1,098	76
Carrie	934	98
David	734	46

6. Customer returns and allowances were 12.5% in the sportswear department. Determine gross sales if net sales totaled $438,418.

$$438,418 = \text{\st{72.5\%}} \text{ of } x$$

7. Set up a skeletal statement, given:

Gross sales	$680,366
Gross margin	$271,251
Customer returns	9.80%
Expenses	41.70%

8. Set up a skeletal statement, given:

Gross sales	$86,536
Customer returns	$ 9,214
Expense	45.64%
Loss	(1.78%)

9. Set up a skeletal statement, given:

Gross sales	$120,000
Customer returns	18,562
Gross margin	45,220
Profit	4,000

10. The home furnishings department of Zachary's Furniture Store had the following sales and returns. Determine the customer return percent (a) for each salesperson and (b) for the department as a whole.

Salesperson	Gross Sales	Customer Returns
Christopher	$33,420	$1,566
Jonathan	40,580	6,410
Kay	20,120	1,020
Suzanne	15,890	750
Zachary	35,420	1,525

Cost of Merchandise Sold

Total cost of merchandise sold is influenced by several factors. Billed cost of merchandise, transportation, cash discounts, and alteration/workroom costs all affect the total cost of merchandise sold. These factors must be controlled in order to maintain or improve profit. Calculation of total cost of merchandise sold will be explained in Chapter 4 and covered in detail in Chapter 7.

Operating Expenses

The various expenses incurred by the operation of the business (excluding cost of merchandise sold) are subtracted from gross margin to determine operating profit. If expenses exceed gross margin, a loss occurs.

The expenses of operating a store include wages for selling and nonselling employees, management salaries, utilities, advertising, supplies, fixtures, taxes, insurance, bad debts, buyers' travel, and so forth. (See Table 3-1 for a comparison between department store and specialty store expenses.)

Table 3-1
Expense Comparisons of Department Stores and Specialty Stores in 1997

Expenses	Department Stores	Specialty Stores
Selling & support	27.0%	34.5%
Property & equipment	16.4	26.1
Sales promotion	14.2	7.3
Service & operations	10.6	5.7
Personnel	6.8	2.6
Credit & accounts receivable	6.4	2.3
Company management	5.1	9.1
Receiving, storage, & distribution	4.7	6.0
Merchandising	4.4	2.3
Accounting & management information systems	4.3	4.1

Note: From *FOR/MOR, The Combined Financial, Merchandising, and Operating Results of Retail Stores in 1997* by Alexandra Moran (Ed.), 1998 (73rd ed.). Copyright 1998 by the National Retail Federation.

There are many ways of classifying expenses. The expense classification system used will depend on the purpose for which expenses are being analyzed. Traditionally, when the buyer was also supervisor of sales personnel, expenses were generally classified as direct and indirect.

Direct expenses are the result of the operation of one specific department and would not occur if the department were eliminated. Before the buying activities were moved to a central office, buyers/department managers had some control over direct expenses. Examples include salaries of sales personnel, department advertising, selling supplies, and buyers' travel.

Indirect expenses benefit the store as a whole and would continue even if a particular department were discontinued. Examples include store maintenance, insurance, salaries of senior executives, and institutional advertising.

In multiunit retail corporations, store managers and sales managers rather than buyers are now responsible for supervision and staffing of the selling floor. Selling personnel may be assigned to an area containing merchandise from several departments. The traditional system of classifying expenses as direct and indirect may not be appropriate. The central organization that includes buyers may be accounted for separately. The *NRF Retail Accounting Manual* points out that there are many different approaches to departmental distribution of expenses.

Moderate- and large-sized stores prepare operating statements for each department and store on a regular basis, perhaps monthly. Companies that classify expenses as direct or indirect may calculate a department's contribution or controllable margin in place of or in addition to departmental profit.

Contribution or controllable margin is the amount left after direct expenses are subtracted from gross margin. This is the amount the department contributes to indirect expenses and profit. Calculation of a contribution figure emphasizes the importance of controlling expenses directly related to the selling department. It provides a better picture of the operation of the department than does the gross margin figure alone.

> Contribution = Gross Margin – Direct Expenses

If a store calculates profit for each department, criteria must be established for allocating or prorating a portion of indirect expenses to each department. Some indirect expenses can be related to the operation of specific selling departments. If detailed accounting records are maintained, these **semi-direct expenses** can be allocated to selling departments on the basis of service provided. For example, expenses associated with maintaining a personnel office could be allocated to selling departments

---

EXAMPLE 3-14

Calculate the contribution percent and profit in percent and dollars for a department with the following figures:

Net sales		$368,430
Cost of merchandise sold		196,005
Direct expenses:		
Wages	$49,264	
Department advertising	12,316	
Wrapping supplies	3,315	
Buyers' travel	4,842	
Other	6,790	
Indirect expenses		77,740

Solution:

Net sales		$368,430	100.00%
Cost of merchandise sold		– 196,005	– 53.20
Gross margin		172,425	46.80
Direct expenses			
Wages	$49,264		
Advertising	12,316		
Supplies	3,315		
Travel	4,842		
Other	6,790		
Total direct expenses:		– 76,527	– 20.77
Contribution margin		95,898	26.03
Indirect expenses		– 77,740	– 21.10
Operating profit		$18,158	4.93%

on the basis of the proportion of employees in each department. Thus, if the sportswear department had 11% of the total employees, 11% of the costs of the personnel function would be allocated to the sportswear department. A department with 7.8% of the store's credit purchases would be allocated 7.8% of the expenses associated with accounts receivable.

Indirect expenses such as general management, general accounting, and telephone service are more difficult to relate to individual selling departments. These indirect expenses are generally allocated on the basis of sales volume, A department contributing 8.5% of total sales would be charged with 8.5% of these indirect expenses.

Today, as a result of mergers, accounting is a corporate level function for the majority of department stores. As was discussed in Chapter 1, centralized buyers are not located in the stores and, therefore, have less control over contribution than decentralized buyers have.

1. Determine (a) contribution percent and (b) profit or loss percent.

Net sales	$178,000
Cost of merchandise sold	91,670
Direct expenses	42,720
Indirect expenses	35,600

2. Calculate (a) contribution percent and (b) profit or loss percent for the sporting goods department.

Net sales	$568,320
Cost of merchandise sold	280,774
Direct expenses	145,490
Indirect expenses	121,621

3. Calculate (a) contribution percent and (b) profit or loss percent.

Cost of merchandise sold	$389,615
Gross margin	353,925
Direct expenses	195,923
Indirect expenses	129,376

4. Calculate (a) contribution percent and (b) profit or loss percent.

Gross sales	$454,645
Customer returns	25,733
Cost of merchandise sold	235,671
Department advertising	12,438
Department selling cost	27,585
Department buying costs	4,652
Department stock and clerical	3,573
General management	19,530
Department supplies and delivery	2,431
Miscellaneous direct expenses	4,870
Maintenance and utilities	12,680
Miscellaneous indirect expenses	50,861

5. Calculate (a) contribution percent and (b) profit or loss percent. (May round dollar amounts to nearest whole dollar.)

Net sales	$689,347	
Cost of merchandise sold		50.98%
Salaries and wages:		
Departmental selling		9.86
Departmental buyer/manager		1.90
General management		6.80
General office and nonselling		2.62
Departmental advertising		3.10
Insurance		0.60
Departmental selling supplies		1.40
Rent		4.16
Utilities and telephone/communication		1.20
Miscellaneous indirect expenses		11.30
Taxes		1.90

6. Using the following figures, calculate (a) contribution percent and (b) profit or loss percent:

Cost of merchandise sold	$567,830
Gross margin	493,460
Direct expenses	203,420
Indirect expenses	273,000

7. Complete the following profit and loss statement:

Net sales	$147,800	
Cost of merchandise sold		53.20%
Gross margin		
Direct expenses		27.30
Contribution	28,822	
Profit		2.18

EXPENSE CONTROL

Compared to typical manufacturing organizations, retailers operate with relatively low gross margins. Low gross margin means it is very important to maintain expenses at the appropriate level. Retailers are experiencing a "profit squeeze." A profit squeeze results from the difficulty in increasing gross margin to keep up with increased expenses. For example, expenses related to energy consumption, travel, and labor have escalated in recent years. Control of expenses and increased productivity are keys to generating an adequate profit.

The concept of control does not mean elimination; control refers to careful monitoring and making adjustments as soon as a factor appears to be slightly out of line. Careful analysis of regular, periodic reports provides information for management decisions that will ensure satisfactory relationships among all factors, thus maximizing profits.

The first step in expense control is planning the appropriate level of expenses. As the season progresses, actual performance is compared to planned figures. Labor is a major expense for all retailers. As a result of increased store hours, increased minimum wage, and improved fringe benefits, payroll costs have escalated. In most large stores, payroll is the largest controllable expense. Retailers must carefully plan and control payroll expense.

Cost of sales personnel has been a major factor in many stores converting to self-selection or self-service. According to *FOR/MOR Results* for 1997, the NRF median figures for selling and support services were the largest component of operating expenses for both department and specialty stores, at 8.27% and 12.84%, respectively.

Selling cost percent is important in scheduling sales assistance. The relationship between sales productivity (net sales) and wages is called **selling cost**. Selling cost can be calculated for an individual salesperson, department, and/or store as a whole.

Selling Cost % = Gross Wages ÷ Net Sales

EXAMPLE 3-15

What would the selling cost percent be for a person who earned $90 during a week when net sales were $1,000?

Solution:

Selling Cost % = Gross Wages ÷ Net Sales
= $90 ÷ $1,000
= 9.0%

EXAMPLE 3-16

Calculate the selling cost percent for a person who worked 38 hours at a wage of $8.10 an hour and had net sales of $2,849.

Solution:

(a) Calculate gross wages.

Gross Wages = Number of Hours Worked × Hourly Pay Rate
= 38 × $8.10
= $307.80

(b) Calculate selling cost %.

Selling Cost % = Gross Wages ÷ Net Sales
= $307.80 ÷ $2,849
= 10.80%

In addition to hourly wages and straight salaries, sales personnel may be compensated by **commission**. **Commission is a percent of net sales paid to the seller of the merchandise.** Retailers like Nordstrom and Neiman Marcus pay commission to encourage excellent customer service. They believe their sales personnel will work harder with the incentive of commission. In wholesale companies, sales representatives may also work on commission. In-house sales representatives who work at corporate headquarters or the company's showroom usually receive a lower percentage commission than road representatives. Road representatives are paid a higher commission percentage if they are expected to cover their travel expenses. Both retailers and wholesalers must pay close attention to selling cost percentage to ensure high profitability.

Commission $ = Net Sales × Commission %

EXAMPLE 3-17

Calculate the commission a salesperson would earn on a net sale of $120 if the commission was 10% of net sales.

Solution:

Commission $ = Net Sales × Commission %
= $120 × 10%
= $12

Sales personnel may calculate average earnings per hour by dividing their total commission by the number of hours they worked.

Average Earnings per Hour = Total Commission ÷ Total Number of Hours Worked

EXAMPLE 3-18

Calculate the average earnings per hour for a salesperson who worked 25 hours and earned total commission of $275.

Solution:

Average Earnings per Hour = Total Commission ÷ Total Number of Hours Worked
= $275 ÷ $25
= $11 per hour

Practice Problems • Exercise 3.4

1. What was the selling cost percent for a person earning $105.60 whose gross sales were $1,049 and customer returns were $79.80?

2. If a department needs to operate with a minimum selling cost of 8.5%, how much would a salesperson need to sell to have earnings of $100?

3. A salesperson who worked 40 hours per week received a wage of $7.75 per hour. If she sold $1,986, what was her selling cost percent?

4. If the salesperson in the previous problem received a raise to $8.00 per hour, what would be the new selling cost percent?

5. A store currently pays all employees $7.50 per hour. For the week, the store has scheduled 164 hours of sales help. If the store desires to maintain the same selling cost percent when minimum wage goes to $8.00, how many hours of sales assistance can be allowed and still maintain the same selling cost?

6. Last year the store had two salespeople who worked 40 hours per week for $6.85 per hour and three salespeople who worked 28 hours per week for $6.75 per hour. With the increase in minimum wage, wages for all salespeople will be increased, but hours will be reduced so selling cost will remain the same. The two people previously earning $6.85 per hour will receive $8.00 per hour, but will work only 37.5 hours per week. The remaining hours will be split evenly among the three part-time employees. The part-time salespeople will be paid $7.25 per hour. How many hours per week can each part-time salesperson work?

7. Calculate the selling cost percent for an entire department with the following information:

Salesperson	Gross Sales	Customer Returns	Basis for Earnings	Hours Worked
Alexandria	$ 8,796	$ 897	8% commission	40
Brian	10,278	1,286	8% commission	36
Charles	7,340	674	$6/hr. + 2% comm.	32
Deidre	6,896	458	$6/hr. + 2% comm.	28
Eve	6,958	573	$7.75 /hr.	32

8. Sales associates in the designer dress department are paid an hourly wage plus commission. Calculate the selling cost percent (a) for each associate and (b) for the entire department under the following conditions:

Sales Associate	Net Sales	Hours Worked	Wage per hour	Commission
Frank	$9,796	38	$7.75	2%
Gwen	9,362	38	7.75	2
Heather	6,854	32	8.00	1
Jason	5,936	28	8.00	3
Kathy	4,815	20	8.00	3
Lacey	5,491	20	8.00	3

9. A store pays employees $7.50 per hour who are scheduled 78 hours per week. The store wants to keep the same selling cost percentage yet increase the hourly wage by 15 cents per hour. How many hours of sales assistance can be allowed and maintain the same selling cost percent?

DEFINITIONS

Commission   A method of compensation in which a salesperson is paid a percent of his/her sales.

Contribution or **Controllable Margin**   The amount remaining after direct expenses are subtracted from gross margin.

Customer Allowance   Deduction from retail price given to a customer when merchandise is not in perfect condition, usually in lieu of return of merchandise.

Direct Expenses   Expenses that specifically relate to the operation of a selling department and would be eliminated if that department were eliminated.

Gross Margin or **Gross Profit**   Difference between net sales and total cost of merchandise sold.

Gross Sales   Total sales before customer returns and allowances have been deducted.

Indirect Expenses   Expenses that do not relate to specific selling departments.

Median   Number that is at the midpoint in an array of numbers when those numbers are ranked according to value.

National Retail Federation   Trade organization for retailers.

Net Sales (also called **Sales Value, Sales Productivity**, or **Operating Income**) Sales after deductions have been made for customer returns and allowances.

Operating Statement (Profit and Loss Statement or **Income Statement)**   Presentation of figures summarizing income, cost of merchandise sold, and expenses for a specific period, usually a month, season, or year.

Operating Profit   Gross margin less operating expenses.

Selling Cost   Relationship, usually expressed as a percent, between gross salary and net sales for a salesperson, department, and/or store.

Chapter 3 • Summary Problems

1. Determine (a) net sales and (b) customer return percent for the handbag department when the following transactions occurred.

Sales:	$ 69.00	$ 50.00	Returns:	$60.00
	85.00	140.00		28.00
	110.00	75.00		98.00
	18.00	69.00		
		36.00		

2. The bath shop buyer anticipates he can sell 150 units if priced at $4.95 or 90 units if priced at $7.95. Which retail will result in larger total dollar sales?

3. Calculate profit or loss percent. Cross out the incorrect word (profit/loss).

Net sales	$317,870
Cost of merchandise sold	181,186
Expenses	169,870

4. Calculate profit or loss percent. Cross out the incorrect word (profit/loss).

Gross sales	$98,340
Customer returns	4,320
Cost of merchandise sold	53,892
Expenses	40,780

5. Set up a skeletal statement with the following figures:

Net sales	$178,000
Cost of merchandise sold	99,680
Profit	8,544

6. Set up a skeletal statement.

Net sales	$589,800
Gross margin	318,050
Expenses	319,600

7. Set up a skeletal statement.

Gross sales	$87,980
Customer returns and allowances	5,430
Gross margin	33,680
Expenses	35,210

8. Set up a skeletal statement.

Cost of merchandise sold		53%
Expenses	$124,558	
Profit	$ 6,850	2.45%

9. Determine the figures necessary to complete a skeletal statement.

Net sales	$679,860	
Gross margin		41.80%
Loss		(1.20%)

10. Set up a skeletal statement.

Gross margin	$37,980	
Expenses		42.3%
Loss		(0.8%)

11. Determine (a) contribution percent and (b) profit percent.

Net sales	$287,600	
Cost of merchandise sold	$152,400	
Direct expenses		21.5%
Indirect expenses		19.80%

12. Calculate profit or loss percent.

Gross sales	$365,400	
Customer returns	$ 14,570	
Cost of merchandise sold		56.60%
Direct expenses		25.20%
Indirect expenses		19.30%

13. For the month of June, the sportswear department has planned net sales of $138,000. The selling cost is not to exceed 8.2%. How much can be spent for selling personnel?

14. A salesperson on commission earns $7.75 per hour plus 2% commission on sales. Last week she worked 38 hours and had net sales of $3,671. Calculate (a) selling cost percent and (b) average earnings per hour.

15. Calculate the selling cost percent for an entire department with the following information:

Salesperson	Gross Sales	Customer Returns & Allowances	Basis for Earnings	Hours
A	$5,876	$ 798	6% commission	38
B	4,935	510	6% commission	38
C	3,810	297	$7.75/hr + 2%	28
D	2,340	167	$7.75/hr + 2%	20
E	2,570	215	$7.15/hr	20

16. Last year the Accessory Shop had net sales of $9,340 with a selling cost of 10.2%. Since the minimum wage has been increased, sales personnel are being paid $7.85 per hour. If sales are expected to increase 8% this year, how many hours of sales assistance can be provided and still maintain a selling cost of 10.2%?

17. Calculate gross sales if net sales are $83,500 and customer returns and allowances are 7.8%.

18. Determine customer return and allowance percent when gross sales are $135,780 and net sales are $127,430.

19. Calculate gross sales if net sales are $532,560 and customer returns and allowances are 3.8%.

20. Calculate gross sales when net sales are $964,300 and customer returns and allowances are 6.8%.

CHAPTER 4

Cost of Merchandise Sold

OBJECTIVES

- To define and calculate different types of discounts offered to the retailer by the vendor, including quantity, trade, and cash discounts.
- To calculate the time period in which a discount may be taken with various forms of dating.
- To define and calculate anticipation rates, loading, and transportation costs.

KEY POINTS

- The amount the retailer actually pays for merchandise is affected by several factors in addition to the cost of the merchandise as quoted by the seller.
- Discounts, transportation charges, and alteration costs affect the total cost of merchandise.
- Although there may be other factors that the vendor and retail buyer negotiate, "terms of sale" specifically refers to cash discounts and dating.

The most important consideration in selecting merchandise for resale to ultimate consumers is the merchandise itself. Is it suitable for the store's clientele? Does it fit in with merchandise already in stock and/or on order? If the answers to these questions are "yes," additional consideration should be given to purchasing the merchandise.

COST NEGOTIATIONS

The amount a retailer actually pays for merchandise is determined by (1) quoted wholesale cost, (2) discounts, and (3) transportation charges. The extent to which a buyer can negotiate the cost of merchandise varies.

The quoted wholesale cost established by the manufacturer covers expenses and a profit. Well-known designers often approach manufacturers to produce goods bearing the designer's label. This is known as **licensing**. The designer is the licensor and the manufacturer is the licensee. In these cases the manufacturer produces and sells the goods and gives a royalty to the designer for using his/her name. Royalties range from a low of 5% upward. This extra expense is added into the wholesale price, making these goods more expensive for the buyer.

For many goods, the cost is established and not open to negotiation; however, buyers of large quantities, especially those who purchase early or late in the season or those doing **specification buying**, may be able to negotiate cost. Specification buying is conducted by very large stores or buying offices representing groups of stores such as Sears, Wal-Mart, Federated Department Stores, and The Limited. Specification buying can vary from asking for a minor change in a product already designed to developing extensive requirements or specifications (specs) for the product and its packaging. Specification buying allows a retailer to offer different, exclusive merchandise not available in competing stores.

Even after the buyer and seller agree on a **wholesale price** (price that is used on the store's order form and vendor's invoice), that quoted cost is rarely the exact amount the store pays for the merchandise. There may be discounts that reduce the cost. In addition, the store generally pays transportation charges associated with getting the merchandise to the store or store's distribution center. These factors—discounts and transportation costs—should be negotiated if at all possible. Other considerations in selection of vendor and merchandise include minimum quantities, reorder availability, exclusivity, packaging, and promotional aids.

DISCOUNTS

A **discount** is a reduction in price allowed by the vendor. Any individual or firm from whom the retailer buys merchandise is referred to as a **vendor**. The vendor may be a manufacturer, wholesaler, or even another retailer.

Many discounts have become standardized through the years. Vendors anticipate such discounts and quote prices accordingly. Retail buyers should attempt to negotiate for the best possible discounts, especially if the discount on desired merchandise is lower than discounts offered by sellers of similar merchandise. It is important for buyers and manufacturers' sales representatives alike to be proficient at negotiating because both are seeking to obtain the best price for their companies. There are numerous reasons for granting discounts. Discussed in this chapter are quantity, trade, and cash discounts.

Quantity (Patronage) Discounts

Quantity discounts are discounts allowed when a large specified quantity is purchased. The amount of discount usually increases as the quantity purchased increases. A quantity discount can also be called a **patronage discount** because it encourages the buyer to concentrate purchases or continue to patronize the same vendor. A quantity discount is allowed when a given quantity is purchased. Such a discount, depending on custom and practice within individual industries, is offered either when a stated quantity is purchased or for accumulated purchases over a specific period of time.

Quantity discounts are seldom available with apparel; however, they are sometimes used in the home furnishings industry. The **Robinson-Patman Act**, which outlaws price discrimination in interstate commerce, does not forbid quantity discounts when the discounts are used to pass on savings that result from manufacturing, selling, and/or packaging of larger quantities. A quantity discount, when offered by a vendor, must be made available to all retailers who qualify. **A quantity discount is deducted prior to any other type of discount and is deducted regardless of when the invoice is paid.**

EXAMPLE 4-1

A carpet manufacturer's discount schedule allows 0.5% discount on orders for 600 to 1,000 square yards, 1% discount on orders for 1,001 to 2,000 square yards, and 2% discount on orders over 2,000 square yards. A furniture store ordered 759 square yards of carpeting costing $6.90 per square yard. After the discount was deducted, how much was remitted to the manufacturer?

Solution: $759 \times \$6.90 = \$5,237.10$

Less 0.5% discount = $\$5,237.10 - \$26.19 = \$5,210.91$

Trade (Functional) Discounts

Trade discounts are a percent deducted from a list price of the manufacturer or supplier. **List price** is referred to as the manufacturer's suggested retail price. The **billed cost** represents the resultant figure after applying the trade discounts to the list price.

List price less a percent or series of percents is a customary way of quoting cost for some types of merchandise. The list price may be, but does not have to be, the same as the retail price. Today, list prices frequently are higher than retail prices. The list price may be set higher than the typical retail price to make customers think they are receiving a special value.

Quoting a discount from an established list price allows a vendor to adjust cost easily. This is an advantage to vendors who picture and describe merchandise in catalogs, such as furniture vendors. A price change can be made quickly by printing new price lists with a change in the discount.

Trade discounts may be expressed as one of a "series" of discounts. For example, the cost may be quoted as "$25.00 less 40% and 15%" or "40 and 15 off." When two or more discounts are quoted in a series, each discount is deducted separately.

EXAMPLE 4-2

A billfold has a list price of $25.00 with a discount of 40% and 15%. What is the final cost of this billfold?

Solution:

List price	$25.00
Less 40%	− 10.00
	15.00
Less 15%	− 2.25
Cost	$12.75

When a series of discounts are to be taken, the numbers in the series cannot be added together. A discount of 40% and 15% results in a different billed cost than does a discount of 55%. (Try it to prove the difference.)

There are several ways series discounts can be calculated. In addition to the direct method shown in the previous example, complement and on-percent methods may be used. Both the complement and on-percent methods use the complement of the discount. Study the following examples.

EXAMPLE 4-3

Find the billed cost of a vacuum cleaner that has a list price of $200 with discounts of 40% and 15%.

Solution: (Use one of the three ways.)

1. **Direct method**: With the direct method, each discount is taken individually and subtracted from the previous balance or preceding net amount.

   $200 less 40% = $200 − $80 = $120
   $120 less 15% = $120 − $18 = $102, billed cost

2. **Complement method**: When the complement of the discount is used, it is not necessary to subtract the amount of the discount from the previous figure. The complement, which is 100% minus the discount, is multiplied by the previous balance or preceding net amount.

   List price = $200
   $200 × 60% (complement of 40%, or 100% − 40%) = $120
   $120 × 85% (complement of 15%, or 100% − 15%) = $102, billed cost

3. **On-percent method**: The on-percent is calculated by multiplying the complements of the discounts. The billed cost is determined by multiplying the list price by the on-percent. With the on-percent method, a lower percent is better since it will provide a lower billed cost.

   On-percent = 60% × 85% = 51% (60% is the complement of 40%) (85% is the complement of 15%)

   Billed cost = $200 × 51% = $102

A trade discount is frequently a **functional discount**. When the amount of discount allowed depends on the "function" of the purchaser (industrial user, wholesaler, retailer, interior designer), the discount is known as a functional discount. Industrial users and wholesalers get larger or additional discounts than retailers because they provide different services in the channel of distribution and generally purchase in much larger quantities. The services provided by middlemen such as wholesalers generally reduce the costs of the manufacturer. A retailer might receive a 30% discount; the wholesaler might receive a discount of 30% and 10%; the industrial user's discount might be 30%, 10%, and 5%.

Cash Discounts

Cash discounts are a percent reduction from quoted cost allowed for prompt payment of the invoice. Cash discounts are the most common type of discount. A cash discount is a percent reduction from quoted cost that can be taken if the invoice is paid within the specified period of time. For many types of merchandise the percent of reduction is standard for regular-priced goods. The buyer of promotional merchandise (goods bought to be sold at a lower price point for a special sale) may be offered a smaller discount than normally associated with that type of merchandise. Anytime the buyer is quoted a discount less than the customary discount, the buyer may be able to negotiate for better terms.

The cash discount percent is written on the store's order form and specified on the vendor's invoice. **"Terms"** refer to the cash discount and dating. **Dating** refers to the time limits for payment of the invoice. "Terms of 8/10" means an 8% cash discount can be taken if the invoice is paid within 10 days from the date of the invoice. The **invoice date** is usually the date on which the merchandise is shipped.

The cash discount is deducted after all other types of discounts have been deducted. The cash discount is taken on **billed cost**. Billed cost is the cost after quantity and/or trade discounts have been deducted, but before the cash discount is taken. Billed cost is shown on the vendor's invoice. Billed cost can also be referred to as **gross cost**. When a cash discount is the only discount allowed on merchandise, the quoted cost is the same as billed cost.

EXAMPLE 4-4

The list price of a bottle of shampoo is $2.00 less 30% and 20%. A 3% cash discount may be taken if paid within 10 days. What is the amount to be paid on an order for 5 dozen bottles when the cash discount is taken? (Remember: 5 dozen is equivalent to 60 units.)

Solution: Total list price, $60 \times \$2.00 = \$120.00$
Less trade discounts:
    $120.00 less 30% = \$84.00$
    $84.00 less 20% = \$67.20$, billed cost
Less cash discount, $67.20 less 3% = \$65.18$, amount due

EXAMPLE 4-5

The coat buyer ordered 18 all-weather coats that cost $39.00 each. An 8% cash discount is deducted. What amount is paid to the vendor?

Solution:

Total billed cost, $18 \times \$39 = \$702$
Less cash discount, $\$702 - (\$702 \times 8\%) = \$702 - \$56.16$
Net cost = $\$645.84$

Technically, in order to receive the cash discount, the retailer must pay for the merchandise within the period of time specified. Large retailers now have a great deal of bargaining power and often extend the period during which they take the discount. This creates friction between the manufacturer and the retailer.

A store should plan its cash flow to be able to take advantage of cash discounts. In most instances, it is cheaper to borrow than lose cash discounts; however, when interest rates are very high, this may not be the case. Retailers need to protect their credit reputations by paying bills on time. Although the buyer is responsible for negotiating the best terms and dating, the buyer does not pay the bills.

Cash discounts act as a profit cushion for the retailer. In 1997, cash discounts earned were 1.45% of retail sales for department stores and 0.36% of sales for specialty stores as reported in *FOR/MOR*. The buyer usually determines retail based on billed cost (gross) of merchandise. When a cash discount is taken, the actual amount the store pays for the merchandise is reduced. The buyer cannot know for certain that cash discounts will be taken because paying invoices is a responsibility of accounts payable and will depend on the cash available at the time the merchandise is received.

On the other hand, cash discounts can be a profit cushion for the manufacturer. Manufacturers include the cost of cash discounts when establishing their wholesale prices. Thus, when the retailer pays after the cash discount period and does not receive a discount, the manufacturer has an extra profit.

Net terms means a cash discount is not allowed. The entire billed cost, as shown on the invoice, is due by the date specified.

Stores keep separate totals for billed cost of merchandise, freight, and cash discounts. On the retailer's operating statement, cash discounts are usually subtracted from gross cost of merchandise sold to determine net cost of merchandise sold. A few stores treat cash discounts as "other income earned" and add it to the operating profit; however, this procedure is not recommended by the National Retail Federation.

There are many other types of discounts and allowances. For example, **seasonal discounts** may be given for ordering and/or accepting merchandise out of season. A **promotional discount** may be given to compensate the retailer for advertising or displaying the product.

ALLOWANCES

Allowances are given by a manufacturer to a retailer to encourage business. For example, a **trade allowance** from a vendor is provided as compensation to the store for stocking and/or displaying merchandise. It is an incentive for retailers and vendors to work together. Trade allowances are typically negotiated during market weeks.

Buying allowances reduce the price of merchandise for a specific, limited time period. The price reduction may be either a dollar amount or a percent off the invoice price—an off-invoice allowance. Buying allowances can also be extra amounts of merchandise—an extra dozen with the purchase of ten dozen.

Manufacturers offer **promotional allowances** to retailers who support the manufacturer's products with promotional activities. Manufacturers develop promotional plans that retailers carry out, such as floor displays, in-store promotions, or advertising programs.

An allowance may be granted as a percent of the cost of the merchandise, but it is more common for an allowance to be granted as a specific dollar amount, specific amount per unit purchased, or percent of service provided. Often stores use an allowance to reduce the cost of the service rather than reduce the cost of the merchandise. For example, an advertising allowance would offset the cost of time or space used for the advertisement. An allowance for display would offset the costs associated with display.

Manufacturers may offer **slotting allowances**, which are also called **stocking** or **introductory allowances** or **street money**, to encourage retailers to stock a product for the first time. These allowances can range from a few hundred to several millions of dollars. Although some feel this is bribery, retailers feel the allowances offset the cost of introducing a new product.

REBATE

Rebate is another term that may be used in connection with an adjustment in the cost of merchandise. Rebate is a refund of part of the cost of the merchandise. For example, a manufacturer might give the retailer a rebate to reduce the cost of merchandise sold during a sale authorized by the manufacturer. This would allow the retailer to reduce the retail price without having to take a markdown or lowering markup.

Practice Problems • Exercise 4.1

1. The accessories buyer placed the following order for small leathergoods. The merchandise cost is list price less 40% and 15%. Calculate billed cost for the entire order.

Quantity (dozen)	Item	List Price ($)	Total Cost of Items
$1\frac{1}{4}$	Cell phone cases	22.50 each	$337.50
$2\frac{1}{2}$	Billfolds	30.00 each	900.00
$1\frac{1}{6}$	French purses	35.00 each	490.00
$\frac{3}{4}$	Card cases	18.00 each	162.00

$1,889.50 × .60 × .85

= $963.65

2. The carpet buyer placed an order for 1,260 square yards of carpet at $11.90 per square yard. A 2% cash discount is taken. Based on the following discount schedule, how much will be paid to the vendor?

$14,994.00

Quantity (yards)	Discount (%)
500–1,000	0.75
1,001–1,800	1.25 → $14,806.58
1,801–2,500	1.75 × .98
Over 2,500	2.00

$14,510.45

3. A cash discount of 6% is allowed on an invoice for $1,654 dated September 16. If the cash discount is taken, how much will be remitted to the vendor?

$1,554.76

4. A manufacturer offers the gift buyer a line of carved wooden items that has trade discounts of 30% and 20%. The buyer orders merchandise that has a total list price of $978. If a 2% cash discount is taken on this order, what will be the amount remitted?

× .70 × .80 = $547.68
× .98

$536.73

5. As a stocking dealer, the Johnson Brothers furniture store buys the Chrome Craft line of furniture for list less 30%, 20%, and 5%. If paid within 15 days, a 2% cash discount is allowed. On the following order, how much should be remitted for all items if the cash discount is taken?

Quantity	Item	List Price ($)	Total Cost of Items
3	215–100 tables	395.00 each	$1,185.00
6	215–201 chairs	159.00 each	954.00
12	215–203 chairs	129.00 each	1,548.00
			$3,687.00

$1,922.25

6. Calculate the on-percent for the series discount in problem 5.

.70 × .80 × .95 = .532
53.20%

7. A textile converter who specializes in drapery fabric sells to furniture stores with discounts of 30%, 20%, and 10%. Individual interior designers are allowed discounts of 30% and 20%. On an order with total list cost of $500, what is the difference in cost for a furniture store compared to an individual designer?

furniture store = $500.00 × .70 × .80 × .90 = $252.00
indiv. designer = $500.00 × .70 × .80 = $280.00

$28.00 difference

8. (a) From the buyer's viewpoint, which is the better series of discounts for the buyer: 25%, 15%, and 10% or 30%, 15%, and 5%? (b) Which would be the better series of discounts for the manufacturer?

(a.) .57375 nd. .56525 ∨ 30%, 15%, $5%

(b.) 25%, 15%, 10%

9. A buyer for Sears is able to negotiate discounts of 30%, 10%, 5%. KiKi's specialty store in Omaha is able to negotiate only a 5% discount. What is the price that each will pay for an item listed at $500?

Sears = $299.25
KiKi = $475.00

10. A buyer places an order totaling $5,460 from a vendor offering trade discounts of 30%, 10% with a 3% cash discount if paid 10 days from the invoice date. If the buyer pays on time, how much should be remitted?

$3,336.61

DATING

Dating refers to the length of time the retailer has to pay the invoice and the time during which the cash discount can be taken. When a cash discount is allowed, two different dates are calculated. One date, known as the **discount date**, is the last day in the discount period; this is the last day on which the discount can be taken. The other date calculated is the **net payment date**. The net payment date is the last day for payment before the bill is overdue and interest might be added to total cost. For example, on an invoice dated July 6 with terms 3/10, n/30, the discount date is July 16. The net payment date is August 5, exactly 30 days from July 6.

Cash on Delivery (COD)

Occasionally a store is not granted credit and must purchase merchandise on a **COD** basis. A new store that does not have a credit rating, a store that is considered a poor credit risk, or a store purchasing internationally might be forced to pay for merchandise when delivered. (In particularly risky situations, cash before delivery (CBD) or cash with order (CWO) may be used, but this is rare.)

Regular (Ordinary or Normal) Dating

Regular dating (also known as **ordinary** or **normal dating**) is calculated from the date of the invoice, which is usually the date the merchandise is shipped. For example, terms of 3/10, n/30 mean a 3% discount can be taken if the invoice is paid within 10 days. If not paid within 10 days, the complete or net amount is due 30 days from the invoice date. If the net period is not specified, it will be 30 days with regular dating.

EXAMPLE 4-6

Calculate discount and net payment dates for an invoice dated October 15 with terms of 2/10, n/30.

Solution: The last day on which the cash discount can be taken is (15 + 10 = 25) October 25.
If not paid by October 25, the full amount is due within 30 days or November 14.
October has 31 days, so days left in October (31 − 15) = 16.
Net payment date (30 − 16 = 14) is November 14.
The invoice is considered overdue if not paid by November 14.

Receipt of Goods (ROG)

When terms are **ROG**, the dating is calculated from the date the merchandise is received at the store rather than from the date of the invoice. A store that is far away from the manufacturer or that selects a slow method of transportation might request ROG dating. When merchandise on an invoice dated March 5 is received on March 12 with terms of 2/10 ROG, the last day for the cash discount is March 22. Net payment date is an additional 20 days, April 11 in this instance, unless some other stipulation is noted.

End of Month (EOM)

With **EOM** dating, the discount date is calculated from the end of the month instead of the date of the invoice. In the apparel industries, 10/EOM is common dating. The last day on which the cash discount may be taken will be the 10th of the month. An invoice dated June 11 with terms of 8/10 EOM has a discount date of July 10 (10 days after the end of June). With EOM dating, the net period is an additional 20 days.

In EOM dating (and only EOM dating), an invoice dated **on or after** the **26th** of the month is considered to be dated the first of the following month.

The last day for taking the cash discount on an invoice dated June 28 with terms of 8/10 EOM will be August 10. The invoice is handled as though its date were July 1; therefore, the last day for taking the cash discount is August 10.

With EOM dating, whether an invoice is dated on the 25th or the 26th makes a great deal of difference in the cash discount date. For example, October 10 is the last day on which the cash discount can be taken on an invoice dated September 25 with EOM terms. However, if the invoice is dated September 26, only one day later, November 10 is the last day for the cash discount.

X-Dating (Extra Dating)

Extra dating extends credit for an additional period. For example, an invoice with terms of 3/10–30X has a cash discount period of 40 days (10 days plus an extra 30 equals 40 days). If the invoice is paid within the 40 day period, the retailer will receive a 3% discount.

EXAMPLE 4-7

On an invoice with terms of 3/10–60X dated May 11, the cash discount period is 70 days (10 plus 60 equals 70). Thus, the cash discount can be taken through July 20.

Solution:

Days left in May (31 – 11)	20
June has 30 days	+ 30
Total days at end of June	50

Additional days needed 70 – 50 = 20

July 20 is the last day on which the cash discount can be taken.

With X-dating the net period ends after an additional 20 days. In Example 4-7, the last day for payment in full (no cash discount) would be August 9 (11 days left in July plus 9 extra to equal 20).

Advanced Dating ("As Of")

Advanced dating and **"as of"** both refer to the same type of dating. Time for payment is calculated from some specified future date that is neither the date of the invoice nor the date the goods are received. Such an invoice might be dated June 12 with terms of 3/10, n/30 as of September 1. The last day for payment with cash discount deducted would be September 11; if not paid by September 11, the entire amount is due by September 31.

Practice Problems • Exercise 4.2

1. A buyer receives an invoice for $500; assuming the buyer paid on time, use the following terms and calculate:

(a) the last day on which the cash discount may be taken

(b) the amount to be remitted if the discount is taken

Invoice Date	Date Merchandise Is Received	Terms	Cash Discount Date	$ Amount Due
a. February 6 +10	February 11	3/10, n/30	2/16	#485.00
b. August 18	August 29 +10	3/10 ROG	9/8	485.00
c. July 10	July 15	8/10 EOM	8/10	460.00
d. October 15 +40 +10 Nov	October 20	6/10–30X	11/24	470.00
e. March 28 Apr 30	April 3	8/10 EOM	5/10	460.00
f. July 5 +70 -26	July 11	6/10–60X	9/13	470.00
g. December 3	December 7	1/10, n30	12/13	495.00
h. September 19	September 30 +10	3/10 ROG	10/10	485.00
i. May 29 June 30	June 5	8/10 EOM	7/10	460.00
j. July 5	July 23	6/10 as of October 1 +10	10/11	470.00
k. May 14	May 21	3/10 EOM	6/10	485.00
l. December 1	December 5	1/10, n/30	12/11	495.00
m. July 25	August 2	6/10 as of November 1	11/11	470.00
n. June 28 +50	July 8	3/10–40X	8/17	485.00
o. January 18	January 24 +10	6/10 ROG	2/3	470.00

ANTICIPATION

In addition to the cash discount, some vendors allow an additional discount, referred to as anticipation, if the invoice is paid before the end of the cash discount period. (This practice is particularly helpful when extra dating or advanced dating is used. With either of these forms of dating, the length of time between the sale and payment to the manufacturer is extended, so the manufacturer offers anticipation as an extra incentive to buyers to pay early.)

Anticipation can be thought of as "interest" deducted from the vendor's payment because the vendor receives payment early. **Anticipation is an additional discount that is based on the number of days remaining between the date of payment and end of the cash discount period.** Anticipation rate will vary somewhat according to prevailing interest rates. When interest rates are high, retailers may not find it advantageous to pay early and take anticipation.

All problems are to be worked with an anticipation rate of 6% per year, which is equivalent to 0.5% per month (half of one percent).

With anticipation it is necessary to calculate the number of days that remain between the date of payment and end of the cash discount period. For example, an invoice for $1,200 with terms of 2/10-60X could have the cash discount deducted if paid within 70 days. If paid in 40 days, there would be 30 days remaining in the cash discount period. The amount of anticipation for these problems is to be calculated at the rate of 6% per year. (A year is assumed to have 360 days rather than 365.) Anticipation for 30 days would be $(30 \div 360) \times 6\% = 0.00499$, which is 0.5%.

The anticipation and cash discount percents are generally added together and taken as one discount. **This is the only instance when two discounts can be added together.**

EXAMPLE 4-8

An invoice for $600 dated July 20 has terms of 8/10-30X, anticipation permitted. How much should be remitted if paid on August 14?

Solution: The cash discount period is 40 days (10 + 30). The bill is paid on the 25th day. (July has 31 days; 31 − 20 = 11; there are 11 days left in July. The invoice is paid on August 14, which is the 25th day (11 + 14 = 25.) There are 15 (40 − 25 = 15) days remaining in the cash discount period. Anticipation may be taken for 15 days.

Anticipation = $(15 \div 360) \times 6\% = 0.2499\% = 0.25\%$

Anticipation + cash discount = $0.25\% + 8\% = 8.25\%$

Net cost = $600 × 8.25% = $49.50
= $600 − $49.50 = $550.50

EXAMPLE 4-9

An invoice for $1,200 dated August 29 has terms of 8/10 EOM, anticipation permitted. If paid on September 16, how much should be remitted?

Solution: Cash discount period expires October 10. If paid on September 16, take anticipation for 24 days.

Anticipation $= (24 \div 360) \times 6\%$
$= 0.00399\ (0.4\%)$

Anticipation + cash discount $= 0.4\% + 8\% = 8.4\%$

Net cost $= \$1,200 \times 8.4\%$
$= \$100.80$
$= \$1,200 - \$100.80$
$= \$1,099.20$

1. An invoice for $960 dated July 15 has terms of 2/10-30X, anticipation permitted. How much should be remitted if paid on August 4?

2. An invoice dated October 12 has a total list price of $1,640 less 40% and 10% with terms of 3/10-40X, anticipation permitted. If paid on November 3, how much should be remitted?

3. The dress buyer purchases with terms of 8/10 EOM, anticipation permitted. An invoice for $860 dated September 28 is paid on October 12. How much should be remitted?

4. An invoice dated March 14 for $640 has terms of 8/10 EOM, anticipation permitted. If paid on April 2, how much should be remitted?

5. An invoice for $1,638 is dated June 16; the merchandise arrived on June 28. Terms are 3/10 ROG, anticipation permitted. If paid on July 2, how much should be remitted?

6. An invoice for $1,200 dated June 15 has terms of 3/10-40X, anticipation permitted. How much should be remitted if paid on July 1?

7. An invoice for $2,500 dated April 15 has terms of 3/10-30X, anticipation permitted. How much should be remitted if paid on April 20?

LOADING

Because cash discounts provide a "profit cushion," a retailer may decide to increase cash discounts by **loading** the invoices. **Loading refers to an increase in the billed cost that is offset by an increased cash discount.**

The retailer's invoice cost is increased to permit a larger cash discount than what is typically available at the vendor's going rate, but results in paying the same amount that the vendor quotes. Thus, the net cost of the merchandise is not changed. Loading is frequently practiced in the purchase of imported merchandise.

Loading may be done by the vendor, or it may be a practice used by the store's accounting office to carry all inventory at the same rate of discount or to provide a profit cushion. Some retailers desire to have all inventory charged to the various departments at the same cash discount rate. When the cash discount percent actually obtained is less than the percent set by the store, the store's accounting office will "load" the cost. It is important to remember that loading does not change the amount the store actually pays for merchandise.

Loaded Cost = Net Cost ÷ Complement of the Cash Discount Desired

Handbags are typically purchased with a 3% discount, whereas sportswear manufacturers typically allow an 8% discount. If the handbag buyer desired to purchase with an 8% cash discount, the vendor might "load" the invoice to allow the larger discount.

EXAMPLE 4-10

A handbag with quoted cost of $36.00 is sold with a 3% cash discount. What is the loaded cost when sold with 8% discount?

Solution:

Net cost = $36.00 less 3% = $34.92

Loaded Cost = Net Cost ÷ Complement of the Cash Discount
= $34.92 ÷ (100% − 8%)
= $34.92 ÷ 92% = $37.96

Check the answer: $37.96 less 8% = $34.92

EXAMPLE 4-11

The neckwear buyer has placed the following order with a manufacturer who quotes terms of 2/10, n/30. Traditionally, neckwear manufacturers have sold with 3% discount, so the buyer asks the manufacturer to load the invoice to allow a 3% discount. What will be the total billed cost of this merchandise when loaded for a 3% discount?

Quantity	Item	Cost
$5\frac{1}{3}$ dozen	Silk scarves	$90.00/dozen
$2\frac{3}{4}$ dozen	Stoles	$14.50 each

Solution:

$5\frac{1}{3}$ dozen (64) × $90/dozen ($7.50 each) = $480.00

$2\frac{3}{4}$ dozen (33) × $14.50 each   = + 478.50

                                                                  $958.50

Net cost = $958.50 − ($958.50 × 2%)

          = $958.50 − $19.17

          = $939.33

Loaded Cost = Net Cost ÷ Complement of the Cash Discount

                   = $939.33 ÷ 97%

                   = $968.38

Practice Problems • Exercise 4.4

1. A handbag that normally costs $49.00 is sold with a 3% cash discount. If the buyer wants to buy with an 8% discount, what is the loaded cost?

2. Merchandise on an order totaling $1,567 is normally sold with a 6% cash discount. What will be the loaded cost if sold with an 8% cash discount?

3. The glove buyer wants to buy with an 8% cash discount. Most of the glove vendors quote 6% cash discounts. What will be the total cost of the following order when loaded for an 8% discount?

Quantity	Style	Cost
5½ dozen	1066	$66.00/dozen
8¾ dozen	1290	$90.00/dozen
2⅓ dozen	1410	$10.50/each

4. An order totals $1,387 for merchandise normally sold with terms of 1/10, n/30. What will be the loaded price if sold with 3/10, n/30 terms?

5. An order totals $2,341 for merchandise normally sold with terms of 2/10, n/30. What will be the loaded price if sold with 4/10, n/30 terms?

6. An order totals $5,667 for merchandise normally sold with terms of 3/10, n/30. What will be the loaded price if sold with 8/10, n/30 terms?

TRANSPORTATION COSTS

Because more companies today are geographically widening their sources for merchandise, and because shipping charges are rising, the negotiation of transportation costs and handling responsibilities is of major importance. This becomes even more important when stores source internationally due to additional costs associated with crating and other costs. In most instances, the store pays the transportation costs associated with getting merchandise to the store.

Transportation costs assumed by the store are considered part of the cost of the merchandise and must be covered in the retail price. Because transportation costs become part of the cost of merchandise, it is important that the retailer negotiate for advantageous shipping charges as a means of reducing the total cost of goods.

The buyer should indicate on the order the type of transportation to be used. Today, shipping costs are high, and the buyer needs to take into consideration both the shipping costs and time required for transportation. If the merchandise is not needed immediately, it may be possible to use a slower method of transportation and reduce freight/transportation costs.

The term that frequently is used in negotiating transportation costs is **FOB (free on board)**. The location specified after the initials FOB indicates **the point at which ownership of the merchandise changes**. The buyer may use more specific locations when determining the actual FOB point. For example, terms such as store, plant, factory, and warehouse are often used for the destination point of the merchandise.

When ordering merchandise, the buyer must consider who will pay the cost of transportation and determine the point of ownership transfer. Transportation terms that can be negotiated between the vendor and retailer may be designated as FOB factory, FOB destination, FOB shipping point, and FOB destination; charges reversed.

FOB Factory.   This arrangement indicates that the buyer takes title to the merchandise at the point of shipment (factory). The buyer pays all transportation charges and assumes all risks for the goods while in transit.

FOB Destination.   This agreement states that the vendor pays all transportation costs and retains title to the merchandise until it arrives at the place designated by the buyer. It can also be written as FOB store or FOB buyer's warehouse.

FOB Shipping (Consolidation) Point.   This agreement means that the vendor pays any crating and transportation costs for getting the merchandise to the shipping company that will transport the goods to the retailer. It can also be written as FOB consolidation point. The retailer takes ownership of the goods at that point and is responsible for cost of getting the goods to the store or receiving point.

FOB Destination, Charges Reversed.   This agreement indicates that the vendor owns the goods until they get to the buyer's designated point; however, the buyer agrees to pay the transportation charges.

In most instances the transportation charges must be prepaid. This means transportation costs are paid by the vendor when the merchandise is delivered to the carrier such as UPS, a freight forwarder, or the U.S. Postal Service. When merchandise is FOB factory and freight has been prepaid, the retailer reimburses the vendor for shipping charges by adding shipping charges to the cost of the merchandise. The amount remitted to the vendor equals the net cost of merchandise plus the cost of transportation.

EXAMPLE 4-12

Merchandise with total quoted cost of $1,312 was billed on an invoice dated March 18 with terms of 8/10 EOM, anticipation not permitted, FOB factory. Transportation costs of $12.87 were prepaid. How much should be remitted to the vendor if the invoice is paid April 10?

Solution:

$1,312 less 8%	$1,207.04
(plus) transportation	+ 12.87
Amount to be repaid	$1,219.91

EXAMPLE 4-13

An invoice for $2,500 was dated June 15 with terms of 6/10, n/30, anticipation not permitted, FOB store. Freight charges were $265. What amount was to be remitted if the retailer paid the bill on June 24?

Solution: FOB store means the vendor is responsible for transportation costs.

$2,500 less 6% = $2,350

Amount to be paid = $2,350

The retailer does not reimburse the vendor for transportation.

FACTORS

The volatile nature of the fashion industry since the 1980s has resulted in numerous retail bankruptcies, leaving retailers without means to pay manufacturers for inventory shipped. Today, retailers and manufacturers generally partner with financial companies called **factors**, which are financial intermediaries that collect manufacturers' receivables from retailers. This also allows the manufacturer to receive payment quickly. When a buyer places an order, the manufacturer calls the factor to receive confirmation that the store is fiscally stable and has the ability to pay promptly. Factors then buy the manufacturer's receivables at a discounted rate that covers their commission and risk. The factor immediately pays a percent of the invoice (usually 80%) to the manufacturer so that the manufacturer has working capital. The factor later collects from the retailer and completes the invoice payment to the manufacturer.

Practice Problems • Exercise 4.5

1. If merchandise is shipped FOB vendor's distribution center, is the retailer or the vendor responsible for paying transportation costs?

2. An invoice for costume jewelry is dated October 22 with terms of 3/10, n/30, FOB Providence, Rhode Island (vendor's warehouse). The total billed cost of the merchandise is $956.20, and shipping charges of $12.80 have been prepaid. If the invoice is paid November 10, how much should be remitted?

3. Merchandise with a total billed cost of $2,230 arrived at the store on May 16. Terms of the invoice dated April 25 were 3/10 ROG, FOB store. No anticipation is permitted. Transportation charges were $128. If paid on May 21, how much should be paid?

4. A jeans manufacturer in Blue Bell, Texas ships all merchandise FOB Dallas. His own trucks take the merchandise into Dallas where it is turned over to the carrier specified by the retail buyer. A store in Kansas has ordered merchandise with a total billed cost of $1,258. Terms are 8/10 EOM. This entire order is shipped August 22 with transportation charges of $26.50 (from Dallas to Kansas City) prepaid. If the store pays for this merchandise on September 10, how much should be paid to the vendor?

5. A sportswear buyer receives a shipment of 40 dozen pairs of pants costing $21 each. The invoice is dated April 29 with terms 6/10 EOM, FOB store. No anticipation is permitted. Shipping charges are $182. If the bill was paid on May 11, how much was remitted to the vendor?

6. A hosiery manufacturer in North Carolina has agreed to extend the dating so the retailer can use a cheaper, but slower method of transportation. Rather than customary terms of 2/10, terms of 2/10-30X, anticipation permitted, have been agreed upon. Transportation is FOB factory. Merchandise with a billed cost of $987.40 was shipped on April 14 with transportation charges of $14.80 prepaid. If the invoice is paid on May 10, how much should be remitted? (Take anticipation.)

7. A buyer for the children's department agreed to order merchandise with terms of 8/10, n/30. The invoice was dated January 25, anticipation not permitted, FOB destination, charges reversed. The total cost of the merchandise was $128,230 and transportation was $251. How much should be remitted if paid on February 14?

8. A buyer for home furnishings orders merchandise from a North Carolina vendor totaling $2,800. The vendor offers two options: (a) 3/10 net 30 FOB destination (buyer's warehouse) or (b) 6/10 FOB factory. If transportation costs are $250, which would be the better option for the buyer?

DEFINITIONS

Allowance   Reimbursement or compensation granted to the retailer by the seller in return for specific services such as advertising or display. For example, the vendor may agree to an advertising allowance whereby the retailer and vendor split the cost of the advertisement.

Anticipation   An additional discount allowed by some vendors if the bill is paid before the expiration of the cash discount period. Traditionally, anticipation has been at the rate of 6% per year, but it varies according to prevailing interest rates. Anticipation is taken on the days between payment and the end of the cash discount period.

Billed Cost/Gross Cost   The price shown on the vendor's invoice after deductions for trade and/or quantity discounts but before cash discounts are taken.

Buying Allowance   A price reduction for buying merchandise during a specified time period.

Dating   The time limits that apply to paying for merchandise. Dating involves two different time periods: (1) the last day on which the cash discount can be taken and (2) the last day for payment before the bill is considered overdue.

> *Advanced Dating/"As Of"*   The time periods are calculated from some future stipulated time.

> *COD*   Cash on delivery means payment is due when buyer receives goods.

> *EOM Dating*   The discount day is calculated from the end of the month. Invoices dated on or after the 26th are considered to be the first of the following month.

> *Extra Dating* (*X-Dating*)   The cash discount period is extended for an additional number of days.

> *Regular/Ordinary/Normal Dating*   The time periods are calculated from the date of the invoice.

> *ROG Dating*   The time periods are calculated from the date the goods are received.

Discount   A reduction in price allowed by the seller.

> *Cash Discount*   A percent reduction in price allowed if the store pays for merchandise before some specified date; a price reduction allowed for prompt payment.

> *Promotional Discount*   An allowance given to compensate a retailer for the expense of promoting a product.

> *Quantity/Patronage Discount*   A reduction in cost that is based on the size of the order.

> *Seasonal Discount*   A discount given for purchasing goods out of season.

> *Trade/Functional Discount*   A percent reduction from list price that may be one or a series of discounts.

Factor   Financial intermediary that collects manufacturer's receivables from retailers.

FOB (Free on Board)   A shipping term placed before a specific location such as factory, origin, store, and so forth. That location is the point at which title (ownership) to the merchandise changes.

> *FOB Destination*   The vendor pays all transportation costs and owns the merchandise until it arrives at the place designated by the buyer. It can also be written as FOB Store or FOB Buyer's Warehouse.

FOB Destination, Charges Reversed   The vendor owns the goods until they get to the buyer's designated point; however, the buyer pays the transportation charges.

FOB Factory   The buyer takes title to the merchandise at the point of shipment (Factory). The buyer pays all transportation charges and assumes all risks for the goods while in transit.

FOB Shipping Point   The vendor pays any crating and costs necessary for getting the goods to a point where they can be turned over to a transportation company. It can also be written as FOB Consolidation Point. The retailer pays transportation costs from the shipping point to the store/distribution center.

Invoice   A bill that is enclosed with a shipment of merchandise or mailed by the seller to the buyer.

Invoice Date   The date on the invoice, which usually is the date the merchandise is shipped.

Licensing   An agreement between a manufacturer and a designer that grants the manufacturer permission to produce under the designer's label in return for a royalty on merchandise sales.

List Price   The manufacturer's suggested retail price. The price or dollar amount to which the trade discount is applied to obtain the billed cost.

Loading   An increase in the billed cost of merchandise that is offset by a larger than normal cash discount. The net cost of the merchandise does not change.

Net Payment Date   Last day on which the buyer can pay for an invoice before it is considered overdue.

Net Price   Resulting figure after applying total discounts to the billed price.

Net Terms   Notation on invoice that indicates a cash discount is not allowed.

Rebate   A refund of part of the cost of the merchandise.

Slotting/Stocking/Introductory Allowance or **Street Money**   Allowance given for stocking a new product.

Specification Buying   A buying process whereby the retailer describes specific product characteristics to the manufacturer that detail how the goods are to be made.

Terms of Sale   Cash discounts and dating applicable to an invoice.

Trade Allowance   Compensation given for stocking or displaying merchandising.

Vendor   Individual or firm from whom retailers buy merchandise.

Wholesale Price   The amount the vendor charges for the goods.

Chapter 4 • Summary Problems

1. An invoice dated May 15 with trade discounts of 40% and 15% has terms of 3/10, n/30. The invoice is for

Quantity	Item	List Price
3$\frac{1}{4}$ dozen	Clutch	$35.00 each
2$\frac{1}{3}$ dozen	Billfold	$30.00 each
1$\frac{1}{6}$ dozen	French purse	$45.00 each
2$\frac{1}{3}$ dozen	Card case	$25.00 each

How much should be remitted if paid on: (a) May 25? (b) June 10?

2. An invoice is dated June 28 for $867.60 with terms of 8/10 EOM, anticipation not permitted. Merchandise was received on July 3. How much is due if paid (a) on or before July 10? (b) on August 10? (c) on August 30?

3. Merchandise received on July 20 is charged to the store on an invoice dated July 8 for $1,254 with terms of 6/10-60X, anticipation permitted.

   (a) What is the last day for taking the cash discount?
   (b) If paid on August 30, how much should be remitted?

4. A vendor who normally sells with a 3% cash discount is asked to sell with an 8% discount. What will be the loaded cost of merchandise normally selling for $968 when loaded to allow the 8% discount?

5. Merchandise costing $2,085 reaches the store on April 2. The invoice is dated March 22 and has terms of 8/10 EOM. This vendor allows anticipation. The invoice is paid on April 10.

   (a) How much should be remitted?
   (b) If the merchandise were shipped FOB New Orleans, Louisiana, charges reversed, with transportation charges of $11.85, how much should be remitted?

6. Merchandise with a total billed cost of $876.48 arrived at the store October 6. Terms of the invoice dated September 22 were 3/10 ROG, FOB store. Transportation charges were $9.82. If paid on October 16, how much should be paid?

7. A wholesaler ordered 14 bolts of drapery fabric at $5.50 per yard. Each bolt had 60 yards. This order qualified for a quantity discount of 2%. The merchandise was shipped FOB factory; freight charges of $21.80 were prepaid. The invoice was dated March 18 with terms of 2/15, n/30. How much should be remitted if paid on March 29?

8. The buyer for the children's department is offered advanced dating and free transportation if the store will accept delivery of winter coats in August. The invoice dated August 1 has a total billed cost of $2,158.60 with terms of 8/10, n/30 as of October 1, anticipation not permitted, FOB store. The coats arrive August 8; transportation costs of $28.70 have been prepaid. If paid on October 11, how much should be remitted?

9. A sportswear buyer placed the following order for coordinates:

Quantity	Item	Cost
$4\frac{1}{2}$ dozen	Blouses	$19.00 each
$3\frac{1}{2}$ dozen	Skirts	$21.00 each
$2\frac{1}{4}$ dozen	Pants	$23.00 each
$3\frac{1}{6}$ dozen	Jackets	$36.00 each

The merchandise is shipped September 15 and received September 22. Invoice terms are 8/10 EOM, FOB factory; transportation charges of $24.79 have been prepaid. How much should be remitted if paid on (a) October 8? (b) October 25?

10. The toy buyer had the option of ordering stuffed animals directly from the manufacturer or from a nearby wholesaler. The manufacturer will not ship orders for less than $1,200 total list price. Delivery typically requires five weeks and freight charges average 2.5% of total billed cost. Trade discounts on this merchandise are 40% and 10%; terms are 2/10, n/30.

A wholesaler, located in the retailer's area, stocks many of the same stuffed animals. He does not require a minimum order and will deliver at no charge in the area if the order has a billed cost of at least $500. The manufacturer and wholesaler base cost on the same list price; however, the wholesaler sells with trade discounts of 40% and 8% and terms of 1/15, n/30.

(a) What is the difference in the total net cost (including freight) of merchandise with a total list price of $1,200 from these two vendors? (Be sure to take the cash discount).

(b) What other considerations will influence the choice of vendors?

CHAPTER 5

Markup as a
Merchandising Tool

OBJECTIVES

- To understand the importance of markup when pricing merchandise.
- To develop skill in calculating dollar markup and markup percent.
- To understand how a buyer averages markup on various items in an attempt to achieve planned markup goals.
- To define and calculate three types of markup: initial, maintained, and cumulative.

KEY POINTS

- Markup refers to the difference between retail price and cost price. Markup serves as a guide in pricing merchandise and in providing the desired operating profit.
- Retailers primarily express markup as a percent because it facilitates analysis and comparison of merchandising and operating statistics.
- Markup percents may vary both within and among classifications and departments.
- It is important to understand basic markup equations in order to make effective buying and pricing decisions.

MARKUP DEFINED

Markup is one of the most important and fundamental concepts used in merchandising operations. It is a major tool used in pricing merchandise but should serve as a guide rather than a determinant in establishing selling prices.

One way to define markup is that it is the amount added to the cost price in order to establish the retail price. Markup serves as a guide in pricing merchandise and in providing the desired operating profit. Careful analysis and planning of prices are necessary in order to achieve a profit. Pricing considerations and strategies are discussed in Chapter 6. Before retailers set prices, it is important to have a basic understanding of markup definitions and calculations. **Another way to define markup is the difference between the retail price of merchandise and its cost.**

> Markup = Retail – Cost

This formula may also be written as:

> Cost = Retail – Markup

and

> Retail = Cost + Markup

Even though retailers are primarily concerned with markup as a percent, markup can be expressed as a dollar figure. The basic formula is the same whether working with dollar figures or percents.

Markup is sometimes referred to as markon. Although the terms **markup** and **markon** are often used synonymously, they may have slightly different meanings. **Markup is most commonly applied to the amount added to cost to determine the retail price for individual items, whereas markon is sometimes used to refer to the total amount added to the cost of all the merchandise in a department.** Furthermore, markon is more frequently used at the manufacturing level and markup at the retail level of the distribution chain. **In this workbook, the term markup will be used.**

MARKUP AS A PERCENT

Retailers find working with percents more meaningful than working with markup dollars because percents allow for comparisons. Comparisons may be made within and/or among classifications and departments. Markup statistics are frequently exchanged among stores within an ownership group and among stores using the same resident buying office. For example, Federated Department Stores might compare the markup figures of Bloomingdale's to those of Macy's. Trade associations such as the National Retail Federation, Retail Hardware Association, and National Association of Chain Drug Stores compile and summarize markup figures as well as other operating statistics.

Markup can be calculated as a percent of cost or of retail price. Most department stores and fashion specialty stores base markup on retail price. The retail base is generally accepted as more meaningful because expenses and profits are figured as percents of net sales. The calculation of markup on retail provides consistency because retailers plan price lines, stock, and sales in retail values. Markup and expense percents cannot be compared if they are based on different figures; both must be based on either retail or cost figures. **In this workbook, all markup problems are to be calculated as a percent of retail price unless otherwise instructed.**

Calculating Markup Percent Based on Retail

To determine markup percent based on retail, divide dollar markup by retail. Dollar markup is equal to retail minus cost. When markup percent is based on retail, retail always equals 100%.

$$\text{\$ Markup} = \text{\$ Retail} - \text{\$ Cost}$$

$$\text{Markup \% Based on Retail} = \text{\$ Markup} \div \text{\$ Retail}$$

EXAMPLE 5-1

What is the markup percent (based on retail) for a dress that costs $40 and retails for $80?

Solution: Markup % = $ Markup ÷ $ Retail
                        = ($80 – $40) ÷ $80
                        = $40 ÷ $80
                        = 0.50
                        = 50% (based on retail)

EXAMPLE 5-2

A coat retails for $200. Find the markup percent based on retail when the cost of the coat is $105.

Solution: Markup % = $ Markup ÷ $ Retail
                        = ($200 – $105) ÷ $200
                        = $95 ÷ $200
                        = 0.475
                        = 47.5% (based on retail)

Calculating Markup Percent Based on Cost

Markup based on cost price is sometimes used by small, independently owned stores. These stores may be reluctant to change because of habit and unwillingness to discontinue old, trusted methods. Large department stores and chain stores seldom base markup on cost.

To determine the markup percent based on cost, divide dollar markup by cost. Because cost is the base, cost equals 100%.

$$\text{Markup \% Based on Cost} = \text{\$ Markup} \div \text{\$ Cost}$$

EXAMPLE 5-3

A man's suit retails for $210 and costs $120. What is the markup percent based on cost?

Solution: Markup % = $ Markup ÷ $ Cost
                        = ($210 − $120) ÷ $120
                        = $90 ÷ $120
                        = 0.75
                        = 75% (markup based on cost)

EXAMPLE 5-4

Determine the markup percent based on cost for a shirt that costs $25 and retails for $40.

Solution: Markup % = $ Markup ÷ $ Cost
                        = ($40 − $25) ÷ $25
                        = 0.60
                        = 60% (markup based on cost)

Comparison of Markup Based on Cost and Retail

Markup percent based on retail is always less than 100%; however, markup percent based on cost may exceed 100%. It is important to understand the difference between markup based on cost and on retail. Markup percent based on cost is always larger than markup percent based on retail (see Table 5-1).

The following table of markup equivalents shows a comparison of markup based on cost and markup based on retail. As you can see, markup percents based on cost are always larger than markup percents based on retail. The retail price remains constant, whereas the markup percent varies according to whether the retail or cost base is used.

Table 5-1
Comparison of Markup Based on Cost and Retail

Markup Based on Cost (%)	Markup Based on Retail (%)
25	20
$66\frac{2}{3}$	40
100	50
150	60
300	75
900	90

> ### EXAMPLE 5-5
>
> Compare the markup percents when based on retail and on cost for a blouse that costs $24 and retails for $40. First, find the dollar markup, which is $16 ($40 − $24).
>
> | **Based on Retail** | **Based on Cost** |
> |---|---|
> | $\dfrac{\$ \text{Markup}}{\$ \text{Retail}} = \dfrac{\$16}{\$40} = 40\%$ | $\dfrac{\$ \text{Markup}}{\$ \text{Cost}} = \dfrac{\$16}{\$24} = 66.67\%$ |

It is important to remember that the base figure is always 100%. **When finding markup based on retail, retail is 100%, and when determining markup based on cost, cost is 100%.**

BASIC MARKUP CALCULATIONS

When working with basic markup calculations, it may be helpful to write the appropriate formula and insert the given dollar and percent figures. This will make the relationships more apparent. **Remember, because you are working with markup based on retail, retail will always be 100%.**

Some students may find the problems clearer by arranging the three factors vertically rather than horizontally.

$$\begin{array}{ccc} \text{Markup} & \text{Retail} & \text{Retail} \\ \underline{- \text{Cost}} & \underline{- \text{Markup}} & \underline{- \text{Cost}} \\ \text{Retail} & \text{Cost} & \text{Markup} \end{array}$$

Markup percent can be calculated when cost and retail are known. Retail can be calculated when cost and markup percent are known, and cost can be calculated when markup percent and retail are known. A buyer works with markup in three different ways:

1. Calculating markup percent when cost and retail are known
2. Calculating retail when cost and markup percent are known
3. Calculating cost when retail and markup percent are known

Calculating Markup Percent When Cost and Retail Are Known

To achieve maximum profits, a buyer must evaluate many factors when purchasing merchandise. When evaluating whether to buy an item, a buyer must consider if markup obtained is adequate to reach the department's ultimate goal. To determine markup percent, find markup dollars ($ retail minus $ cost) and divide by retail dollars. When given the dollar cost and dollar retail, the markup percent can be determined by using the formula.

> Markup % = $ Markup ÷ $ Retail

EXAMPLE 5-6

What is the markup percent on a jacket that costs $66 and retails for $120?

Solution:

		$	%
Retail	=	$120 =	100%
– Cost	=	– 66 =	
Markup		$ 54	?

Markup % = Markup $ ÷ Retail $
= $54 ÷ $120
= 45%

EXAMPLE 5-7

What is the markup percent on a shirt that costs $18 and retails for $34?

Solution: Markup $ = $ Retail – $ Cost
= $34 – $18
= $16

Markup % = Markup $ ÷ Retail $
= $16 ÷ $34
= 47.06%

Note: Remember the rule from Chapter 2, round off percents so that the answers are correct to two decimal places; for example, in this previous example 0.470588 = 47.0588% is rounded off to 47.06%.

Calculating Retail When Cost and Markup Percent Are Known

When making purchases, buyers must evaluate the retail prices that will be placed on merchandise considering the cost price and the markup percent needed. Buyers need to consider the retail prices to determine if customers would be willing to buy merchandise at these prices.

To determine the retail price when given the cost and markup percent, find the cost complement (100% – markup %) and divide dollar cost by cost complement percent. **The cost complement or cost percent is the difference between retail percent (100%) and markup percent.** For example, the cost complement of a 40% markup is 60% (100% minus markup %). This is the same as saying that cost is 60%. The following formulas are helpful for finding retail when the cost and markup percents are known:

Cost Complement % = Retail % – Markup %

$ Retail = $ Cost ÷ Cost %

EXAMPLE 5-8

Calculate the retail price on a sofa table that costs the store $420 and has a 52% markup.

Solution:

		$	%
Retail	=		100
− Markup	=		− 52
Cost	=	$420	48%

$$\$\text{ Retail } = \$\text{ Cost} \div \text{Cost \%}$$
$$= \$420 \div 48\%$$
$$= \$875$$

Calculating Cost When Retail and Markup Percent Are Known

Buyers must be able to determine the price they can afford to pay for each item purchased in order to achieve their planned markup goal. To determine the cost when retail dollars and markup percent are known, find the cost complement percent and multiply retail (dollars) times cost complement percent.

$$\$\text{ Cost} = \$\text{ Retail} \times \text{Cost \%}$$

EXAMPLE 5-9

Determine the cost of a dress that retails for $180.00 and has a 55% markup.

Solution:

$$\text{Cost Complement } = \text{Retail \%} - \text{Markup \%}$$
$$= 100\% - 55\%$$
$$= 45\%$$

$$\$\text{ Cost } = \$\text{ Retail} \times \text{Cost \%}$$
$$= \$180 \times 45\%$$
$$= \$81$$

EXAMPLE 5-10

An alternate solution to determine cost dollars is to find markup dollars and subtract markup dollars from retail dollars.

Solution:

$$\$\text{ Cost } = \$\text{ Retail} - \$\text{ Markup}$$
$$= \$180 - (\$180 \times 55\%)$$
$$= \$180 - \$99$$
$$= \$81$$

When working with markup, you are applying the same basic percent calculations that were reviewed in Chapter 2. For example, when determining retail, you are using the same calculation as finding the base figure. Retail is 100% because it is the base figure.

Practice Problems • Exercise 5.1

Fill in the blanks for questions 1 through 15.

	Retail ($)	Cost ($)	Markup (%)	Cost (%)
1.	$149.00	_____	$67\frac{1}{4}\%$	_____
2.	$25.00	$12.75	_____	_____
3.	_____	$45.98	50%	_____
4.	$440.00	_____	75%	_____
5.	$150.00	$100.00	_____	_____
6.	_____	$80.00	$65\frac{1}{2}\%$	_____
7.	$30.00/dozen	_____/unit	54%	_____
8.	$22.98	_____	42.5%	_____
9.	_____	$120.00	48%	_____
10.	$14.50	$7.83	_____	_____
11.	_____	$100.00	44%	_____
12.	$3.80	_____	$52\frac{1}{5}\%$	_____
13.	_____/unit	$100.80/dozen	60%	_____
14.	$650.00	$375.00	_____	_____
15.	$95.50	_____	58%	_____

16. Hand-tooled belts for the men's department cost $180 a dozen. If a 47.5% markup is required, what unit retail would achieve this markup? $15.00 $CC\% = 0.525$

$28.57

17. Find the cost of a dress that retails for $185 and has a 55% markup. $185.00 × .45

$83.25

18. What retail price on a walnut entertainment center that costs $2,500 would provide a 58% markup?

$2,500.00 ÷ .42 = $5,952.38

133

19. Determine the markup percent on a child's hand-smocked dress that costs $45 and retails for $110.

$$\frac{\$110.^{00} - 45.^{00}}{\$110.^{00}} = 59.09\%$$

20. A buyer of men's furnishings paid $168 per dozen for jute belts. What unit retail will provide a 52.25% markup?

$14.^{00}

CC% = .4775

$14.^{00} ÷ .4775 = $29.^{32}

21. A furniture store's feature of the week is a cherry table that retails for $1,200 with a 64% markup. Find the cost of the table.

36%

$1,200.^{00} × .36 = $432.^{00}

22. The paint department received a shipment of brushes that cost $4.50 each and retail for $9.75 each. Find (a) the cost percent and (b) the markup percent.

46.15%   53.85%

23. What were (a) the cost percent and (b) dollar cost for a scarf that retails for $18 and was marked up 40.5%?

59.50% $18.^{00} × .5950 = $10.^{71}

24. Determine the markup percent for hand-blown wine glasses costing $132 a dozen and retailing for $22 each.

$11.^{00}

50.00%

25. Determine the markup percents (a) based on retail and (b) based on cost for an antique mirror that the buyer purchased for $850 and priced at retail for $1,500.

(a.) $650.^{00} ÷ 1,500 = 43.33%

(b.) $650.^{00} ÷ 850 = 76.47%

MARKUP PERCENT ON A GROUP OF ITEMS

At times it is necessary to determine the markup percent on an order or shipment of merchandise that includes items with different cost and retail values.

To compute the markup percent on an entire order (merchandise with varying cost and/or retail values), determine the total cost and total retail, then subtract to determine total markup dollars.

EXAMPLE 5-11

Find the markup percent on the following order:

Quantity	$ Cost	$ Retail
14 skirts	20 each	45 each
25 blouses	18 each	40 each
10 belts	16 each	30 each

Solution: Find total cost and total retail.

Cost	Retail
$14 \times \$20 = \$280$	$14 \times \$45 = \$\ \ 630$
$25 \times \$18 = \$450$	$25 \times \$40 = \$1{,}000$
$10 \times \$16 = \underline{\$160}$	$10 \times \$30 = \underline{\$\ \ 300}$
Total cost $\ \ \$890$	Total retail $\ \ \$1{,}930$

Find total markup dollars.

$$\begin{aligned} \$ \text{ Markup} &= \$ \text{ Retail} - \$ \text{ Cost} \\ &= \$1{,}930 - \$890 \\ &= \$1{,}040 \end{aligned}$$

Find markup percent.

$$\begin{aligned} \text{Markup \%} &= \$ \text{ Markup} \div \$ \text{ Retail} \\ &= \$1{,}040 \div \$1{,}930 \\ &= 0.53886 \\ &= 53.89\% \end{aligned}$$

EXAMPLE 5-12

Determine the markup percent on the following group of merchandise:

Quantity	$ Cost	$ Retail
120 pr socks	36.00/dozen	6.50 each
120 pr socks	2.50 each	5.50 each

Solution: Find total cost and total retail.

Cost	Retail
$120 \times \$3.00 = \$360$	$120 \times \$6.50 = \$\ \ 780$
$120 \times \$2.50 = \underline{\$300}$	$120 \times \$5.50 = \$\ \ \underline{660}$
Total cost $660	Total retail $1,440

Find total markup dollars.

$$
\begin{aligned}
\$\ Markup &= \$\ Retail - \$\ Cost \\
&= \$1,440 - \$660 \\
&= \$780
\end{aligned}
$$

Find markup percent.

$$
\begin{aligned}
Markup\ \% &= \$\ Markup \div \$\ Retail \\
&= \$780 \div \$1,440 \\
&= 0.54166 \\
&= 54.17\%
\end{aligned}
$$

Practice Problems • Exercise 5.2

1. Determine the markup percent on the following order:

Quantity	$ Cost	$ Retail
18 belts	$90.⁰⁰ 60.00/dozen	80.⁰⁰ 10.00 each
11 scarves	121.⁰⁰ 11.00 each	220.⁰⁰ 20.00 each
14 stickpins	63.⁰⁰ 4.50 each	140.⁰⁰ 10.00 each

$274.⁰⁰ $540.⁰⁰

49.26%

2. A buyer coordinated a special purchase of men's shirts from a manufacturer. Determine the markup percent on this purchase:

Quantity	$ Cost	$ Retail
14 white shirts	210.⁰⁰ 15 each	476.⁰⁰ 34 each
24 plaid shirts	480.⁰⁰ 20 each	912.⁰⁰ 38 each
45 oxford shirts	630.⁰⁰ 14 each	1350.⁰⁰ 30 each
10 knit shirts	100.⁰⁰ 120/dozen	250.⁰⁰ 25 each

$1,420.⁰⁰ $2988.⁰⁰

52.48%

3. Find the markup percent on this order, which a buyer purchased for a special sale:

100 hand towels costing $22.80/dozen to sell at $3.50 each

116 9²/₃ dozen washcloths costing $1.20 each to sell at $2.10 each

85 bath towels costing $4.25 each to sell at $8.00 each

27 2¹/₄ dozen beach towels costing $5.50 each to sell at $10.98 each

$C
190.⁰⁰
$838.95 139.²⁰
361.²⁵
148.⁵⁰

#R
$350.⁰⁰
243.⁶⁰ $1,570.⁰⁰   46.57%
680.⁰⁰
296.⁴⁶

4. Determine the markup percent on the following purchase for a handbag department:

Quantity	$ Cost	$ Retail
24 2 dozen	264.⁰⁰ 132/dozen	480.⁰⁰ 20 each
14 1¹/₆ dozen	210.⁰⁰ 15 each	392.⁰⁰ 28 each
40 3¹/₃ dozen	480.⁰⁰ 12 each	1,000.⁰⁰ 25 each

$954.⁰⁰ $1,872.⁰⁰

49.04%

5. What is the markup percent on the following order?

Quantity	$ Cost	$ Retail
30 brass lamps	3,570 119 each	5,940 198 each
24 crystal lamps	4,536 189 each	9,600 400 each
18 porcelain lamps	2,862 159 each	5,850 325 each
	$10,968.00	$21,390.00

48.72%

$3,360.00 $1,920.00

6. The buyer needs a group of T-shirts for a special sale. He buys 40 dozen at $84/dozen, 20 dozen at
$1,800.00
$96/dozen, and 15 dozen at $120/dozen. If he marks them all at a sale price of $18.00 each, what markup
percent is realized on the merchandise?   75 dozen total = 900

Total Cost = $7,080.00
Total Retail = $16,200.00

56.30%

AVERAGING MARKUP

When pricing merchandise, retailers do not apply the same markup percent to all merchandise. Even in the same classification, not all merchandise will have identical markups. For instance, the buyer may take a lower markup on promotional goods, whereas it may be possible to obtain a higher markup on exclusive or unique items.

Merchandise must be priced to sell in a competitive environment. To achieve maximum sales, buyers may have to use markups that are considerably more or less than the desired overall markup goal. That is, buyers must balance markups that are below average with above average markups to achieve the planned department markup goal.

The use of averaging markup is common in apparel and home furnishings departments because of the rapid change in fashion. The buyer usually has less control over markups on staple items, but increased promotional emphasis can be given to lines carrying the higher markups.

Averaging markup can apply to the markup on an entire stock of goods, a single purchase, or a group of purchases.

An average markup is determined by working with total cost and total retail. The example below illustrates how to find total cost and total retail.

EXAMPLE 5-13

A buyer has placed an order for 20 shirts that cost $14 each and will retail for $24 each. She also purchases 18 shirts costing $12 each and retailing for $21 each. Find the total cost and total retail.

Solution:

Units	× Cost price	=	Total cost
20	× $14	=	$280
18	× $12	=	$216
			$496

Units	× Retail price	=	Total retail
20	× $24	=	$480
18	× $21	=	$378
			$858

The average markup cannot be determined by averaging the markup on individual items. **An average markup is determined by working with the total cost and total retail. Remember, individual percents cannot be averaged unless the quantities are exactly the same.**

The sections that follow illustrate three types of averaging markup problems:

1. Calculating markup percent needed on balance of purchases when planned markup percent is known
2. Averaging costs when retail and markup percent are known
3. Averaging retail when cost and needed markup percent are known

Each section begins with an explanation indicating the circumstances under which such a problem might occur in a retail store.

The following examples will help you understand the process used in averaging problems. When working word problems, it is important to understand clearly what you are trying to find. In solving these word problems, the first steps are to determine information given and identify information needed to complete the problem. Several steps are required to solve each problem.

Calculating Markup Percent Needed on Balance of Purchases When Planned Markup Percent is Known

Buyers must be able to determine the markup percent needed on balance of purchases in order to achieve the planned markup goal (an average). This requires working with total cost and total retail values. The following examples illustrate calculating markup percent needed on a balance of purchases when planned markup percent is known.

EXAMPLE 5-14

A buyer for a children's department needs $12,000 worth of merchandise at retail for the month. She has already purchased 200 dresses that cost $18.00 each and will retail for $30.00 each. What markup percent must she obtain on the remaining purchases in order to average a 54% markup for the month?

	Total Needs	Purchases	Balance
Retail	$12,000	200 at $30 (b) $6,000	(d) $6,000
Cost	(a) $5,520	200 at $18 (c) $3,600	(e) $1,920
Markup %	54%		Markup balance (f) 68%

First ask: What are you trying to find? Markup percent on balance.

Solution: (a) Find total needs at cost.

$$\text{Cost} = \$\text{ Retail} \times \text{Cost \%}$$
$$= \$12,000 \times (100\% - 54\%)$$
$$= \$12,000 \times 46\% = \$5,520$$

(b) Find retail value of purchases.
$$\text{Retail} = 200 \times \$30 = \$6,000$$

(c) Find cost value of purchases.
$$\text{Cost} = 200 \times \$18 = \$3,600$$

(d) Find balance at retail.
$$\text{Retail Balance} = \text{Total Retail} - \text{Retail of Dresses Purchased}$$
$$= \$12,000 - \$6,000 = \$6,000$$

(e) Find balance at cost.
$$\text{Cost Balance} = \text{Total Cost} - \text{Cost of Dresses Purchased}$$
$$= \$5,520 - \$3,600 = \$1,920$$

(f) Find markup percent needed on balance.

$$\text{Markup \% Balance} = \frac{\text{Retail Balance} - \text{Cost Balance}}{\text{Retail Balance}}$$

$$= \frac{\$6,000 - \$1,920}{\$6,000} = \frac{\$4,080}{\$6,000} = 68\%$$

EXAMPLE 5-15

The buyer for the children's department plans to purchase approximately $3,800 (retail) worth of sweaters. She will operate with a 52.5% markup. Her first purchase is for 6 dozen sweaters costing $14.60 each that she plans to retail for $24.90 each. What percent markup must be obtained on the balance of sweaters in order to average a 52.5% markup?

	Total Needs	Purchases	Balance
Retail	$3,800	6 dozen at $24.90 (c) $1,792.80	(d) $2,007.20
Cost	(a) $1,805	6 dozen at $14.60 (b) $1,051.20	(e) $753.80
Markup %	52.5%		Markup balance (f) 62.45%

Solution:

(a) Find total needs at cost.

$$\text{Total Cost} = \$ \text{ Retail} \times \text{Cost \%}$$
$$= \$3,800.00 \times (100\% - 52.5\%)$$
$$= \$3,800.00 \times 47.5\%$$
$$= \$1,805.00$$

(b) Find cost value of purchases.

6 dozen = 72 units
$72 \times \$14.60$ each = $1,051.20 cost

(c) Find retail value of purchases.

$72 \times \$24.90$ each = $1,792.80 retail

(d) Find balance at retail.

$$\text{Retail Balance} = \text{Total Retail} - \text{Retail of Sweaters Purchased}$$
$$= \$3,800.00 - \$1,792.80 = \$2,007.20$$

(e) Find balance at cost.

$$\text{Cost Balance} = \text{Total Cost} - \text{Cost of Sweaters Purchased}$$
$$= \$1,805.00 - \$1,051.20 = \$753.80$$

(f) Find markup percent needed on balance.

$$\text{Markup \%} = \text{Markup \$ on Balance} \div \$ \text{ Retail Balance}$$

$$= \frac{\$2,007.20 - \$753.80}{\$2,007.20} = \frac{\$1,253.40}{\$2,007.20} = 62.45\%$$

Averaging Costs When Retail and Markup Percent Are Known

Many times a buyer will have a retail price line that consists of merchandise with different costs. This means buying merchandise at close but different costs and marking the goods at the same retail price. The following examples illustrate the calculation of averaging costs when retail dollars and markup percents are known.

EXAMPLE 5-16

A buyer plans to purchase 300 pairs of slacks for an Anniversary Sale to retail for $26.00 each. The buyer has already placed an order for 170 pairs at $12.00 each (cost). What is the most he can pay for each remaining pair of slacks if he is to achieve the department's markup goal of 52%?

	Total Needs	Purchases	Balance
Retail	300 at $26 (a) $7,800		
Cost	(b) $3,744	170 at $12 (c) $2,040	(d) $1,704 (total) (e) $13.11 (unit)
Markup %	52%		

First ask: What are you trying to find? Unit cost on balance.

Solution: (a) Find total retail.
$$300 \times \$26 = \$7,800$$

   (b) Find total cost.
$$\begin{aligned} \text{Cost} &= \$\,\text{Retail} \times \text{Cost \%} \\ &= \$7,800 \times (100\% - 52\%) \\ &= \$7,800 \times 48\% \\ &= \$3,744 \end{aligned}$$

   (c) Find the cost of slacks purchased.
$$170 \times \$12 = \$2,040$$

   (d) Find the balance that can be spent on slacks.
   Total Cost – Cost of Slacks Purchased = Balance
   $3,744   – $2,040   = $1,704

   (e) Find unit cost of slacks to be purchased.
   Number of slacks still needed = 300 – 170 = 130
   Cost Balance ÷ Number of Slacks Still Needed = Unit Cost
   $1,704 ÷ 130 = $13.11 each

EXAMPLE 5-17

A sportswear buyer needs to average a 48% markup. He needs 120 skirts to retail at $21.00 each and 80 jackets to retail at $38.00 each. If he pays $20.00 for each jacket, how much can he pay for each skirt in order to achieve his planned markup percent?

	Total Needs	Purchases	Balance
Retail	80 at $38		
	120 at $21		
	(a) $5,560		
Cost	(b) $2,891.20	80 at $20	Total (d) $1,291.20
		(c) $1,600	Unit (e) $10.76
Markup%	48%		

First ask: What are you trying to find? Cost per skirt.

Remember: You must find totals before determining unit cost.

Solution:

(a) Find total retail for the merchandise.

80 (jackets) × $38 = $3,040

120 (skirts) × $21 = $2,520

$5,560 total retail needed

(b) Find total cost for the merchandise.

$$Cost = \$ Retail \times Cost \%$$
$$= \$5,560 \times (100\% - 48\%)$$
$$= \$5,560 \times 52\%$$
$$= \$2,891.20$$

(c) Find cost of the jackets purchased.

80 × $20 = $1,600 cost

(d) Find the balance cost that can be spent on skirts.

Total Cost – Cost of Jackets = Cost of Skirts

$2,891.20 – $1,600 = $1,291.20

(e) Find the unit cost of each skirt.

Cost Balance ÷ Number of Skirts to be Purchased = Unit Cost

$1,291.20 ÷ 120 = $10.76 unit cost

Averaging Retail When Cost and Needed Markup Percent Are Known

In order to achieve a planned markup goal, buyers must determine an average retail price for purchases made at two or more different cost prices. The following examples involve finding an average retail price when costs and markup percents are known.

EXAMPLE 5-18

A buyer for the men's department purchased a group of shirts that consisted of 10 shirts at $11.00 each; 20 shirts at $12.00 each; and 12 shirts at $14.00 each. He plans to sell all the shirts at the same price. What unit retail price will result in a 58% markup?

Markup %	Cost	Retail
58%	10 at $11	Total retail (b) $1,233.33
	20 at $12	Unit retail (c) $29.37
	12 at $14	
	42	
	Total cost	
	(a) $518	

First ask: What are you trying to find? Retail per shirt.

Solution: (a) Find total cost.

$10 \times \$11 = \$110$

$20 \times \$12 = \$240$

$12 \times \$14 = \underline{\$168}$

$\$518$ total cost

(b) Find total retail needed to obtain a 58% markup.

Retail = $ Cost ÷ Cost %

= $518.00 ÷ 42%

= $1,233.33

(c) Find retail for each shirt.

Retail per Shirt = Total Retail ÷ Number of Shirts

= $1,233.33 ÷ 42

= $29.37

Each shirt should retail for at least $29.37 to obtain a 58% average markup.

EXAMPLE 5-19

The sportswear buyer purchased 30 corduroy jackets that cost $34.75 each and 48 tweed jackets that cost $39.75 each. She wants a 55.5% overall markup. If she retails the corduroy jackets for $60.00 each, what must the average retail price be for each tweed jacket in order to achieve the planned markup percent?

Markup %	Cost	Retail
		(b) Total retail = $6,630.34
55.5%	30 at $34.75	(c) 30 corduroy at $60 = $1,800
	48 at $39.75	(d) 48 tweed = $4,830.34
		(e) unit $100.63
	Total cost	
	(a) $2,950.50	

First ask: What are you trying to find? Retail per tweed jacket.

Solution:

(a) Find total cost.

$30 \times \$34.75 = \$1,042.50$
$48 \times \$39.75 = \underline{\$1,908.00}$
$\$2,950.50$ total cost

(b) Find total retail needed to obtain a 55.5% markup.

Retail = $ Cost ÷ Cost %
= $2,950.50 ÷ 44.5%
= $6,630.34

(c) Find retail contributed by corduroy jackets.

$30 \times \$60$ each = $1,800

(d) Find retail needed for tweed jackets.

Retail for Tweed = Total Retail – Retail of Corduroy
= $6,630.34 – $1,800.00
= $4,830.34

(e) Find retail for each tweed jacket.

Retail for Each = Total Retail ÷ Number of Tweed Jackets
= $4,830.34 ÷ 48
= $100.63

Each tweed jacket should retail for at least $100.63 to achieve a 55.5% average markup.

Practice Problems • Exercise 5.3

1. A buyer purchased the following rugs:

25 Persian floral rugs	$1,210 each	$30,250.00
30 Aubusson rugs	$1,290 each	38,700.00
22 Kurdish rugs	$1,250 each	27,500.00
77		$96,450.00

The average markup percent must be 52%. What should be the retail price for each rug if all rugs are to be sold at the same price?

 $R is to be placed on each item

$$\$R = \$96,450 \div (1 - .52)$$
$$= \$200,937.50$$
$$\div 77$$
$$\$2,609.58$$

2. A buyer plans to purchase 400 skirts that will retail for $120 each. She has already placed an order for 320 skirts at $48 each (cost). What is the most she can pay for each of the remaining skirts if she is to obtain the departmental markup of 56.5%?

$C on balance of order

MU% 56.50%

	$R	$C
Total	$48,000.00	$20,880.00
On order (320)		$15,360.00
Balance (80)		$5,520.00

$$\$5,520.00 \div 80 = \$69.00$$

3. The owner of The Perfect Florist Shop intends to buy vases with a retail value of $14,000. He has purchased 200 vases at $14 each that will retail for $32 each. What markup should he obtain on the remaining vases in order to achieve a 62% markup goal?

MU% on balance

	$R	$C	MU%
Total	$14,000.00	$5,320.00	62.00%
Purchased 200	6,400.00	$2,800.00	
Balance	$7,600.00	$2,520.00	

$$MU\% \text{ on balance} = \frac{(\$7,600.00 - 2,520.00)}{\$7,600.00}$$
$$= \frac{\$5,080.00}{\$7,600.00}$$
$$= 66.84\%$$

$R your unit

4. For a holiday catalog, a buyer purchased the following decorative items at a manufacturer's closeout sale:

10 foot baths	$125 each	$1,250.00
15 ginger jars	$110 each	1,650.00
25 tureens	$ 75 each	1,875.00
14 planters	$ 90 each	1,260.00
		$6,035.00

If all decorative pieces are to be retailed at the same price, what unit retail price will result in a 61.25% markup?

$R $C   MU%.
                        $6,035.00   61.25%

$R = $6,035.00 ÷ .3875   C% = .3875
   = $15,574.19 ÷ 64
   = $243.34   or → $243.35

MU% or balance

5. A buyer for a small sporting goods store needs to purchase merchandise with a cost of $10,000. She has purchased football jerseys costing $8,000 that will retail for $14,000. If she is to achieve a 51.5% markup goal, what markup percent will be needed on the remainder of the goods?

	$R	$C	MU%.	C%
Total	$20,618.56	$10,000.00	51.50%	.485
Purchased	14,000.00	8,000.00		
Balance	$6,618.56	2,000.00	49.78%	

$C for balance

6. A buyer plans to purchase 150 blouses for a special sale that will retail for $48 each. She has already ordered 80 blouses at $20 (cost) each. What is the most she can pay for each remaining blouse if she is to achieve the department's average markup goal of 60%?

	$R	$C	MU%.
Total (150)	$7,200.00	$2,880.00	60.00%
On Order (80)		1,600.00	
Balance (70)		$1,280.00	

$18.29

$C for balance

7. For a Christmas catalog, a buyer plans to purchase 500 bird feeders to retail for $45 each. He placed an order for 350 feeders that cost $25 each. What is the most he can pay for each of the remaining feeders if he wishes to average a 42% markup?

	$R	$C	MU%.
Total (500)	$22,500.00	$13,050.00	42.00%
Order (350)		8,750.00	
Balance (150)		$4,300.00	

$28.67

8. A buyer for women's sportswear purchased 10 cotton sweaters at $52 each and 22 linen sweaters at $66 each. If all sweaters are to be retailed at the same price, what average retail price will provide a 52% markup?

$R per unit

$R $C   MU%.

Cotton 10 $520.00

linen 22   1,452.00

Total 32 $4,108.33 $1,972.00   52%.

$128.39

9. During the month, a buyer plans to purchase damask tablecloths that cost $8,000. He has purchased tablecloths that cost $2,000 and will retail for $3,800. What markup percent should the buyer obtain on the balance of his purchases in order to obtain a markup of 60%?

MU% on balance

$R $C   MU%.

Total   20,000.00 $8,000.00   60.00%.

Purch.   3,800.00   2,000.00

Balance $16,200.00 $6,000.00

62.96%

10. A buyer needs to purchase 200 scarves to sell for $25 each. He has ordered 140 scarves at $10 each (cost). What is the most he can pay for each of the remaining scarves to obtain an average markup of 54%?

$C on balance

$R $C   MU%.

Total (200) $5,000.00 $2,300.00   54.00%.

On order (140)   1,400.00

Balance (60) $ 900.00

$15.00

11. A buyer needs to average a 57% markup. He has purchased 50 silk jackets that cost $78 each and 38 wool jackets that cost $60 each. If he plans to retail the silk jackets for $175 each, what must be the average retail price for each of the wool jackets in order to maintain the planned markup percent?

$R price or balance

$R $C   MU%.

silk (50) $8,750.00 $3,900.00

Wool (38)   5,622.00   2,280.00

Total $14,372.00 $6,180.00   57.00%

$147.95

12. The buyer in the junior department plans to purchase $45,000 (retail) worth of jackets. She has purchased 5¼ dozen jackets costing $80 each, which she plans to sell for $140 each at retail price. What markup percent must be obtained on the balance of jackets in order to average a 53% markup?

MU% or balance

$R $C   MU%.

Total $45,000.00 $21,150.00   53.00%.

Purch.   8,820.00   5,040.00

Balance $36,180.00 $16,110.00   55.47%

MU% on balance

13. A buyer plans to purchase $30,000 (retail) worth of comforters. She purchased $9\frac{1}{2}$ dozen comforters costing $90 each, which she plans to sell for $180 each at retail price. What markup percent must be obtained on the balance of comforters in order to average a 48% markup?

	#R	#C	MU%
Total	$30,000.00	$15,600.00	48.00%
Purch.	20,520.00	10,260.00	
Balance	$9,480.00	$5,340.00	43.67%

MU% on balance

14. During July a buyer plans to buy suits with a retail value of $120,000. He has purchased 300 suits at $90 each that will retail for $200 each. What markup percent should he obtain on the remaining suits in order to achieve a 57% markup goal?

	#R	#C	MU%
Total	$120,000.00	$51,600.00	57.00%
Purch	60,000.00	27,000.00	
Balance	$60,000.00	$24,600.00	59.00%

#R for balance

15. A buyer needs to average a 60% markup. She has purchased 54 cashmere sweaters that cost $58 each and 48 merino wool sweaters that cost $32 each. If she plans to retail the cashmere sweaters for $139 each, what must be the average retail price for each of the merino wool sweaters in order to maintain the planned markup percent?

	#R	#C	MU%
Total	$11,670.00	$4,668.00	60.00%
Cashmere	7,506.00	3,132.00	
wool	$4,164.00	1,536.00	
	÷ 48		

$= \$86.75$

INITIAL MARKUP

The markup that is placed on merchandise as it is received into the store is initial markup. Initial markup can be planned by working with either dollar figures or percents. It is important to keep in mind that initial markup is based on the first or original retail price of the goods. Initial markup should be large enough to cover expenses and reductions and to provide a profit. A loss will occur if the initial markup does not cover expenses and reductions.

Initial Markup is the difference between billed cost of merchandise and the original retail price placed on an item or group of items.

Remember that billed cost is the price of the goods as stated on the vendor's invoice. When transportation charges are available, they are added to billed cost in calculating initial markup.

Billed Cost is the cost after quantity and/or trade discounts are deducted but before cash discounts are deducted.

$$\text{Initial Markup \%} = \frac{\text{Expenses} + \text{Profit} + \text{Reductions}}{\text{Net Sales} + \text{Reductions}}$$

As shown in the above formula, reductions must be added to both the numerator and denominator. Because markup must cover expenses, reductions, and profit, these factors are in the numerator. (Adjustments for alteration costs and cash discounts will be explained later.) The denominator represents the original retail value, that is, net sales plus reductions. Remember, initial markup is based on the first retail price.

Not all items in an assortment sell at the original retail owing to markdowns, discounts to employees and customers, and shortages. Because markdowns, employee discounts, and shortages reduce the sales that can be obtained from an assortment of merchandise, they are called retail reductions.

Retail Reductions are factors that reduce the retail value of a merchandise assortment. These factors include markdowns, employee discounts, special customer discounts, and stock shortages.

EXAMPLE 5-20

What should be the initial markup percent in a department having the following figures?

Net sales	$170,000
Profit	6,000
Expenses	80,000
Employee discounts	400
Markdowns	5,200
Shortages	600

Solution:

$$\text{Initial Markup \%} = \frac{\text{Expenses} + \text{Profit} + \text{Reductions}}{\text{Net Sales} + \text{Reductions}}$$

$$= \frac{\$80,000 + \$6,000 + (\$400 + \$5,200 + \$600)}{\$170,000 + (\$400 + \$5,200 + \$600)}$$

$$= \frac{\$80,000 + \$6,000 + \$6,200}{\$170,000 + \$6,200}$$

$$= \frac{\$\ 92,200}{\$176,200}$$

$$= 52.33\%$$

Other factors that can affect the initial markup are workroom/alteration costs and cash discounts. Whereas employee discounts, markdowns, and shortages reduce the retail value, workroom/alteration costs increase the retail value of goods. Some examples are garment alterations and construction of draperies, curtains, and furniture slipcovers. Retailers are sometimes required to assemble products that are not fully assembled by the vendor. These additional costs are included in the retail value of the goods because the value added by the retailer increases the value of the goods. Workroom and alteration costs can include expenses for labor, supplies, and services that are not offset by customer fees. Cash discounts are subtracted from the numerator when calculating initial markup percent because they represent a reduction in the cost of the merchandise. Therefore, the modified initial markup percent equation is as follows:

$$\text{Initial Markup \%} = \frac{\text{Expenses} + \text{Profit} + \text{Reductions} + \text{Alterations} - \text{Cash Discounts}}{\text{Net Sales} + \text{Reductions}}$$

EXAMPLE 5-21A

Determine the necessary initial markup percent for a department having these planned figures:

Net sales	$100,000
Expenses	40,000
Reductions	10,000
Alteration costs	900
Cash discounts	750
Profit	5,000

Solution: Initial Markup %

$$= \frac{\text{Expenses} + \text{Profit} + \text{Reductions} + \text{Alterations} - \text{Cash Discounts}}{\text{Net Sales} + \text{Reductions}}$$

$$= \frac{\$40,000 + \$5,000 + \$10,000 + \$900 - \$750}{\$100,000 + \$10,000}$$

$$= \frac{\$55,150}{\$110,000} = 50.14\%$$

Retailers may plan initial markup with percents of net sales rather than in specific dollar amounts. (Remember that net sales = 100%.) The same equation can also be used when working with percents.

EXAMPLE 5-21B

Determine initial markup percent.

Net sales	$100,000	100.00%
Expenses	40,000	40.00
Reductions	10,000	10.00
Alteration costs	900	0.90
Cash discounts	750	0.75
Profit	5,000	5.00

Solution: Initial Markup %

$$= \frac{\text{Expenses} + \text{Profit} + \text{Reductions} + \text{Alteration Costs} - \text{Cash Discounts}}{\text{Net Sales} + \text{Reductions}}$$

$$= \frac{40\% + 5\% + 10\% + 0.9\% - 0.75\%}{100\% + 10\%}$$

$$= \frac{55.15\%}{110\%} = 50.14\%$$

Reduction figures are frequently given individually and must be added together. The following example reports all items needed for calculating initial markup in percents.

EXAMPLE 5-22

Determine the initial markup percent that will be required to achieve a 4% profit, using the following figures:

Expenses	39.1%
Employee discounts	6.8
Markdowns	4.2
Shortages	1.0
Alterations	0.5
Cash discounts	0.6
Profit	4.0

Solution:

Initial Markup %

$$= \frac{\text{Expenses} + \text{Profit} + \text{Reductions} + \text{Alterations} - \text{Cash Discounts}}{\text{Net Sales} + \text{Reductions}}$$

Reductions = Employee Discounts + Markdowns + Shortages
= 6.8% + 4.2% + 1%
= 12%

Initial Markup % $= \dfrac{39.1\% + 4\% + 12\% + 0.5\% - 0.6\%}{100\% + 12\%}$

$$= \frac{55\%}{112\%}$$

$$= 49.11\%$$

Note: Net sales always equal 100% because all other percents are based on net sales.

To determine initial markup, it may be necessary to convert percents into dollar amounts. In the following example, some items are reported in dollars and others are listed as percents. Before working the problem, convert the items listed as percents into dollars figures.

EXAMPLE 5-23

Calculate the initial markup percent that will enable the department to achieve a 9% profit.

Net sales	$220,000	
Markdowns		4%
Employee discounts	2,100	
Shortages	1,900	
Expenses	95,000	
Profit		9%
Cash discounts	5,400	
Alteration costs	2,600	

Solution:

First determine the markdown and profit dollars.

Markdowns $= 4\%$ of net sales $= 0.04 \times \$220,000 = \$8,800$

Profit $\quad= 9\%$ of net sales $= 0.09 \times \$220,000 = \$19,800$

Reductions $=$ Employee Discounts + Markdowns + Shortages

$\qquad\qquad= \$2,100 + \$8,800 + \$1,900$

$\qquad\qquad= \$11,800$

Initial Markup %

$$= \frac{\text{Expenses + Profit + Reductions + Alteration Costs - Cash Discounts}}{\text{Net Sales + Reductions}}$$

$$= \frac{\$95,000 + \$19,800 + \$11,800 + \$2,600 - \$5,400}{\$220,000 + \$11,800}$$

$$= \frac{\$124,800}{\$232,800}$$

$$= 53.61\%$$

Practice Problems • Exercise 5.4

1. What should be the initial markup percent in a department having these planned figures?

Net sales	$55,000
Markdowns	3,000
Shortages	700
Employee discounts	400
Expenses	15,000
Profit	9,000

$4,100.00

$$IMU\% = \frac{\$15,000 + 9,000 + 4,100}{\$55,000 + 4,100}$$

$$= \frac{\$28,100}{\$59,100}$$

$$= 47.55\%$$

2. Determine the initial markup percent needed based on the following figures:

Net sales	$21,000
Profit	2,300
Expenses	7,500
Shortages	300
Employee discounts	200
Alteration costs	150
Cash discounts	280

500

$$\frac{\$2,300 + 7,500 + 500 + 150 - 280}{\$21,000 + 500.00}$$

$$= \frac{\$10,170.00}{\$21,500.00}$$

$$= 47.30\%$$

3. Determine what initial markup percent will be required to achieve a 4.25% profit.

Expenses	42.0%
Markdowns	2.8
Shortages	1.0
Employee discounts	0.5
Cash discounts	0.3
Alteration costs	0.2
Profit	4.25%

4.30

$$= \frac{42.0\% + 4.30 + 4.25 + .20 - .30}{100.00\% + 4.30}$$

$$= \frac{50.45\%}{104.30\%}$$

$$= 48.37\%$$

4. What should be the initial markup percent in a department having these planned figures?

Net sales	$420,000	
Expenses	159,600	38%
Markdowns	8,500	
Alteration costs	950	
Shortages	2,500	
Cash discounts	1,600	
Employee discounts	1,900	
Profit	33,600	8%

RR = $12,900

$$\frac{\$159,600 + 950 + 12,900 - 1,600 + 33,600}{\$420,000 + 12,900}$$

$$= \frac{\$205,450}{\$432,900} = 47.46\%$$

5. A department has planned net sales of $220,000, expenses of $85,000, reductions of $18,000, cash discounts of $1,800, and alteration costs of $3,200. Determine what initial markup percent will result in a 7% profit.

$15,400.00

$$\frac{\$85,000 + 18,000 - 1,800 + 3,200 + 15,400}{\$220,000 + 18,000}$$

$$= \frac{\$119,800}{\$238,000}$$

$$= 50.34\%$$

CUMULATIVE MARKUP

Although cumulative markup is an average markup, it is discussed in a separate section because it is a special type of markup. Cumulative markup is the average markup resulting from the markup on the beginning inventory and the purchases received during a specified period. Cumulative markup is calculated on a season-to-date basis. It is an average figure because it is the markup on merchandise that has accumulated over a period of time.

Cumulative Dollar Markup is the difference between total delivered cost and total retail price of all merchandise handled during a given period of time.

Total value of goods handled is calculated by adding beginning inventory and net purchases throughout the period. Total merchandise handled must be calculated at retail and at cost in order to find cumulative markup percent. Cumulative markup percent is determined by dividing the cumulative dollar retail into the cumulative dollar markup.

Cumulative Dollar Retail is the beginning inventory plus receipts.

Cumulative Markup % = $ Cumulative Markup ÷ $ Cumulative Retail

FOR/MOR data for 1997 showed a median cumulative markup percent among all departments in department stores of 50.1%. Overall cumulative markup for specialty stores in 1997 was 51.4%.

EXAMPLE 5-24

The shoe department showed an opening inventory of $80,000 at retail with a markup of 48%. During the month, purchases were received in the amount of $30,000 at cost that were marked up 52%. Find the cumulative markup percent for the department.

	Opening Inventory	Purchases	Total Merchandise Handled
Retail	$80,000	(a) $62,500	(c) $142,500
Cost	(b) $41,600	$30,000	(d) $71,600
Markup %	48%	52%	(e) 49.75%

Solution:

(a) Find the retail value of purchases.
Retail = $30,000 ÷ (100% − 52%) cost %
        = $30,000 ÷ 48%
        = $62,500

(b) Find the cost value of opening inventory.
Cost   = $80,000 × (100% − 48%) cost %
        = $80,000 × 52%
        = $41,600

(c) Find the total retail value for all goods handled.
Total retail value = $80,000 + $62,500 = $142,500

(d) Find the total cost value for all goods handled.
Total cost value = $41,600 + $30,000 = $71,600

(e) Find the markup % on the total goods handled.
$ Markup = $142,500 − $71,600
         = $70,900

Markup % = $70,900 ÷ $142,500
         = 49.75%

Practice Problems • Exercise 5.5

1. The children's department had an opening inventory on May 1 of $48,500 at cost with a markup of 42%. During the month, the buyer purchased additional merchandise that cost $38,000 with a 46% markup. Calculate the cumulative markup percent for the department at the end of May.

	$R	#C	MU%
OI	$83,620.69	$48,500.00	42%
Purch.	70,370.37	38,000.00	46%
TMH	$153,991.06	$86,500.00	

43.83%

2. The buyer in the fashion jewelry department received a report showing an opening inventory for September 1 of $58,000 at cost with a markup of 47%. Merchandise with a retail value of $50,000 with a 51% markup was received into the department during the month. Find the cumulative markup percent for September.

	$R	#C	Mu%
OI	$109,433.96	$58,000.00	47%
Purch	50,000.00	24,500.00	51%
TMH	$159,433.96	$82,500.00	

48.25%

3. On August 1 the home furnishings department showed an opening inventory of $192,000 (retail) with a markup of 54%. During the month, merchandise costing $59,048 with a 60% markup was received into the department. What was the cumulative markup percent?

	$R	#C	Mu%
OI	$192,000	$88,320	54%
Purch	147,620	59,048	60%
TMH	$339,620	$147,368	

56.61%

4. A sporting goods store had an opening inventory of $42,000 at cost and $95,000 at retail. Purchases during
the month totaled $64,000 at cost and $138,000 at retail. Determine the cumulative markup percent.

	$R	$C	MU%
OI	$95,000.00	$42,000.00	
Purch	138,000.00	64,000.00	
TMH	$233,000.00	$106,000.00	

54.51%.

5. On July 1 the housewares department showed an opening inventory of $90,000 at retail with a 54%
markup. During July, purchases were received in the amount of $40,000 at cost and were marked up 51%.
Find the cumulative markup percent.

	$R	$C	MU%
OI	$90,000.00	$41,400	54%
Purch	81,632.65	40,000	51%
TMH	$171,632.65	$81,400	

52.57%.

MAINTAINED MARKUP

Maintained markup is the final markup obtained by a retail store when the merchandise is sold. It is based on the actual sale of goods rather than on planned sales.

Maintained Markup is the difference between gross cost of the goods sold and the actual retail price obtained (net sales).

The markup initially planned by the buyer may be quite different from the maintained markup actually realized when the goods are sold to the customer. Retail reductions (markdowns, stock shortages, and discounts) reduce the retail value that can actually be achieved. Maintained markup is based on results and is usually figured on the activity of an entire classification, department, or store for a given period of time rather than on an individual purchase or few items. It is calculated whenever an operating statement is prepared and is reported as a percent of net sales and does not reflect deductions for cash discounts and workroom costs.

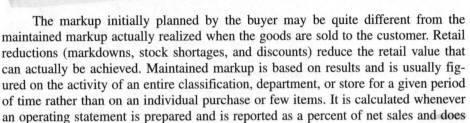

Maintained markup and initial markup percents are both calculated on a retail base, but they are not based on the same retail figure. Initial markup is based on the first retail price placed on merchandise, and maintained markup is calculated on net sales. Initial markup is planned in advance and is calculated on merchandise as it is received in the store.

The buyer cannot determine maintained markup in advance because it is based on actual retail sales and, therefore, is the result of merchandising activities. Maintained markup is a more meaningful percentage than initial markup because it is an accurate reflection of actual business.

EXAMPLE 5-25A

Determine the maintained markup percent using the following operating results:

Net sales			$250,000
Cost of merchandise sold			
Opening inventory		$ 35,000	
Gross purchases	$155,000		
Less, returns to vendor	– 7,500		
Net purchases		$147,500	
Freight inward		+ 3,500	
Total merchandise handled		$186,000	
Closing inventory		– 41,000	
Gross cost of merchandise sold		$145,000	
Cash discounts earned		– 8,000	
Net cost of merchandise sold		$137,000	
Net alteration/workroom costs		+ 2,500	
Total cost of merchandise sold			– 139,500
Gross margin			$110,500

Solution:

Maintained Markup $ = Net Sales – Gross Cost of Merchandise Sold
= $250,000 – $145,000
= $105,000

Maintained Markup % = Maintained Markup $ ÷ Net Sales
= $105,000 ÷ $250,000
= 42%

Maintained markup and gross margin both represent the markup achieved after the merchandise is sold. Both percents are based on the net sales figure rather than on original retail prices. As will be emphasized in Chapter 7, gross margin is the difference between net sales and **total cost of goods sold**. Maintained markup, as just illustrated, is the difference between net sales and **gross cost of merchandise sold**.

Gross Margin $ = Net Sales – Total Cost of Merchandise Sold

Gross Margin % = Gross Margin $ ÷ Net Sales

Maintained markup differs from gross margin in that gross margin takes into consideration cash discounts and alteration/workroom costs. If there are no cash discounts or alterations costs, maintained markup and gross margin are identical.

When a retailer does not incur cash discounts or alteration and workroom costs, gross margin and maintained markup are the same. Most stores do, however, encounter both cash discounts and alteration costs; therefore, these factors must be considered in figuring gross margin. Example 5-25B demonstrates how this works.

EXAMPLE 5-25B

Using the same numbers from Example 5-25A, find gross margin and gross margin %.

Net sales			$250,000
Cost of merchandise sold			
Opening inventory		$ 35,000	
Gross purchases	$155,000		
Less, returns to vendor	– 7,500		
Net purchases		$147,500	
Freight inward		+ 3,500	
Total merchandise handled		$186,000	
Closing inventory		– 41,000	
Gross cost of merchandise sold		$145,000	
Cash discounts earned		– 8,000	
Net cost of merchandise sold		$137,000	
Net alteration/workroom costs		+ 2,500	
Total cost of merchandise sold			–139,500
Gross margin			$110,500

Solution:

$$\text{Gross Margin \$} = \text{Net Sales} - \text{Total Cost of Merchandise Sold}$$
$$= \$250,000 - \$139,500$$
$$= \$110,500$$

$$\text{Gross Margin \%} = \text{Gross Margin \$} \div \text{Net Sales}$$
$$= \$110,500 \div \$250,000$$
$$= 44.2\%$$

In some instances, when total cost of merchandise sold is not available, gross margin can be determined using another method

Gross Margin = Maintained Markup + Cash Discounts - Alteration/Workroom Costs

Applying this formula in Examples 5-25A and 5-25B, gross margin ($110,550) = $105,000 + $ 8,000 - $2,500.

1. Given the following figures, determine (a) the maintained markup percent and (b) the gross margin percent:

Net sales	$200,000
Gross cost of merchandise sold	102,500
Cash discounts	3,500
Alteration costs	1,500

$MMU\% = NS - GCOMS$
$= 200,000 - 102,500$
$= \$97,500 \div 200,000$
$= 48.75\%$

$GM\% = NS - TCOMS$
$= NS - (104,500 - 3,500 + 1,500)$
$= 200,000 - 100,500$
$= 49.75\%$

2. Calculate (a) the maintained markup percent and (b) the gross margin percent with the following figures:

Net sales	$890,000
Cash discounts	6,000
Alteration costs	2,500
Gross cost of merchandise sold	420,000

(a.) $MMU\% = 52.81\%$

(b.) $GM\% = 53.20\%$

3. Calculate the maintained markup percent for a department under the following conditions:

Net sales	$75,000
Opening inventory	37,000
Closing inventory	38,000
Net purchases	46,000
Freight inward	1,400
Cash discounts	2,400

✳✳ $MMU\%$

$MMU\% = \dfrac{NS - GCOMS}{NS}$

$GCOMS = OI - CI + P + T$
$= \$46,400.\cdot$

38.13%

4. The housewares department had a gross margin of $88,200, cash discounts of $6,200, and alteration costs of $2,400. If the net sales were $220,000, what was the maintained markup percent?

$GM = NS - TCOMS$
$MMU = NS - GCOMS$
$GM = MMU + CD - AWC$
$88,200 = MMU + 6,200 - 2,400$
$MMU = 88,200 - 6,200 + 2,400$
$= \$84,400.^{00} \div NS = 38.36\%$

To go from GM + MMU, you have to deduct CD & add AWC

5. Determine (a) the maintained markup percent and (b) the gross margin percent for a department with the following figures:

Net sales	$320,000
Opening inventory	85,000
Closing inventory	105,800
Net purchases	185,000
Freight inward	3,800
Cash discounts	5,400
Alteration costs	2,100

(a.) $MMU\% = (NS - GCOMS) \div NS$

$$= \frac{320,000 - 168,000}{320,000}$$

$$= 47.50\%$$

(b.) $GM = (NS - TCOMS) \div NS$

$$= \frac{320,000 - 164,700}{320,000}$$

$$= 48.53\%$$

$$MMU = NS - \overset{GM}{\overline{(GCOMS}} - CD + awk$$

DEFINITIONS

Billed Cost   The cost after quantity and/or trade discounts are deducted but before cash discounts are deducted.

Cost Complement   The difference between retail percent (100%) and markup percent.

Cumulative Dollar Markup   The difference between total cost price and total retail price of all merchandise handled during a specific period. Cumulative markup is an average figure for merchandise classifications, departments, or the entire store.

Cumulative Dollar Retail   The difference between total delivered cost and total retail price of all merchandise handled during a given time.

Gross Margin   The difference between net sales and the total cost of merchandise sold. Because cash discounts and workroom costs are taken into consideration in computing gross margin, the figure is not the same as maintained markup.

Initial Markup   The difference between the cost price and the original retail price of merchandise. Initial markup does not reflect markdowns and stock shortages.

Maintained Markup   The difference between net sales and the gross cost of merchandise sold. Maintained markup is expressed as a percent of net sales and does not reflect cash discounts and workroom costs. Maintained markup represents the actual markup achieved for a selling period.

Markon   A term often used interchangeably with markup. Markon most often indicates the total amount added to the cost of the total merchandise in a department rather than to the amount added to individual items. The term markon is used more often in manufacturing, whereas markup is used in retail merchandising.

Markup   The difference between the cost price and the retail price of merchandise. Markup may be expressed in dollars or as a percent. If stated as a percent, it may be based on either cost price or retail price. Most retailers base markup on the retail price.

Retail Reductions   Factors that reduce the retail value of a merchandise assortment. These factors include markdowns, discounts to employees and special customers, and stock shortages.

Chapter 5 • Summary Problems

1. Determine the cost of a jacket that retails for $249 and has a 49% markup.

    $126.99

2. Find the retail price of a sofa that costs $900 and was marked up 62%.

    $2,368.42

3. What is the markup percent for braided belts that cost $78 a dozen and retail for $12 each?

    $6.50

    45.83%

4. Find the markup percent on a suit that costs $350 and retails for $680.

    48.53%

5. Determine the markup percent for the following group of merchandise:

Item Quantity	$ Cost	$ Retail
15 chains 330.00	$22.00 each 750.00	$50.00 each
27 bracelets 216.00	$96.00 per dozen 486	$18.00 each
2¼ dozen pins 121.50	$54.00 per dozen 216	$ 8.00 each
30 charms 195.00	$ 6.50 each 360	$12.00 each
$862.50	$1,812.00	

    52.40%

6. What is the markup percent on an item that costs $183 a dozen and retails for $30 each?

    49.17%

169

7. A buyer purchased a group of ties at $90 a dozen. What would be the retail price for each tie to achieve a 48% markup?

$14.42

8. The following figures have been planned for a department. Calculate the initial markup percent that should be used in order to arrive at the planned figures.

Shortages	1.0%
Employee discounts	2.0
Markdowns	4.6
Expenses	30.0
Profit	6.0
Alteration costs	0.9
Cash discounts	1.4

7.67.

$$\frac{43.1\%}{107\,6\%} = 40.06\%$$

9. The home furnishings department had net sales of $420,000 and gross cost of merchandise sold of $187,500. The department's cash discounts were $3,800 and alteration costs were $2,450. Determine the maintained markup percent and the gross margin percent.

$232,500

MMU% = ($420,000 - 187,500) ÷ 420,000 = 55.36%

GM% = $233,850 ÷ 420,000 = = 55.68%

GM = MMU + CD - awn

10. A buyer plans to purchase $25,000 (retail) worth of children's coats for a back-to-school sale. He has already purchased 180 coats that cost $45 each and will retail for $80 each. What markup percent must be obtained on the balance of coats in order to average a 44.5% markup?

Total Purch.	$R $25,000.00 14,400.00 $10,600.00	$C $13,875.00 8,100.00 $5,775.00	MU% 44.50% 45.52%

11. Determine the initial markup percent that will enable the department to achieve a 5.5% profit, using the following figures:

Markdowns	5.3%
Expenses	35.2
Employee discounts	2.8
Cash discounts	2.5
Shortages	1.4
Alterations	1.1
Profit	5.5

9.5RR

$$\frac{48.8\%}{109.5\%} = 44.57\%$$

361-857 7900 (Honda

12. Calculate the initial markup percent that will be required to achieve a 6% profit, using the following figures:

Net sales	$540,000
Employee discounts	2,900
Expenses	180,000
Markdowns	8,250
Alteration costs	6,486 1.2%
Cash discounts	6,550
Shortages	1,800
Profit	32,400 6%
rr	12,950

$$\frac{\$225,280}{\$552,950} = 40.74\%$$

13. A menswear buyer needs 84 shirts to retail at $18 each and 52 pairs of slacks to retail at $35 each. He needs to average a 47.5% markup. If he pays $9.50 for each shirt, how much can he pay for each pair of slacks in order to achieve his planned markup percent?

	$R	$C	MU%
Total	$3,332.00	$1,749.30	47.5%
84 Shirts	1,512.00	798.00	
52 slacks	1,820.00	$951.30 ÷ 52 =	
		$18.29	

14. A buyer needs to average a 44% markup. She has purchased 25 flannel robes that cost $18.50 each and 32 fleece robes that cost $24 each. If she retails the flannel robes for $29 each, what must be the average retail for each fleece robe in order to achieve the planned markup percent?

	$R	$C	MU%
Total	$2,197.32	$1,230.50	44.00%
25 Flannel	725.00	462.50	
32 Fleece	$1,472.32 ÷ 32 =	768.00	
	$46.01		

15. The housewares department had an opening inventory for March 1 of $95,000 at cost with a markup of 45.5%. During the month the buyer for the department purchased additional merchandise with a retail value of $50,000 with a 48% markup. Calculate the cumulative markup percent for March.

	$R	$C	MU%
OI	$174,311.92	$95,000.00	45.5%
Purch.	50,000.00	26,000.00	48.00%
TMH	$224,311.92	$121,000.00	46.06%

16. Determine the initial markup percent for a children's department with these figures:

Net sales	$270,000
Expenses	92,500
Profit	13,500 5%
Employee discounts	2,100
Shortages	1,550
Cash discounts	5,500
Markdowns	8,100 3%
Alteration costs	3,500

RR = $11,750

$$\frac{\$115,750}{\$281,750} = 41.08\%$$

17. A buyer plans to purchase 250 towels for the store's Harvest Sale and plans to retail each towel for $7.50. He has placed an order for 128 towels that cost $3.25 each. What is the most he can pay for each of the remaining towels if he wishes to average a 42% markup?

250 Total $R $C   MU%
128 Purch.   #1,875.00 $1,087.50   42.00%
122   416.00
                                           671.50 ÷122 = $5.50

18. The sportswear buyer purchased 22 blouses at $15.00 each, 15 blouses at $12.50 each, and 27 blouses at $126 per dozen. The average markup must be 50%. What should be the retail price for each blouse if all blouses are to be sold at the same price?

$C
64 units $330.00
                     187.50
                     283.50
                    $801.00 ÷ .50 = $1,602.00 ÷ 64 = $25.03

19. The opening inventory on March 1 for the boys' department was $150,000 at cost and $260,000 at retail. During the month, the department received merchandise that cost $95,000 with a 51% markup. Find the cumulative markup percent.

           $R $C   MU%
OI $260,000.00 $150,000.00
Purch.   193,877.55   95,000.00   51%
          $453,877.55 $245,000.00   46.02%

20. During July a buyer plans to buy gowns with a retail value of $10,000. She has purchased 150 gowns at $15.00 each that will retail for $35.00. What markup should she obtain on the remaining gowns in order to achieve a 47.5% markup goal?

           $R $C   MU%
Total $10,000.00 $5,250.00   47.50%
150   5,250.00   2,250.00
Bal $4,750.00 $3,000.00   36.84%

21. The following items were purchased by the menswear buyer:

28 shirts at $9.50 each $266.00
32 shirts at $132.00 per dozen   352.00
10 shirts at $12.50 each   125.00
                                 $743.00

70 units   If all shirts are to be retailed at the same price, what retail price will result in a 48% markup?

$20.41

22. Find the markup percent on the following order of table runners purchased for a midnight sale:

Quantity	$ Cost	$ Retail
20	$290.00 $14.50 each	$500.00 $25.00 each
18	324.00 $18.00 each	576.00 $32.00 each
10	220.00 $22.00 each	480.00 $48.00 each
	$834.00	$1,556.00

46.40%

23. Using the following departmental markups, find the cost of an item in each department that retails for $25.50.

Department	Markup %
(a) Children's	47
(b) Junior sportswear	48.5
(c) Costume jewelry	42
(d) Furniture	53.5

(handwritten) $13.52
13.13
14.79
11.86

24. The net sales for the shoe department were $650,000. Calculate the maintained markup percent for the department with the following figures:

Net purchases	$350,000
Opening inventory	175,000
Closing inventory	220,000
Cash discounts	8,500
Alteration costs	4,200
Freight inward	5,000

(handwritten) 52.31%

25. A sportswear buyer purchased a group of blouses at a closeout sale. The group consisted of 60 blouses costing $12.50 each, 42 blouses costing $10.50 each, and 82 blouses costing $11.00 each. He plans to retail the entire lot at a 48% markup. If the buyer decides to mark all blouses the same price, what minimum retail price must be placed on each blouse to achieve the planned 48% markup?

(handwritten) 184 units

(handwritten)
$750.00
441.00
902.00
————
$2,093.00

(handwritten) $21.88

CHAPTER 6

Retail Pricing for Profit

OBJECTIVES

- To understand the importance of pricing in the operation of a successful retail business.
- To understand the factors that affect retail pricing.
- To analyze the causes of markdowns and understand the importance of using markdowns and other price changes in profitable merchandising.
- To calculate dollar markdown and markdown percent.
- To calculate markdown cancellation and determine net markdown.
- To calculate discounts to employees and special customers.

KEY POINTS

- One of the important factors in successful merchandising is offering merchandise at the right price.
- Retail pricing serves as a major tool in selling goods.
- Maximizing profit requires consideration of the relationships between customer demand, retail price, and expenses.
- Pricing policies relate to many variables that contribute to store image.

RETAIL OBJECTIVES AND PRICING

One of the major objectives in successful retailing is to offer merchandise at the right price. Retailers must be familiar with many pricing strategies when providing goods to the consumer. Careful planning and analyzing of prices of merchandise are necessary for retailers to provide consumers with the right merchandise and obtain a desirable profit. Today's consumers are faced with the availability of a diverse group of retail formats for purchasing merchandise. With increased competition in the industry, price often serves as a major motivation factor for consumer buying practices.

PRICING POLICIES AND STORE IMAGE

Pricing policies impact the success of a retail establishment. Careful analysis and planning of prices are necessary by retailers in order to achieve a profit. The right price for a retailer should be one that covers both the cost of the merchandise and operating expenses and provides a profit. In some instances the retail price may not provide "typical" profit, but the goods are carried because they generate traffic and contribute to the sale of other merchandise.

All retailers operate with pricing policies that serve as guidelines in making sure that a reasonable profit will be accomplished. Pricing policies are used to determine the price levels at which retailers sell their merchandise. Pricing policies vary among stores depending on what type of image the store wishes to project and are important guidelines in determining the types of customers the stores will attract. There are numerous pricing policies; only the five most common will be mentioned here. These pricing strategies are:

1. Prestige pricing
2. Leader pricing
3. Competitive pricing
4. Everyday low pricing (EDLP)
5. High/low pricing

Pricing and other issues, such as store image, level of personal service, and the variety of goods and services offered, are important strategic variables when consumers decide where to shop.

Prestige pricing, or above-the-market pricing, is used by some retailers to feature elite, innovative, or exclusive merchandise projecting a prestigious image. Stores that carry exclusive items and high-quality goods and offer a high level of personal service are looking to attract prestige or status-minded consumers. This type of customer is willing to pay a higher price in order to receive specialized attention and purchase unique, fashionable items. Therefore, this type of retailer may use prestige pricing, where prices are higher than competitors. Upscale department stores and speciality stores are often successful with this pricing policy.

Leader pricing occurs when a retailer offers brand-name merchandise at special, reduced prices. The purpose is to attract consumers to the store because of well-known products with the hope that they will purchase additional, regularly priced items. Discount department stores, toy stores, supermarkets, and home centers are some of the retailers that utilize leader pricing to attract customers. If merchandise is priced below cost, it is referred to as a **loss leader**. Loss leaders are low-priced goods on which retailers make little or no profit. While customers are in the store for these lower priced goods, retailers hope that other merchandise at regular prices will be purchased.

Competitive pricing, also known as at-the-market pricing, involves retailers pricing products exactly at or near the same price as competitors. Stores with competitive pricing have average prices and offer solid service. Because of the increased number of choices, customers are willing to shop around in order to obtain the lowest price. This is especially important for nationally distributed brand names, which can be readily compared by customers. Traditional department stores, supermarkets, and many drug stores use this type of pricing strategy.

Everyday low pricing (EDLP) is a way that retailers can achieve increased sales volume and markup dollars. Everyday low pricing can be defined as a pricing policy that sets prices somewhere between the lowest discounted sale price and the regular, non-sale price of competitors. A better term for this type of strategy would be stable pricing because prices often do not vary. Retailers are able to obtain a satisfactory profit by reducing expenses and limiting assortments of merchandise at a lower markup. A small difference in price may make a big difference in sales volume and profits. However, retailers claiming everyday low prices—such as Wal-Mart, Home Depot, and Amazon.com—do not necessarily have the lowest prices.

High/low pricing is another policy retailers may use depending on their particular strategy. High/low pricing consists of retailers providing prices above the EDLP of competitors and offering special sales that decrease these prices. These special sales usually occur frequently and for short periods to increase consumer interest.

FACTORS THAT AFFECT PRICING

Because pricing has a major impact on the retailer's operations and store image, merchandisers carefully consider factors that influence prices. Many retailers continue to sell designer brands and national brands (manufacturers' brands that are available nationwide). Private-label merchandise is often priced below manufacturers' brands, which allows the retailer to be more competitive. The private-label merchandise has higher markups, which increases profits. In addition, private-label merchandise offers customers more distinctive assortments of goods and allows retailers to have greater control over their merchandise. Several other factors that influence the determination of retail prices include:

1. Type of merchandise—the quality of the goods, markdown risks, and perishableness.
2. Competition—the price of identical or similar merchandise at competitive stores.
3. Manufacturer's policies—prices suggested by the manufacturer.
4. Selling costs—the need for a professional salesperson or for a large commission to sell the merchandise.
5. Demand and supply—availability of goods and customer interest.
6. Handling costs—expenses involved in warehousing and delivery.

PRICING RELATED TO CONSUMER DEMAND

Although most buyers have an initial markup percent goal, maximizing dollar markup must not be overlooked. Expenses are paid in dollars, and a trade-off may be made between taking a higher markup percent and selling larger quantities.

The following example illustrates a theoretical situation, whereby a lower markup percent stimulates customer demand and increases markup dollars and profit:

EXAMPLE 6-1

Retail	100 units at $22 =	$2,200	300 units at $15 =	$4,500
Cost	100 units at $10 =	− 1,000	300 units at $10 =	− 3,000
Markup	(54.55%)	1,200	(33.33%)	1,500
Expenses		− 1,050		− 1,250
Profit		$ 150		$ 250

Increasing total profit dollars by decreasing markup percent is appropriate for merchandise that has great elasticity of demand. In other words, units sold will increase dramatically as retail price is lowered. It is important to remember that in this low-margin philosophy, expenses must not increase proportionally to an increase in sales.

PRICE-CONSCIOUS CONSUMERS

Retailers must price merchandise carefully in order to satisfy customers and to achieve a profit. The retail price of merchandise serves to attract and maintain customer patronage. However, the type of customer that is attracted is dependent on the store's proposed image and consumers' perceptions of price-quality relationships.

The Right Price for the Consumer

Often, consumers associate prices with the degree of product quality. If a price is low, the consumer may associate the low price with poor quality. Conversely, if a price is high, consumers may perceive the product as a high-quality item. However, most shoppers are searching for a good value.

Good value varies according to the consumer's own expectations; therefore, it is difficult to define. **Good value is defined generally as a quality-made product with an appropriate price that reflects the degree of quality.** Most customers are looking for the best quality at the right price. However, this judgment is based on the consumer's individual subjective opinion; therefore, finding the correct mix of quality and price is quite difficult.

Today's consumers are well-informed, educated shoppers. They have access to many resources to help determine which purchases are a good value. Many consumers have access to the World Wide Web. Virtually all large store-based retailers have Web sites. With the Web's popularity, many consumers have an increased price awareness and tend to do more comparison shopping. Many of today's consumers use technology to make informed purchasing decisions. Some manufacturers are bypassing retailers and selling directly to consumers through the Internet and direct mail. With increased competition, customers have more choices from where to buy their goods. Therefore, retailers need to be aware of competitors' merchandise offerings and pricing policies.

The Right Price for the Retailer

The right price for a retailer should be one that covers the cost of the merchandise plus operating expenses while still providing a fair profit. Sometimes low markup goods are carried by retailers because they generate traffic and contribute to the sale of other merchandise. Stores may offset this low markup by placing higher markups on other goods. However, the retailer has to find the right balance. What the retailer would like to charge is not always what customers are willing to pay. Ideally, to determine the best price, retail buyers should ask themselves, "What is my customer willing to pay for this item?"

PRICE LINES AND ZONES

Pricing structure is set by management as part of the company's established merchandising policies. Management must first decide who will be the target customer and then establish price lines and/or price zones to appeal to this customer. **Price lining is a technique used by retailers to determine the particular prices at which the**

store's merchandise is offered for sale. In this process the pricing structure is related to the buying power of the target customers, who are divided into groups. Some customers may prefer to purchase merchandise priced in the lower price zone, others shop in the middle price zone, and some seek the highest price zone.

The retailer develops price lines, price ranges, and price zones for the different merchandise classifications carried in the store. In pricing, it is important to understand the following terminology:

> **Price Line or Price Point.**   A specific predetermined price at which an item is offered for sale. For example, if a store offers women's dresses at $89, $99, $129, and $159, each specific price represents a price line or price point.
>
> **Price Range.**   The spread between the highest and lowest price line offered for sale. In the previous example of women's dress price lines, the price range is $89 to $159.
>
> **Price Lining.**   The practice of predetermining the price points at which an assortment of merchandise will be offered for sale. The buyer does not price the merchandise at all possible prices but seeks merchandise that can be sold to the customer at predetermined prices.
>
> **Price Zone**.   A series of price lines that are relatively close together and tend to appeal to a certain group of customers. Most stores maintain two or three of the following price zones: promotional (lower price lines), moderate (middle price lines), and prestige (higher price lines). Merchandise is offered for sale at several price lines within each of the price zones.

There should be enough spread between the different price lines so customers can see the quality-price relationships of various merchandise assortments. The best-selling price lines provide a greater share of the total dollar and unit sales.

PRICE CHANGES

Retailers would prefer to sell most goods at the original retail price. However, a decrease or an increase in prices is sometimes necessary to provide successful merchandising operations.

Several major types of price changes are used by retailers. These include:

1. Markdowns
2. Markdown cancellations
3. Additional markups
4. Markup cancellations
5. Employee discounts

Every price change has an impact on markup and, therefore, on gross margin and net profit. Any change in retail prices, whether a decrease or an increase of the original retail price, is used in calculating the value of the inventory on hand. Price changes, including both increases and decreases in retail, are classified according to whether they affect the net markdown figure or the total value of merchandise handled. Price revisions that affect the total value of merchandise handled are discussed in more detail at the end of this chapter.

Markdowns

Markdowns are the most common type of price change. Markdowns can be a very effective tool for increasing sales and providing for new merchandise. Failure to take markdowns when warranted results in inventory that does not sell and the inability to buy current merchandise. Markdowns should be used as a merchandising tool. With today's advanced technology, retailers are able to track merchandise sales and identify slow-selling merchandise that should be marked down. An analysis of markdowns enables buyers to locate trouble spots and adjust future assortments. For example, styles that require excessive markdowns indicate merchandise that failed to attract sufficient customers and should be avoided in the future.

Markdown refers to a reduction from the original or previous retail price.

Purpose of Markdowns.   Markdowns serve several purposes:

1. Stimulating sales of slow-moving or inactive stock.
2. Disposing of broken assortments, discontinued lines, and damaged or shop-worn merchandise.
3. Providing additional open-to-buy for the purchase of new merchandise.
4. Meeting competitors' prices of the same or similar merchandise.
5. Increasing customer traffic.

Markdowns are used by retailers to move merchandise. These reductions in price will lower the amount of the final markup that will be obtained. Because maintained markup and gross margin represent the retailer's final markup, it is important that these be planned in relation to the initial or original markup.

As discussed in Chapter 5, the initial markup represents the first markup placed on an item to provide the original retail price that the retailer hopes to receive. However, the original retail price placed on merchandise will usually be reduced by such reductions as markdowns, employee discounts, and stock shortages. The original retail price of an item must be large enough to cover the planned reductions and still provide the desired gross margin and maintained markup. Therefore, markdowns are important factors in determining gross margin and maintained markup. Markdowns reduce the retail price, causing a decrease in gross margin that is further reflected in a decrease and/or elimination of profit. Retailers should carefully plan for and control markdowns because of their significant impact on achieving profits.

Reasons for Markdowns.   Because markdowns are the most common type of price change, it is important to recognize the reasons for taking markdowns. Some markdowns are caused by errors in buying, pricing, and selling; other markdowns are taken to stimulate sales.

Buying Errors.   Buying errors can result in having to take markdowns. Markdowns may be necessary when the wrong styles, colors, sizes, materials, and/or quantities have been purchased. Buying errors can be minimized by careful planning of sales and purchases. Pretesting merchandise by buying in small quantities before ordering in large amounts may help eliminate excessive markdowns. The frequency of fashion change may not allow for testing of fashion merchandise. Another buying error may relate to late delivery of merchandise. Merchandise that is received after the peak of customer demand may require excessive markdowns.

Pricing Errors.   Errors in pricing are another reason for markdowns. The initial retail price may be set too high or too low. When merchandise is priced too high, the customer may turn to a lower-priced competitor. When merchandise is priced too low, a retailer may be losing revenues that another retailer is earning.

Selling Errors.   A major error in selling merchandise that leads to markdowns is the failure to display and show merchandise. Goods may be slow sellers simply because they are in the wrong location. Careless selling or high-pressure selling may lead to customer returns, causing markdowns. Returned goods may be past the peak of customer acceptance. A large proportion of returned merchandise ends up having to be reduced. Markdowns may also result from careless handling of merchandise in the department. Uninformed salespersons and poor stockkeeping contribute to shopworn and damaged merchandise that will have to be reduced in price.

Special Sales.   Regular stock may be marked down for special sales events, or the retailer may buy special purchase goods to sell at promotional prices. Special purchases include merchandise that is offered to retailers by vendors at lower than regular prices. Merchandise is often of lower than usual quality and may include broken sizes or end-of-season goods. Special purchase merchandise is sometimes marked at higher prices when first placed on the sales floor and then marked down for a sales event. Retailers frequently find that even higher markdowns must be taken on special purchase goods following a sale in order to move the unsold merchandise.

Broken Assortments and Out-of-Season Goods.   Markdowns must also be taken to weed out merchandise that is unsalable because of broken assortments or to clear goods to provide more space for new merchandise. In some departments, such as piece goods and floor coverings, remnants are reduced to encourage sales.

Amount and Timing of Markdowns.   Markdowns are a necessary part of retailing. The timing and amount of markdowns are important factors in achieving profit. The timing of markdowns relates to the amount of the markdowns needed in order to sell merchandise and to protect the gross margin or profit potential. The size of the markdown relates to the timing of the markdown. Appropriate timing of markdowns can have a positive impact on turnover in that markdowns decrease the value of the inventory and increase sales.

Depending on the type of store, the policies governing the timing and amount of markdowns vary. With many stores, the amount and timing of markdowns are related. The markdown timing sequence varies with different retailers and with the type of merchandise. For instance, fashion goods typically require higher, more frequent markdowns than staple goods. Staple goods may stay in stock with little or no price reduction. Markdowns in cosmetics are virtually nonexistent.

Traditionally, retailers postponed their markdowns until the end of the season. Storewide markdowns were usually taken twice a year, January and July (after the peak selling seasons of Christmas and Fourth of July). Today, many retailers believe that a small markdown taken early in the season is more likely to move merchandise than a drastic reduction in prices late in the season. The first markdown should be sufficient to move the majority of goods. Late-in-the-season markdown policies are commonly used by upscale department stores and specialty stores. In addition, specific departments, such as furniture, often use late-season markdowns.

Many successful merchants believe that merchandise should be marked down as soon as the rate of sales slows down. These markdowns are usually small because the merchandise at this time is still in demand. A small markdown taken soon in the season will not only help sell slow-moving goods, but will also provide more open-to-buy for newer merchandise. Bringing in new styles during the middle of the season also tends to increase customer traffic.

Some retailers use monthly sales to encourage customers to purchase slow-moving goods. Many department stores organize special sales each month to encourage the sale of slow-moving and inactive stock and to pull customer traffic into the store.

Some retailers maintain an **automatic markdown policy**. This involves reducing the price of merchandise according to a predetermined schedule. The policy establishes the amount of markdown as well as the length of time the merchandise is in stock before the markdown is taken.

Retailers often request **markdown money** from vendors to cover lost gross margin dollars that result from markdowns. In this agreement, the vendor shares the loss from markdowns, enabling the retailer to achieve a specific maintained markup percent. According to the Robinson-Patman Act, markdown money should be provided to all retailers on a proportionally equal basis, usually on a percentage of purchases.

Markdowns as a percent of sales also vary according to the type of merchandise. Table 6-1 presents a comparison of markdown percents in various merchandise categories.

Table 6-1
Markdown Percents by Merchandising Category

Merchandise Category	Markdown % Specialty Stores	Markdown % Department Stores
Female apparel	42.6%	42.6%
Men's/boys' apparel and accessories	19.8%	29.3%
Infants'/children's clothing and accessories	39.0%	34.4%

Note: From *FOR/MOR, The Combined Financial, Merchandising, and Operating Results of Retail Stores in 1997* by Alexandra Moran (Ed.), 1998 (73rd ed.). Copyright 1998 by the National Retail Federation.

Calculating Markdown Percent.   For planning and control purposes, markdowns are expressed as a percent of net sales. Because markdowns are based on net sales, markdown percents cannot be calculated until the merchandise is sold. Although this workbook contains some problems requiring calculation of the markdown percent on one style or group of merchandise, markdown percents are usually calculated for a period of time rather than on individual items and are based on sales for that period of time.

With today's point-of-sale technology, retailers no longer have to mark each item of merchandise to indicate the markdown price. Price changes are programmed into the stores' computers so that markdowns are recorded at the time customers purchase the goods.

To calculate markdown percent, first find the dollar markdown and then divide the net sales into the dollar markdown.

Markdown $ = Previous Price – New, Reduced Price

Markdown % = $ Markdowns ÷ $ Net sales

EXAMPLE 6-2

The designer department received 4 dresses in style 1436 that retailed for $200. All 4 dresses were reduced to $140 before they were sold. What was the markdown percent on this style?

Solution:

Markdown $	= Previous price – New, Reduced Price
	= 4 × ($200 – $140)
	= 4 × $60 = $240
Sales from this style	= 4 × $140 = $560
Markdown %	= $ Markdown ÷ Net Sales
	= $240 ÷ $560
	= 42.86%

EXAMPLE 6-3

The net sales for a department during the month of June were $28,000. If markdowns for June amounted to $7,280, what was the markdown percent?

Solution:

Markdown %	= $ Markdowns Taken in June ÷ Net Sales for June
	= $7,280 ÷ $28,000
	= 26%

At times it may be necessary to determine net sales when given the dollar markdowns and the markdown percent, as shown in Example 6-4. The solution for this type of problem (finding base) was covered in Chapter 2. The dollar amount ($5,400) is divided by the rate (30%). The following example shows how to determine net sales when given the markdown dollar amount and markdown percent.

EXAMPLE 6-4

Determine the net sales if markdowns for May were 30% of net sales and the markdown dollar amount was $5,400.

Solution:

Net sales	= $ Markdown ÷ Markdown %
	= $5,400 ÷ 30%
	= $18,000

Markdowns Used in Advertising. When merchandise is advertised to the public, markdowns are expressed as a percent of the original retail. This is done because it is how consumers perceive markdowns.

	Advertised Reduction	Internal Records
Original retail	$200.00	$200.00
Reduction	− 40.00	− 40.00
Sale price	$160.00	$ 160.00
Markdown %	$40 ÷ $200 = 20%	$40 ÷ $160 = 25%

All problems in this workbook requiring calculation of markdown percents are to be calculated with sales as the base.

Practice Problems • Exercise 6.1

1. During January the markdowns for rugs at Jossett's Designs were $15,200. Rug sales during this month were $95,000. What was the markdown percent for January?

$$\frac{\$15,200}{\$95,000} = 16.00\%$$

2. For a three-month period the Bath Shop had net sales of $110,000. If the markdowns for this period amounted to $16,775, determine the markdown percent.

$$\frac{\$16,775}{\$110,000} = 15.25\%$$

3. The merchandise plan for the children's department indicated planned sales of $850,000 and planned markdowns of 30.2%. Find the planned dollar markdowns.

$$\$850,000 \times .302 = \$256,700.00$$

4. Last year markdowns for case goods in a design shop were 15.5%. If markdowns amounted to $84,475, determine the net sales for the year.

$$\$84,475 \div .155 = \$545,000.00$$

5. During June the sales for a sporting goods store were $320,000 and markdowns amounted to $59,200. What was the markdown percent for June?

$$\frac{\$59,200}{\$320,000} = 18.50\%$$

Markdown Cancellation and Net Markdowns

Frequently, merchandise is reduced for a special sale, and after the sale is over, the remaining goods are returned to or toward their original price. This upward price change on merchandise previously marked down is a cancellation of a markdown. **Markdown Cancellation is the upward price adjustment that is offset against a former markdown.**

Cancellations usually occur after a special sale if the remaining merchandise is repriced upward. The remaining merchandise may be repriced to its original price or repriced to a different price. However, the new price should not exceed the original retail price.

Today, markdown cancellations are entered into a computer, thus eliminating the need to manually mark merchandise and to record the cancellations. However, the student should understand how markdown cancellations are calculated.

Net Markdown is the difference between the total markdown and the markdown cancellation.

Net Markdown = Total Markdown – Markdown Cancellation

EXAMPLE 6-5

For a midnight sale, 24 blazers were reduced from \$80 to \$60. During the sale, 14 blazers were sold. After the sale, the remaining 10 blazers were remarked to the original \$80 price. Determine the total markdown, markdown cancellation, and net markdown.

Solution:

Total markdown	24 blazers × (\$80 – \$60) =	\$480
– Markdown cancellation	10 blazers × (\$80 – \$60) =	– 200
Net markdown		\$280

Net Markdown Percent is the net markdown divided by the sales actually obtained.

Net Markdown % = Net Markdown ÷ Actual Sales

In order to calculate the net markdown percent, it is necessary to determine the sales actually obtained. The net markdown divided by the total sales will provide the net markdown percent.

EXAMPLE 6-6

Using the same information from Example 6-5, assume that 36 blazers were received and 12 blazers were sold prior to the midnight sale. As stated earlier, 14 blazers were sold during the sale. The remaining 10 blazers were eventually sold at the full $80 price. Determine the net markdown percent.

Solution:

First determine the actual sales:

Sales prior to the sale	12 blazers × $80 =	$ 960
Sales during the sale	14 blazers × $60 =	$ 840
Sales after the sale	10 blazers × $80 =	$ 800
Total sales actually obtained	36 =	$2,600

$$\text{Net Markdown \%} = \text{Net \$ Markdown} \div \text{Actual Sales}$$
$$= \$280 \div \$2,600$$
$$= 10.77\%$$

Merchandise in Example 6-6 was remarked to the original price. After a sale, the remaining goods may be priced toward the original price, instead of being priced at the exact original price.

EXAMPLE 6-7

The buyer for the Music Shop received 200 CDs priced at $15.95 each. Fifty CDs sold at this price. The remaining CDs were marked down to $11.95 for a special sales event. During the sale, 85 CDs were sold. After the sale, the buyer repriced the remaining CDs to $14.95 and sold all of them.

Determine:

    a. Total markdown
    b. Markdown cancellation
    c. Net dollar markdown
    d. Net markdown percent

Solution:

    a. Total markdown (prior to the sale) 150 CDs reduced from $15.95 to $11.95

$$\text{Total markdown} = 150 \times (\$15.95 - \$11.95)$$
$$= 150 \times \$4.00$$
$$= \$600$$

    b. Markdown cancellation (after the sale) 65 CDs were repriced to $14.95.

$$\text{Markdown cancellation} = 65 \times (\$11.95 - \$14.95)$$
$$= 65 \times \$3.00$$
$$= \$195$$

    c. Net $ Markdown = Total Markdown − Markdown Cancellation
$$= \$600 - \$195$$
$$= \$405$$

    d. To find net markdown %, first determine total sales.

Sales prior to sale	= 50 CDs × $15.95 each =	$ 797.50
Sales during the sale	= 85 CDs × $11.95 each =	$1,015.75
Sales after the sale	= 65 CDs × $14.95 each =	$ 971.75
Total sales	=	$2,785.00

$$\text{Net Markdown \%} = \text{Net \$ Markdown} \div \text{Total Sales}$$
$$= \$405 \div \$2,785$$
$$= 14.54\%$$

Practice Problems • Exercise 6.2

1. For a special two-day sale a sportswear buyer reduced 30 blouses from \$40 to \$32. Twenty-one of the blouses were sold during the sale. After the sale was over, the remaining 9 blouses were returned to their original retail price. Determine (a) the markdown cancellation and (b) the net dollar markdown. MDC & NMD

$$(a.) \; MDC = 9 \times (40 - 32) = \$72.00$$
$$\$8.00$$

$$(b.) \; MD = \$8.00 \times 30.00 = \$240.00$$
$$NMD = \$240.00 - 72.00 = \$168.00$$

2. A buyer reduced 62 shirts from \$28 to \$20 for a special three-day sale. During the sale, 44 shirts were sold. After the sale, the remaining shirts were priced at \$25 each. Determine the markdown cancellation. MDC

$$MDC = (62 - 44) \times (\$20 - 25) =$$
$$= 18 \times \$5.00$$
$$= \$90.00$$

3. A buyer reduced 42 jackets from \$85 to \$60 for a one-day sale. Forty jackets were sold during the event. After the sale, the remaining jackets were marked up to \$75. All the jackets were sold at this price. Determine (a) the markdown cancellation and (b) net dollar markdown. MDC & NMD

$$(a.) \; MDC = (42 - 40) \times (\$75 - 60) = 2 \times 15 = \$30.00$$

$$(b.) \; NMD = (42(\$85 - 60)) - \$30.00 = \$1,050 - 30.00 = \$1,020.00$$

4. During March, the Camera Shop had a net markdown of \$529. If the total markdowns amounted to \$830, determine the markdown cancellation. MDC

$$MD = \$830.00$$
$$NMD = -529.00$$
$$\overline{MDC = \$301.00}$$

5. The buyer for the boys' department had received 4 dozen all-weather jackets that retailed for \$68 each. After several weeks 8 of the jackets were sold and the remaining 40 jackets were marked down to \$50 for a one-day sale. Twelve jackets were sold during the one-day sale. All remaining jackets were remarked to \$61 and eventually sold at this price. Determine the net markdown percent. NMD%

$$Sales = 8 \times \$68.00 = \$544.00$$
$$MD = 40(\$68 - 50) = \$720.00$$
$$12 \times \$50.00 = \$600.00$$
$$MDC = 28(\$61 - 50) = -\$308.00$$
$$(48 - 20) \times \$61.00 = \$1,708.00$$
$$\overline{\$412.00}$$
$$\overline{\$2,852.00}$$
$$NMD =$$
$$NMD\% = \$412.00 \div \$2,852.00 = 14.45\%$$

191

MDC & NMD

6. A buyer reduced the price on 135 blouses from $49.99 to $39.99 for an anniversary sale. After the sale, the remaining 54 blouses were returned to the presale price. Determine (a) the markdown cancellation and (b) the net $ markdown.

(a.) MDC = 54 x ($10.00) = $540.00

(b.) NMD = 135 x ($10.00) = $1,350.00 − 540.00 = $810.00

MDC

7. Six hundred shirts were purchased at a cost of $15.75 each. The buyer decided to retail the shirts for $34.99 each. After a month, 123 shirts were sold at $34.99. The remaining shirts were marked to $24.99 for a store-wide sale. After the sale, 192 shirts were left and were repriced to $29.99. Determine the markdown cancellation.

MDC = 192 x ($29.99 − 24.99) = $960.00

NMD

8. A buyer received 5 dozen blazers retailing for $150 each. After several weeks only 8 of the blazers had been sold. The remaining 52 blazers were reduced to $110 for a promotion. During the promotion, 10 of the blazers sold at the reduced price. After the promotion, the remaining 42 blazers were repriced to $140 and sold. Determine the net markdown percent.

MD = 52 x ($150.00 − 110.00) = $2,080.00   Sales = 8 x $150.00 = $1,200.00

MDC = 42 x ($140.00 − 110.00) = $1,260.00   10 x 110.00 = 1,100.00

NMD =   42 x 140.00 = 5,880.00

$820.00 ÷ 8,180.00 = 10.02% $8,180.00

9. A buyer had 68 coats in stock at a retail price of $485 each. They were marked down to $399 for a special sale. When the special sale ended, the buyer marked the 39 remaining coats back to their original price. Determine the markdown cancellation.

MDC

MDC = 39 ($485.00 − 399.00) = $3,354.00

MDC

10. For a Veterans Day Sale, a buyer reduced 72 shirts from $49 each to $35 each. The following day, the 48 shirts that remained were repriced to $45. What was the amount of the markdown cancellation?

MDC = 48 ($45 − 35) = $480.00

Additional Markup and Markup Cancellations

In addition to markdowns and markdown cancellations, there are two other types of price changes used by many stores: additional markups and markup cancellations.

Additional Markup is a price revision that increases selling price above the initial retail price.

An additional markup is used to correct an error made by the buyer or by the marking room personnel, which resulted in the initial price being marked too low. Another reason for an additional markup is to increase retail to coincide with an increase in cost. An additional markup might be taken on merchandise already in stock when reordered merchandise is retailed at a higher price. Most department and specialty stores want to avoid the confusion that occurs when the same style is marked at different retails.

Markup Cancellation is a reduction in the price of an item that previously had an additional markup.

A markup cancellation is a downward price adjustment that offsets the original or additional markup. It is used to adjust the markup on the purchase in accordance with the original intent and is not to be used to manipulate stock values. By definition, a markup cancellation never exceeds the amount of additional markup applied to an item.

Some stores do not recognize markup cancellations and classify all downward price changes as markdowns. Markup cancellations are infrequent, except in highly promotional departments/stores. Stores that do allow markup cancellations must be very careful in determining which downward revisions are markup cancellations. Markup cancellations and markdowns affect valuation of merchandise differently. Markup cancellations should be limited to correction of an error and cancellations of an additional markup. The cancellation of additional markup should never reduce the retail price lower than the original retail.

Discounts to Employees and Special Customers

As illustrated in Chapter 5, retail reductions influence the initial markup needed. Most stores give employees a discount, which is usually stated as a percent off the retail price. Discounts are an important fringe benefit for employees. Many stores allow larger discounts for management personnel. For instance, a manager or buyer may receive a 30% discount, whereas a salesperson in the same store may receive a 20% discount.

Some retailers in the home furnishings field offer independent interior designers discounts on purchases such as fabric, accessories, and case goods. In rare instances, educational institutions and charitable organizations may be given a discount by some retailers.

On a profit and loss statement, employee discounts are usually combined with markdowns and shortages to show total retail reductions. As seen in Chapter 5, retail reductions, including employee discounts, are important factors in determining initial markup.

EXAMPLE 6-8

An employee purchases a lamp that retails for $439. The employee discount is 15%. How much should the employee pay for the lamp (not including taxes)?

Solution:

$$\text{Employee discount} = \$439 \times 15\%$$
$$= \$65.85$$

$$\text{Employee purchase price} = \$439 - \$65.85$$
$$= \$373.15$$

Alternate Solution:

$$\text{Employee discount complement} = 100\% - 15\%$$
$$= 85\%$$

$$\text{Employee Price} = \text{Retail Price} \times \text{Discount Complement}$$
$$\$373.15 = \$439 \times 85\%$$

Practice Problems • Exercise 6.3

1. A store gives its employees a 25% discount on all merchandise purchased. If a salesperson buys a coat that retails for $249, (a) what is the amount of employee discount in dollars? (b) If sales tax is 8%, what will the employee pay for the coat?

(a.) Discount = $249.⁰⁰ × .25 = $62.²⁵

(b.) Total pd. = ($249.⁰⁰ × .75) × 1.08 = $201.⁶⁰

2. The lawyers for a store receive a 10.5% discount on all merchandise purchased. The tax on all purchases is 12%. If a store's lawyer bought a suit that retails for $500 and a shirt that retails for $50, determine the total amount of the purchase, including tax.

.895
$500.⁰⁰ + 50.⁰⁰ = $550.⁰⁰ × (1-.105) × 1.12 = $551.³²

3. As manager for a store, Mr. Thomas receives a 33⅓% discount on clothing and a 20% discount on furniture. He decides to purchase two suits retailing for $350 and $285 and a set of lawn furniture priced at $549. What will be his total bill, including a 6.5% tax on all items?

× (2)
Rounding error from 33⅓%

Suits = $350.⁰⁰ + 285.⁰⁰ = $635 × (1-.3333) = $423.³⁵

Lawn furniture = $549.⁰⁰ × (1-.20) = $439.20

Total pd. = ($423.35 + 439.20)(1.065) = $918.62   ($918.59)

4. Jane receives a 16⅔% employee discount on all merchandise. Determine her total payment for a group of items that retails for $25.00, $19.00, $49.99, $15.99, and $11 (include 7% tax).

× (1)

16.677.
Total purchase = $120.98
            × (1-.1667)
            _____
            $100.81
            × (1.07)
            _____
            $107.87

5. As a frequent customer at a small decorative fabric store, a local interior designer receives a 20% discount on all purchases. She bought 12 finials at $32 each, 6 fluted drapery rods at $42 each, and 12 metallic tassels at $48 each. Include a 9% tax on the purchase and calculate her total payment.

Total purchase = $384.⁰⁰ + 252 + 576 = $1,212.⁰⁰ × .80 × 1.09 = $1,056.86

DEFINITIONS

Additional Markup Price revision that increases selling price above the original retail price.

Competitive Pricing A pricing policy retailers use that sets prices exactly at or near the same price as competitors. Also called **at-the-market pricing**.

Everyday Low Pricing (EDLP) A pricing policy that sets prices somewhere between the lowest discounted sale price and the regular, non-sale price of competitors.

High/Low Pricing A pricing policy that sets prices above the EDLP of competitors and uses frequent special sales for short periods to increase consumer interest.

Leader Pricing A pricing policy where a retailer offers brand name merchandise at special, reduced prices to attract consumers with the hope that they will purchase other, regularly priced items.

Loss Leaders Well-known, name brand products priced below cost and used in leader pricing.

Markdown A reduction from the original or previous retail price of merchandise.

Markdown Cancellation Upward price adjustments that are offset against former markdowns.

Markdown Money Money obtained from manufacturers to cover lost gross margin dollars that result from markdowns occurring late in the season.

Markup Cancellation A reduction in the price of an item after it has been subject to additional markup.

Net Markdown The difference between the total markdown and the markdown cancellation.

Prestige Pricing A pricing policy used in retail stores that wish to project a prestigious image. Prices are set higher than competitors to reflect exclusivity, personal service, and high-quality merchandise. Also called **above-the-market pricing**.

Price Line A specific price at which merchandise is offered to the customer. Also called **price point**.

Price Lining The practice of predetermining the retail points at which an assortment of merchandise will be offered for sale.

Price Range The spread between the highest and lowest price line offered for sale.

Price Zone A series of price lines that are relatively close together and tend to appeal to a certain segment of customers.

Retail Reduction A reduction in the retail value of merchandise, such as markdowns, stock shortages, and employee and customer discounts.

Special Purchase Merchandise purchased by the retailer at a lower than regular price.

Chapter 6 • Summary Problems

1. During July, sales for the junior sportswear department were $575,000 and markdowns amounted to $161,000. What was the markdown percent for July?

$$\frac{\$161,000}{\$575,000} = 28.00\%$$

2. The men's department had sales of $50,000 for December. During the month, the buyer reduced 40 suits from $685 to $450 and 22 suits from $475 to $325. What was the markdown percent for the month?

$$MD = 40 \,(\underset{235}{\$685} - 450) = \$9,400.^{00}$$
$$22 \,(\underset{150}{\$475} - 325) = \underline{3,300.^{00}}$$
$$\$12,700.^{00}$$

$$MD\% = \$12,700.^{00} \div 50,000$$
$$= \underline{25.40\%}$$

3. A salesperson purchased the following items from a store that allows employees a 20% discount:

Quantity	Retail (each)
2 blouses	$25
1 jacket	$82
3 skirts	$40
2 belts	$10

$50.^{00}$
$82.^{00}$
$120.^{00}$
$20.^{00}$
$\underline{\$272.^{00}}$

Determine the total cost to the employee including a 7.5% sales tax.

$$\$272.^{00} \times .80 \times 1.075 = \underline{\$233.92}$$

4. The shoe department had gross sales of $320,000 and customer returns of $19,000. Determine the markdown percent if the dollar markdowns amounted to $54,180.

$$NS = \$301,000.^{00}$$

$$MD\% = \$54,180 \div 301,000$$
$$= \underline{18.00\%}$$

5. During October, the markdowns for a department were $12,550. This amounted to 32% for the month. Determine the net sales during the month.

$$NS = \$12,550 \div .32$$
$$= \$39,218.75$$

6. Determine the markdown percent for July if sales were $28,000 and the buyer for home furnishings made the following markdowns:

Quantity	Original Retail		Markdown Price	
10 table lamps	$225	80	$145	$800.00
15 silk plants	$ 79	35	$ 44	525.00
8 vases	$125	55	$ 70	440.00
20 pictures	$289	90	$199	1,800.00
5 floor lamps	$254	127	$127	635.00

Total MD = $4,200.00

MD% = $4,200.00 ÷ 28,000 = 15.00%

7. The reports for the junior department indicated that net sales for April totaled $540,000 and markdowns were 41%. Determine the dollar amount of markdowns.

$$\$MD = \$540,000 \times .41 = \$221,400.00$$

8. A retail store allows groups and organizations from the local high school a 15% discount on all purchases. If cheerleaders from the local high school purchase 32 yards of fabric retailing for $5.98 a yard and 12 yards of trim at $2.98 a yard, how much will they pay, including a 8% sales tax?

Purchase = $191.36 + 35.76 = $227.12 × .85 × 1.08 = $208.50

9. The sportswear buyer reduced 20 belts from $20 to $12 for a four-day sale. Ten of the belts were sold. After the sale, the remaining belts were priced at $15 each. Calculate the markdown cancellation.

$$MDC = 10 \times (\$15 - 12) = \$30.00$$

10. The markdowns for a three-month period in the children's department amounted to $133,000. If the net sales for this period were $380,000, determine the markdown percent.

$$MD\% = \$133,000 \div 380,000 = 35.00\%$$

11. Employees of a specialty store receive a 25% discount. Determine a salesperson's bill if she purchased the following items (include an 11% sales tax):

Quantity	Retail (each)	
1 designer suit	$850	$850.00
3 wool skirts	$ 85	255.00
2 wool blend blazers	$145	290.00
2 silk blouses	$ 65	130.00

$$\$1,525.00 \times .75 \times 1.11 = \$1,269.56$$

12. During May, the Radio Shop had a net markdown of $850. If the total markdowns were $1,550, determine the markdown cancellation.

$$MDC = \$1,550.00 - 850.00 = \$700.00$$

13. A buyer received 40 skirts retailing for $45 each. For a Moonlight Madness Sale the 40 skirts were reduced to $30. During the sale 28 skirts were sold. After the sale was over the remaining 12 skirts were returned to their original price. All these skirts were sold for $45. Find the markdown cancellation, net markdown, and net markdown percent.

$$MDC = 12 \times (\$45 - 30) = \$180.00 \quad (a.)$$
$$Sales = (28 \times 30) + (12 \times 45)$$
$$= 840 + 540$$
$$= \$1,380.00$$

$$MD = 40 \times (\$45 - 30) = \$600.00$$
$$NMD = \$600.00 - 180.00 = \$420.00 \quad (b.)$$
$$NMD\% = \$420 \div 1,380$$
$$= 30.43\% \quad (c.)$$

14. A tea table retailing for $550 in the furniture department was reduced 20.5%. Calculate the new selling price of the table after the markdown was taken.

$$\$550.00 (1 - .205) = \$437.25$$

15. A buyer had 64 knit shirts in stock at a retail price of $32 each. He marked them down to $28 for a five-day sale. After the sale 21 shirts remained. The buyer marked the remaining shirts back to the original price of $32. Determine the markdown cancellation.

$$MDC = 21 \times (\$32.00 - 28.00)$$
$$= 21 \times (\$4.00)$$
$$= \$84.00$$

16. A giftware buyer received 40 crystal clocks that retailed for $69 each. Five clocks sold at that price before a special sales event. The remaining 35 clocks were marked down to $50. Twenty-one of the clocks were sold during the sale, and the remaining clocks were marked to the original $69 price. The remaining clocks were eventually sold at full price. Calculate the net markdown percent.

$$MD = 35 \times (\$69.00 - 50.00) = \$665.00$$
$$MDC = (35 - 21)(\$69.00 - 50.00) = 14 \times \$19.00 = \$266.00$$
$$NMD = \$665.00 - 266.00 = \$399.00$$
$$Sales = (5 \times 69) + (21 \times 50) + (14 \times 69) = \$345.00 + 1,050.00 + 966 = \$2,361.00$$
$$NMD\% = \$399.00 \div 2,361.00 = 16.90\%$$

17. The buyer for accessories received 130 silk scarves priced at $30 each. For a two-day sale the remaining 120 scarves were reduced to $20. Of this group, 40 scarves were sold. After the sale, the buyer marked the remaining scarves to $25, and all these scarves were sold for $25 each. Calculate the net markdown percent.

$$MD = 120 \times \$10 = \$1,200.00$$
$$MDC = 80 \times \$5 = 400.00$$
$$NMD = \$800.00$$

$$Sales = 10 \times \$30 = \$300.00$$
$$40 \times \$20 = 800.00$$
$$80 \times \$25 = 2,000.00$$
$$\$3,100.00$$

$$NMD\% = \$800.00 \div 3,100.00 = 25.81\%$$

CHAPTER 7

Inventory Valuation

OBJECTIVES

- To define and determine retail deductions.
- To explain the differences between book inventory, physical inventory, and estimated physical inventory.
- To define and calculate shortage based on book and physical inventory figures.
- To understand why department and specialty stores use the retail method of inventory (RIM).
- To calculate maintained markup and gross margin using the retail method of inventory.

KEY POINTS

- A book inventory provides information on the value of the inventory between physical inventories.
- The amount of shortage that has occurred cannot be calculated without both book and physical inventories.
- The retail method of inventory provides information that allows calculation of gross margin at frequent intervals.

A merchant must know how much stock is on hand in order to determine how much to purchase and to calculate profit. The actual counting of merchandise, a physical inventory, is time-consuming and expensive; consequently, most stores take a complete physical inventory only once or twice a year. In between physical inventories, the value of merchandise on hand can be determined from accounting records.

In all but the smallest stores, the accounting or statistical department maintains separate records for each department. The inventory at the beginning of the period is adjusted to reflect purchases, sales, returns, price changes, and so forth, as they occur. This provides the retailer with a **perpetual inventory** because the value of the inventory can be determined at any time.

A perpetual inventory is also referred to as a **book inventory** because it is based on the accounting books or records. This book or statistical inventory requires a day-to-day recording of all movements of merchandise in and out of the department. It gives the buyer the total retail value of the stock at any time. It is important to remember that the terms stock and inventory are used interchangeably.

In order to maintain a book inventory, one copy of each transaction affecting the value of the inventory—sales, purchases, price changes, transfers, returns to vendors, customer returns—must be sent to the accounting office. In actual practice, the book inventory is reported to buyers and major executives at predetermined intervals such as every seven days, ten days, or every month.

CALCULATION OF BOOK INVENTORY

The disadvantage of utilizing a perpetual inventory is that extensive records must be maintained because everything that affects the value of the inventory must be reported. Care must be taken that purchases, returns to vendors, sales, customer returns, employee discounts, special customer discounts, transfers, markdowns, markdown cancellations, and additional markups are accurately reported. **Transactions that increase the value of the inventory** include purchases, transfers in, customer returns, markdown cancellations, and additional markups. **Transactions that reduce the value of the inventory** include sales, returns to vendors, markdowns, revisions downward, transfers out, and employee discounts

> Book Inventory = Total Merchandise Handled – Total Retail Deductions

Total Merchandise Handled

Total merchandise handled is the sum of beginning inventory plus **net** receipts (both transfers and purchases) and adjustments for additional markup and markup cancellations. (When they occur, additional markup and markup cancellations must be kept separate from markdowns and markdown cancellations.) The section on the retail method of inventory explains why it is important to classify price changes accurately. Total merchandise handled is affected by the following:

> **Beginning Inventory.**   When a physical inventory figure is available, it is used, because a physical inventory is more accurate than a book inventory value.
>
> **Net Purchases.**   Returns to vendors (RTV) are subtracted from gross purchases.
>
> **Net Transfers.**   Merchandise is frequently transferred between stores and may be transferred between departments. A transfer in is treated like a purchase; a transfer out is treated like a RTV.
>
> **Net Price Revisions.**   Additional markup and markup cancellations (also known as downward revisions) are price changes that affect the value of total merchandise handled.

EXAMPLE 7-1

Determine the value of total merchandise handled from the following figures:

Opening inventory	$20,000
Gross purchases	10,000
RTV	450
Transfers out	350
Transfers in	150
Additional markup	48

Solution:

		Merchandise Handled	
	Opening inventory		$20,000
	Gross purchases	$10,000	
(minus)	RTV	− 450	
	Net purchases		9,550
	Transfers out	$ 350	
(minus)	Transfers in	− 150	
	Net transfers *out*		− 200*
	Additional markup		48
	Total merchandise handled		$29,398

*Note: Transfers out exceeded transfers in.

Retail Deductions

It is important to use net figures in determining total deductions. Sales are adjusted by the amount of customer returns and allowances; markdowns are reduced by markdown cancellations.

Net Sales.   Customer returns and allowances are subtracted from gross sales.

Net Markdowns.   Markdown cancellations are subtracted from markdowns.

Discounts to Employees (and any other special customers).   These discounts reduce the amount of sales that can be achieved from an inventory; they must be treated as deductions from total merchandise handled.

EXAMPLE 7-2

Calculate the total deductions and closing book inventory from the following figures:

Total merchandise handled	$29,398
Gross sales	9,870
Customer returns	642
Employee discounts	380
Markdowns	936
Markdown cancellations	76

Solution:

Total merchandise handled			$29,398
Deductions:			
Gross sales	$9,870		
(minus) Customer returns	– 642		
Net sales		$9,228	
Markdowns	$ 936		
(minus) Cancellations	– 76		
Net markdowns		$ 860	
Employee discounts		380	
Total deductions			– 10,468
Closing book inventory			$18,930

Maintaining a book inventory requires time and constant monitoring of all records. Failure to record any information involving an increase or decrease in the value of an item of merchandise will result in an error in the valuation of book inventory. For example, 36 dresses that originally retailed for $80 are marked down to $58. This is a markdown of $22 per dress. If only 30 are reported to have been reduced, the accounting records will overstate the inventory by $132 ($22 × 6 = $132). Discrepancies of inventory figures can be caused by errors in completing forms and in posting information to accounting records.

Stores that use computerized sales registers can check for the correct price, regular or reduced, according to style number; consequently, they have fewer markdown errors. Problems still occur as a result of incorrect ticketing, missing tags, incorrect handling of customer returns, incorrect entry of information into the computer, and so forth.

Practice Problems • Exercise 7.1

1. Calculate closing book inventory.

Opening inventory	+ $287,219
Gross purchases	+ 122,756
RTV	− 3,176
Net transfers in	+ 4,320
Additional markup	+ 170
Net sales	− 126,970
Markdowns	− 10,835
Markdown cancellations	+ 720
Employee discounts	− 4,540

$269,664.00

2. Calculate (a) total merchandise handled and (b) closing book inventory.

Opening inventory	+ $ 76,346
Net purchases	+ 168,754
Transfers in	+ 1,346
Transfers out	− 1,896
Gross sales	− 180,920
Customer returns	+ 10,240
Markdowns	− 16,710
Markdown cancellations	+ 496
Employee discounts	− 2,080

(a.) $244,550.00

$188,974

(b.) $55,576.00

3. Calculate (a) total merchandise handled and (b) closing book inventory. (Factors may not be listed in the order to be used.)

Opening inventory	+ $36,728
Gross purchases	+ 87,317
RTV	− 1,117
Transfers in	+ 984
Transfers out	− 1,576
Additional markup	+ 96
Gross sales	87,843
Customer returns	4,981
Markdowns	6,516
Markdown cancellations	423
Employee discounts	2,015

(a) TMH = $122,432

$90,970

$31,462.00 = CBI

4. Calculate closing book inventory.

Gross purchases	+ $567,416
Opening inventory	+ 117,260
Transfers in	+ 9,368
Transfers out	− 11,980
RTV	− 5,424
Markdowns	− 32,968
Markdown cancellations	+ 976
Gross sales	− 582,390
Employee discounts	− 2,956
Customer returns	+ 49,203

$108,505

CALCULATION OF SHORTAGE

When the retailer takes a physical inventory, the actual value of the inventory, as determined by the physical count, is compared with book inventory, and **books are adjusted to agree with the physical inventory**.

Shortage or shrinkage refers to the difference between physical and book inventory when the physical inventory is less than book inventory. If the physical inventory is larger than book inventory, an overage exists.

Shortage or shrinkage.   Occurs when book inventory is larger than physical inventory.

Overage.   Occurs when physical inventory exceeds book inventory.

The amount of shortage or overage that has occurred can be determined only by comparing physical and book inventories. Of course, the most common situation is for the physical inventory to be smaller than book inventory. Nearly all overages are caused by clerical errors. For example, when a customer returns merchandise, an overage will result if the return is not recorded.

As you learned in Chapter 6, shortages are caused by physical loss of merchandise and clerical errors. Most of the physical loss is the result of theft; however, merchandise can be lost through breakage, incorrect measuring/weighing, and giving samples. Improper handling of sales transactions, incorrect counting of merchandise, and failure to record merchandise on loan can also contribute to shortage.

Merchandise shortage is a major drain on profit. Many stores have found that loss from internal theft (pilferage by employees) can be as large as loss from external theft. Shortage in excess of what is considered "normal" indicates a need for careful evaluation of security procedures and record keeping. The University of Florida conducts an annual National Retail Security Survey. The 1998 survey found that shortage represented 1.72% of total retail sales. "Most loss-prevention executives in the NRSS (National Retail Security Survey) felt employee theft was their biggest problem, representing 42 percent of all losses. Shoplifting was another 34.4 percent, while 17.6 percent was administration error and 5.3 percent, vendor fraud."[1]

Shortage Percent = Amount of Shortage ÷ Net Sales

EXAMPLE 7-3

During the spring season (February 1 through July 31), the lingerie department had net sales of $350,000. On July 31, a physical inventory showed $87,110. The book inventory showed $92,610. What was the shortage percent for the season?

Solution:

Book inventory	$92,610	Shortage %	= $5,500 ÷ $350,000
Physical inventory	− 87,110		= 1.57%
Shortage	$ 5,500		

---

[1]Silverman, D. (1999, May 24). Who's minding the store theft? *DNR*, pp. 8–9.

EXAMPLE 7-4

Determine the shortage or overage percent for a department with the following figures:

Opening inventory	$ 75,000	Net transfers in	$ 520
Gross purchases	548,000	Additional markup	86
Returns to vendors	10,200	Gross sales	531,800
Customer returns	27,000	Markdowns	33,100
Employee discounts	2,450	Markdown cancellations	900
		Closing physical inventory	68,014

Solution:

Opening inventory		$ 75,000	
Gross purchases	$548,000		
RTV	− 10,200		
Net purchases		$537,800	
Net transfers in		520	
Additional markup		86	
Total merchandise handled			$613,406
Deductions:			
Gross sales	$531,800		
Customer returns	− 27,000		
Net sales		$504,800	
Markdowns	$ 33,100		
Markdown cancellations	− 900		
Net markdowns		$ 32,200	
Employee discounts		2,450	
Total deductions			− 539,450
Closing book inventory			$ 73,956
Physical inventory			− 68,014
Shortage			$ 5,942

Shortage % = $5,942 ÷ $504,800 = 1.18%

1. Based on the following figures, determine the shortage or overage percent.

Opening inventory	$190,000
Gross purchases	315,000
RTV	21,000
Transfers in	10,500
Transfers out	8,400
Customer returns	21,500
Gross sales	311,000
Markdowns	12,600
Markdown cancellations	1,600
Employee discounts	3,400
Closing physical inventory	176,700

(handwritten annotations)

TMH = $486,100.00

$289,500

RD = $303,900

CBI = ~~~~ 182,200

Shortage = $5,500.00
Shortage % = $5,500.00 ÷ 289,500
= 1.90%

2. Determine the shortage or overage percent under the following conditions:

Opening inventory	$ 78,000
Gross purchases	117,500
RTV	6,000
Additional markon	280
Gross sales	62,400
Customer returns	5,900
Markdowns	11,340
Markdown cancellations	780
Closing physical inventory	123,180

(handwritten annotations)

TMH = $189,780.00

RD = $67,060.00

CBI = $122,720

overage = $460.00
overage % = $460.00 ÷ 56,500.00
= 0.81%

3. Calculate shortage or overage percent, given the following: (Factors may not be in the order to be used.)

Opening inventory	$ 36,842
Gross purchases	102,351
Transfers in	8,526
Transfers out	9,893
Markdowns	14,618
Markdown cancellations	976
Additional markup	134
RTV	3,239
Gross sales	96,527
Customer returns	9,827
Employee discounts	1,068
Closing physical inventory	34,319

Handwritten work:

TMH = $36,842 − 3,239 + 102,351 + 8,526 − 9,893 + 134

= $134,721.00

RD = $96,527 − 9827 + 14,618 − 976 + 1,068

= $101,410.00

CBI = $33,311

$86,700

Overage = $1,008

Overage % = $1,008 ÷ 86,700

= 1.16%

ESTIMATED SHORTAGE

When calculating the book inventory of merchandise that typically has large shortages, the **amount of shortage that probably has occurred** is estimated, based on past experience. When a physical inventory is taken, it is important to calculate the shortage that actually has occurred.

The term **estimated physical inventory** is used to describe the value of the inventory as determined from records **after an adjustment has been made for estimated shortage**. Adjustments for shortage are calculated as a percent of net sales. For example, during a period of time when net sales totaled $186,000 and shortage was estimated at 1.4%, the estimated amount of shortage was $2,604 ($186,000 × 1.4%).

EXAMPLE 7-5

Calculate (a) estimated shortage and (b) estimated physical inventory using the following information:

Opening inventory	$16,400
Net purchases	84,300
Net sales	76,000
Net markdowns	3,600
Employee discounts	2,200
Estimated shortage	1.6%

Solution:

Opening inventory	$16,400	
Net purchases	84,300	
Total merchandise handled		$100,700
Deductions:		
Net sales	$76,000	
Net markdowns	3,600	
Employee discounts	2,200	
Total deductions		− 81,800
Closing book inventory		$ 18,900
Estimated shortage ($76,000 × 1.6%)		− 1,216 (a)
Estimated physical inventory		$ 17,684 (b)

It is important to understand the differences between the following terms:

Book Inventory. The value of the inventory as determined from records rather than a physical count.

Physical Inventory. The value as shown by an actual count of the merchandise.

Estimated Shortage. The amount of shortage that probably has occurred based on past experience.

Estimated Physical Inventory. The value of the inventory as determined by book inventory after an adjustment has been made for estimated shortage.

It is unrealistic to expect that shortages can be eliminated completely; however, if a satisfactory profit is to be earned, shortages must be controlled.

Practice Problems • Exercise 7.3

1. GIVEN:

Net sales	$^{+}$$84,055
Markdowns	$+$ 2,520
Employee discounts	$-$ 864
Opening inventory	$+$ 30,420
Net purchases	$+$91,350
Net transfers out	$-$ 670
Estimated shortage	1.4%

$RD = \$87,439$

$TMH = \$121,100$

$1.4\% = \$1,176.77$

FIND: (a) Estimated physical inventory and (b) actual shortage percent if closing physical inventory was $32,800.

$CBI = \$87,439 - 121,100$
$= \$33,661$

(a.) $EPI = \$33,661 - 1,176.77$
$= \$32,484.23$

(b.) shortage % $= \$33,661.^{00} - 32,800$
$= \$861$
$\dfrac{\$861}{\$84,005} = 1.02\%$

2. A retail store had an opening inventory of $34,000. Net purchases totaled $7,800; gross sales were $14,250; customer returns amounted to $1,115; and net markdowns totaled $480. FIND: (a) Closing book inventory and (b) estimated physical inventory if shortages were estimated to be 1.2%.

$13,135$

$TMH = \$34,000 + 7,800 = \$41,800$
$RD = \$14,250 - 1,115 + 480 = 13,615$

(a.) $\overline{\$28,185}$

$E. Shortage = \$13,135 \times .012 = \$157.^{62}$

$EPI = \$28,185 - 157.^{62}$
$= \$28,027.^{38}$

3. GIVEN:

Opening inventory	$15,860
Gross purchases	35,200
Additional markon	36
Transfers in	870
Transfers out	520
RTV	980
Gross sales	29,846
Markdowns	3,116
Markdown cancellations	48
Customer returns	180
Employee discounts	710

$TMH = \$50,466$

$RD = \$33,444$

$CBI = \$17,022$

$NS = \$29,666$

FIND: (a) Closing book inventory, (b) actual shortage or overage percent if physical inventory is $17,326, and (c) estimated physical inventory when shortages are estimated to be 0.85%.

(a.) $17,022

(b.) overage % = ($17,326 − 17,022) ÷ 29,666
= 1.02%

(c.) EPI = $17,022 − 252.14
= $16,769.84

METHODS OF INVENTORY VALUATION

Sales are made and reported in retail values; yet calculation of profit and loss requires **knowing the cost value** of opening and closing inventories so cost of merchandise sold can be calculated. There are two basic ways to value inventory—retail method and cost method. Management must decide which method of inventory valuation is to be used.

Retail Method of Inventory Valuation

Today most moderate- and large-sized department and specialty stores use the retail method of inventory (also known as **RIM**, retail inventory method) to determine the cost value of their inventories. The merchandise in a department typically includes some items that have been marked down. The retail method of inventory valuation allows this depreciation in retail to be reflected in the cost value of the inventory.

> **Retail Inventory Method (RIM).** **A procedure whereby the approximate cost value is determined from the retail value.**

In almost every department there are items that have been marked down. One advantage of the retail method is that this reduction (markdown) in retail value results in a corresponding reduction in the cost value of the inventory. The retail method of inventory valuation results in an inventory figure that is the **lower of cost or market value**.

The retail method of inventory requires the maintenance of a book inventory in addition to records that allow for calculation of the cost of total goods handled. Advantages and limitations of RIM will be easier to understand after using the procedure.

Many of the steps in the retail method of inventory involve concepts already learned. (Do not be confused by thinking this is something entirely new.) It may be helpful to review cumulative markup, cost of merchandise sold, and book inventory.

Steps:

1. Calculation of total value of merchandise handled at both retail and cost.
2. Calculation of cost percent of total merchandise handled. (Cumulative markup can be calculated.)
3. Calculation of closing book inventory at retail.
4. Calculation of approximate cost value of the closing book inventory.

Inventory valuation at cost, using the retail method, is complete; however, two more steps are necessary for determination of gross margin.

5. Calculation of gross cost of merchandise sold. (Maintained markup can now be calculated.)
6. Calculation of total cost of merchandise sold and gross margin.

Example 7-6 shows the correct way to set up a problem. The numbers in parentheses correspond to the steps in the procedure. Refer to the solution as each step is presented.

> *Suggestion:* **In order to avoid confusion, it is very important to keep cost and retail values in separate columns. It may be helpful to draw a line between the cost and retail columns and to work these problems on lined paper.**

EXAMPLE 7-6

Calculate gross margin percent.

	Cost	Retail		Cost	Retail
Opening inventory	$15,000	$25,000	Additional markup		$ 24
Gross purchases	6,000	10,000	Gross sales		8,750
RTV	300	500	Customer returns		435
Freight	240		Markdowns		189
Cash discounts	199		Markdown cancellations		39
Alteration costs	37		Employee discounts		55

Solution:

	Cost		Retail	
Opening inventory		$15,000		$25,000
Gross purchases	$6,000		$10,000	
RTV	− 300		− 500	
Net purchases		5,700		9,500
Freight		240		xx
Additional markup		xx		24
(1) Total merchandise handled		$20,940		$34,524
(2) Cost % = $20,940 ÷ 34,524 = 60.65%				
Deductions:				
Gross sales			$ 8,750	
Customer returns			− 435	
Net sales			$ 8,315	
Markdowns			189	
Markdown cancellations			− 39	
Net markdowns			150	
Employee discounts			55	
Total deductions				− 8,520
Closing book inventory		− 15,771 (4)		$26,004 (3)
Gross cost of merchandise sold		$ 5,169 (5)		
Cash discounts		− 199		
Net cost of merchandise sold		$ 4,970		
Alteration costs		+ 37		
Total cost of merchandise sold		$ 5,007 (6)		

Gross margin % = ($8,315 − $5,007) ÷ $8,315 = 39.78%

Step 1.   Calculation of cost and retail values of total merchandise handled.

Earlier in this chapter, you learned to calculate the retail value of merchandise handled. This step requires using the cost value of these same factors plus consideration of freight charges. As discussed in Chapter 4, transportation charges required to get merchandise to the store are part of the cost of the merchandise. Some factors, such as purchases and transfers, affect both cost and retail values, whereas other factors affect only cost or only retail.

Remember, price revisions such as additional markup and markup cancellations affect the value of goods handled, whereas markdowns and markdown cancellations are retail deductions.

Step 2. Calculation of cost percent of total merchandise handled.

Cost percent can be calculated directly from the cost and retail values of total merchandise handled. In Example 7-6, the cost percent is 60.65%.

> Cost % = Cost of Total Merchandise Handled ÷ Retail of Total Merchandise Handled

$$\text{Cost \%} = \$20{,}940 \div \$34{,}524 = 60.65\%$$

Step 3. Calculation of closing book inventory, a retail value.

Retail deductions (net sales, net markdowns, and employee discounts) are deducted from the total merchandise handled to provide the retail value of the closing book inventory. In the example, closing book inventory is $26,004.

> Closing Book Inventory = Total Merchandise Handled – Total Retail Deductions

$$\text{Closing book inventory} = \$34{,}534 - \$8{,}520 = \$26{,}004$$

Note: When a physical inventory is taken, **the value of the actual physical inventory is used** in Step 4, rather than the book inventory. Also, at that time it is possible to calculate the actual shortage or overage.

Step 4. Calculation of approximate cost value of the closing book inventory.

The retail value of the closing book or physical inventory (when available) is converted to its approximate cost value by multiplying the retail value by the cost percent calculated in Step 2. In the example, the cost value of the closing inventory is $15,771.

> Cost of Closing Book Inventory = Retail Value of Closing Book Inventory × Cost %

$$\text{Cost value of closing book inventory} = \$26{,}004 \times 60.65\% = \$15{,}771$$

Step 5. Calculation of gross cost of merchandise sold.

Gross cost of merchandise sold is the difference between the cost value of total merchandise handled and cost value of the ending inventory. In the example, gross cost of merchandise sold is $5,169.

> Gross Cost of Merchandise Sold = Cost of Merchandise Handled – Cost of Ending Inventory

$$\text{Gross cost of merchandise sold} = \$20{,}940 - \$15{,}771 = \$5{,}169$$

Step 6.   Calculation of total cost of merchandise sold and gross margin.

To arrive at total cost of merchandise sold, the gross cost of merchandise sold is adjusted by cash discounts and alteration costs; cash discounts are subtracted and alteration costs are added. In our example:

Net Cost of Merchandise Sold = Gross Cost of Merchandise Sold – Cash Discounts

Net cost of merchandise sold = $5,169 – $199 = $4,970

Total Cost of Merchandise Sold = Net Cost of Merchandise Sold + Alteration Costs

Total cost of merchandise sold = $4,970 + $37 = $5,007

Remember, gross margin is the difference between net sales and total cost of merchandise sold.

Gross Margin = Net Sales – Total Cost of Merchandise Sold

Gross margin $ = $8,315 – $5,007 = $3,308
Gross margin % = $3,308 ÷ $8,315 = 39.78%

The main purpose of RIM is to determine the cost value of the ending inventory so cost of merchandise sold and, consequently, gross margin can be calculated without having to take a physical inventory. This allows for frequent, perhaps monthly, calculation of cost of merchandise sold and gross margin without taking a physical inventory each time. Use of an estimated physical inventory value (closing book inventory adjusted for probable shortage) results in a gross margin that is adjusted for shortage.

Review the six steps:

1. Calculation of total value of merchandise handled at both retail and cost.
2. Calculation of cost percent of total merchandise handled.
3. Calculation of closing book inventory at retail value.
4. Calculation of approximate cost value of closing inventory. (Use the physical inventory when this value is known.)
5. Calculation of gross cost of merchandise sold.
6. Calculation of total cost of merchandise sold and gross margin.

The retail method of inventory is an important merchandise management tool because it provides information for regular and frequent evaluation. Potential problems can be identified and adjustments made prior to the end of the season or year. Figure 7-1 is an example of a form that might be used by a smaller store for calculation of gross margin. The form allows for calculation of gross margin every three months rather than every month. When an actual physical inventory is taken, that

Line #	Department Stock Ledger			Per 1	Per 2	Per 3	Per 4	Year
	Store							
	Department							
	Cost:							
1	Beginning inventory			$15,000				
2	Purchases			5,700				
3	Transportation			240				
4	Transfers in (plus)							
5	Transfers out (minus)							
6	Total Merchandise Handled			20,940				
	Retail:							
7	Beginning inventory			25,000				
8	Purchases			9,500				
9	Markups			24				
10	Transfers in (plus)							
11	Transfers out (minus)							
12	Total Merchandise Handled			34,524				
13	Cost % (Line 6 ÷ Line 12)			60.65%				
14	Cumulative markon %			39.35%				
	(100% – Line 13)							
15	Net sales			8,315				
16	Markdowns			150				
17	Shrinkage provision							
18	Sales discounts			55				
19	Total Retail Deductions			8,520				
20	Ending inventory (Line 12 – Line 19)			26,004				
21	Ending inventory at cost (Line 20 × Line 13)			15,771				
	Gross Margin							
22	Gross cost of merchandise sold			5,169				
	(Line 6 – Line 21)							
23	Maintained markup $			3,146				
	(Line 15 – Line 22)							
24	Maintained markup %			37.84%				
	(Line 23 ÷ Line 15)							
25	Cash discounts earned			199				
26	Alteration/Workroom costs			37				
27	Total cost of merchandise sold			5,007				
	(Line 22 – Line 25 + Line 26)							
28	Gross margin (Line 15 – Line 27)			3,308				
29	Gross margin %			39.78%				
	(Line 28 ÷ Line 15)							

Figure 7-1. Form for calculation of gross margin by a small store.

figure will be used on line 20. This form allows for estimated shortage for each period (every three months); see line 17.

Original-Cost Method of Inventory Valuation

The cost method of inventory valuation may be used by firms where turnover is slow or where inventory is small in comparison to sales volume. Stores with slow turnover and/or large unit sales may use a cost method based on maintenance of a book inventory at cost. A store that has high-priced items, such as a furniture or appliance store, might put the cost on the price ticket by using a code. When the item is sold, this portion of the price ticket is retained in order to maintain a book inventory at both cost and retail.

An alternative method of maintaining book inventory at cost is to refer to the vendor's invoice for cost information as items are sold. This method is appropriate only when the number of transactions is limited and items have a high unit value.

Advantages and Disadvantages of the Retail Method of Inventory (RIM)

The extensive record keeping that is necessary for a book inventory can be a disadvantage. As you learned in the section on book inventory, any transaction affecting the retail value of the inventory must be recorded. All transactions that affect the value of the inventory must be reported to the information management/statistics office. Some small retailers, especially those that sell very high-priced items, believe the retail method is too complex and time consuming. Because RIM uses a cost percent that is the average over a period of time, it may result in a closing cost value that is not an exact figure. If markup on merchandise has varied, as might be the situation when some merchandise is brought into the store for a special sale, the merchandise sold first may be the merchandise on which the lowest markup was taken. The actual goods left in the inventory may be goods on which a higher, more typical, markup was taken. This is not a major concern to most stores. However, it does point out the importance of maintaining separate records for each department or, in some instances, major classifications.

Moderate- and large-size department and specialty stores consider the retail method superior to the cost method for the following reasons:

- It allows for more efficient merchandise management.
- It is more accurate.
- It may be less expensive.
- It is more flexible.[2]

Suggestions for Working RIM Problems

Example 7-7 introduces two new factors that influence the calculation of gross margin when they occur. In this example, a rebate has been received from a manufacturer. The rebate reduces the cost of the merchandise handled, just as a consumer rebate ultimately reduces the cost of a purchase for the consumer.

Also, in Example 7-7 there is a markup cancellation that reduces the retail value of the total merchandise handled. A markup cancellation affects only the retail value and must be subtracted.

The factors in Example 7-7 have **not been separated** according to whether they affect the total merchandise handled or deductions. Before starting to work a problem, determine in which part of the problem each factor will be used.

In many schools, students are doing RIM problems with a computer spreadsheet. The authors recommend that at least two of the practice problems in Exercise 7.4 be worked on lined notebook paper to ensure that calculations are understood. Unless the class has access to a computer lab during class time, any quiz or test will have to be done with pencil and paper. RIM problems can be done in any computer lab or on a home computer. Example 7-7 illustrates how RIM problems can be set up on a spreadsheet.

Utilizing a computer spreadsheet makes it easy to do "what if" problems. For instance, how much would the gross margin percent in Example 7-7 increase if net

[2]National Retail Merchants Association. (1971). *Retail inventory made practical.* New York: Author, p. 3.

markdowns were reduced from $6,626 to $4,800? When the individual values and correct formulas have been entered in a spreadsheet, a change in any one value immediately changes all the other numbers that utilized the revised value (see Example 7-8).

With the exception of net markdowns, Example 7-8 uses the same information as Example 7-7. A comparison of the two examples shows that gross margin improves by 1.3% (42.45% vs. 43.75%) if net markdowns can be reduced to $4,800.

EXAMPLE 7-7

Calculate gross margin, given:

	Cost	Retail		Cost	Retail
Opening inventory	$31,458	$56,680	Gross Sales		$80,760
Gross purchases	41,860	84,320	Customer returns		6,920
Returns to vendors	440	820	Markdowns		6,843
Cash discounts	621		Markdown cancellations		217
Rebate*	180		Employee discounts		934
Additional markup		360	Freight	$970	
Markup cancellation*		90	Alteration costs	417	
*Must be deducted.					

Solution:

	Cost				Retail	
Merchandise Handled:						
Opening inventory		$31,458			$56,680	
Gross purchases	$41,860			$84,320		
Returns to vendors	440			820		
Net purchases		41,420			83,500	
Freight		970				
Rebate		−180				
Additional markup				360		
Markup cancellation				−90		
Net additional markup					270	
Total Merchandise Handled			$73,668			$140,450
Cost %		52.45%				
Deductions:						
Gross sales				80,760		
Customer returns				6,920		
Net sales					73,840	
Markdowns				6,843		
Markdown cancellation				217		
Net markdowns					6,626	
Employee discounts					934	
Total Deductions						81,400
Closing Book Inventory			30,973			$59,050
Gross Cost of Merchandise Sold			$42,695			
Cash discounts (minus)			621			
Net cost of merchandise sold			$42,074			
Alteration/workroom costs (plus)			417			
Total Cost of Merchandise Sold			$42,491			
Gross Margin $			$31,349			
Gross Margin %		42.45%				

EXAMPLE 7-8

Calculate gross margin, given:

With the exception of net markdowns, all values are the same as in Example 7-7.

	Cost	Retail		Cost	Retail
Opening inventory	$31,458	$56,680	Gross Sales		$80,760
Gross purchases	41,860	84,320	Customer returns		6,920
Returns to vendors	440	820	Net markdowns		4,800
Cash discounts	621				
Rebate*	180		Employee discounts		934
Additional markup		360	Freight	$ 970	
Markup cancellation*		90	Alteration costs	417	
*Must be deducted.					

Solution:

		Cost			Retail	
Merchandise Handled:						
Opening inventory		$31,458			$56,680	
Gross purchases	$41,860			$84,320		
Returns to vendors	440			820		
Net purchases		41,420			83,500	
Freight		970				
Rebate		−180				
Additional markup				360		
Markup cancellation				−90		
Net additional markup					270	
Total Merchandise Handled		$73,668				$140,450
Cost %		52.45%				
Deductions:						
Gross sales				80,760		
Customer returns				6,920		
Net sales					73,840	
Markdowns						
Markdown cancellation						
Net markdowns					4,800	
Employee discounts					934	
Total Deductions						79,574
Closing Book Inventory			31,930			$60,876
Gross Cost of Merchandise Sold			$41,738			
Cash discounts (minus)			621			
Net cost of merchandise sold			$41,117			
Alteration/workroom costs (plus)			417			
Total Cost of Merchandise Sold			$41,534			
Gross Margin $			$32,306			
Gross Margin %		43.75%				

Practice Problems • Exercise 7.4

Work problems on lined paper. In some practice problems, factors will not be given in the order in which they need to be used.

1. Calculate (a) closing book inventory, (b) cost value of closing inventory, and (c) gross cost of merchandise sold.

   GIVEN:

	Cost	Retail
Opening inventory	$39,500	$ 77,400
Gross purchases	69,000	136,000
RTV	640	1,200
Additional markup		800
Markup cancellation		320
Freight	3,260	
Gross sales		117,000
Customer returns		2,500
Markdowns		9,300
Markdown cancellations		460

2. Calculate (a) closing book inventory, (b) shortage percent, and (c) gross cost of merchandise sold.

   GIVEN:

	Cost	Retail
Opening inventory	$16,400	$34,600
Net purchases	10,800	21,300
Freight	580	
Additional markup		180
Rebate from vendor	230	
Gross sales		24,700
Customer returns		1,080
Net markdowns		2,120
Closing physical inventory		29,860

3. Determine (a) gross cost of merchandise sold, (b) total cost of merchandise sold, and (c) gross margin percent. (Factors may not be in the order to be used.)

GIVEN:

	Cost	Retail
Opening inventory	$31,680	$ 58,426
Gross purchases	86,780	168,342
RTV	2,320	4,127
Freight	1,018	
Additional markup		345
Markdowns		11,136
Markdown cancellations		476
Employee discounts		480
Transfers out	2,324	4,470
Transfers in	1,550	2,980
Gross sales		168,050
Customer returns		12,378
Closing physical inventory*		53,672
Cash discounts	2,957	
Alteration costs	832	

*When the closing physical inventory is available, it is converted to cost in place of the closing book inventory.

4. Determine gross margin percent, given:

	Cost	Retail
Opening inventory	$147,460	$ 289,130
Gross purchases	452,660	1,005,780
Cash discounts	6,470	
Additional markup		540
Freight	29,730	
Returns to vendors	2,690	5,380
Gross sales		870,430
Markdowns		216,910
Markdown cancellations		13,680
Customer returns		81,760
Employee discounts		2,780
Alteration costs	720	
Closing physical inventory		282,771

REVIEW OF CUMULATIVE AND MAINTAINED MARKUP

Information that allows the calculation of cumulative and maintained markup is available from RIM records. As you learned in Chapter 5, cumulative markup is based on **total merchandise handled**, and maintained markup is based on **gross cost of merchandise sold**. (You may want to review Chapter 5.)

Refer back to Example 7-7. In this example, cumulative markup is 47.55%.

Cumulative Markup \$ = Retail of Total Merchandise Handled – Cost of Total Merchandise Handled
= \$140,450 – \$73,668
= \$66,782

Cumulative Markup % = Cumulative Markup \$ ÷ Retail of Total Merchandise Handled
= \$66,782 ÷ \$140,450
= 47.55%

Also, cumulative markup percent can be calculated as the complement of the cost percent. (100% – 52.45% = 47.55%).

Maintained markup is calculated using **gross cost of merchandise sold**.

Maintained Markup \$ = Net Sales – Gross Cost of Merchandise Sold
= \$73,840 – \$42,695
= \$31,145

Maintained Markup % = Maintained Markup \$ ÷ Net Sales
= \$31,145 ÷ \$73,840
= 42.18%

Practice Problems • Exercise 7.5

For these problems, refer back to Exercise 7.4.

1. Using the information given in problem #1, calculate (a) cumulative markup percent and (b) maintained markup percent.

(a.) 47.75%

(b.) MMU% = ($114,500 - 64,440) ÷ 114,500
= 43.72%

2. Using the information given in problem #2, calculate (a) cumulative markup percent and (b) maintained markup percent.

(a.) 50.87%

(b.) 45.47%

$\frac{NS-GCo\text{ns}}{NS}$

3. Using the information given in problem #3, calculate (a) cumulative markup percent, and (b) maintained markup percent.

(a.) 47.46%

(b.) 43.35%

$\frac{NS-GCo\text{ns}}{NS}$

4. Using the information given in problem #4, calculate (a) maintained markup percent and (b) gross margin percent, if net markdowns were reduced to $180,000. (Disregard using the physical inventory given in the problem.)

$\frac{NS-GCo\text{ns}}{NS}$ $\frac{NS-TCo\text{ns}}{NS}$

(a.) 40.12%

(b.) 40.85%

DEFINITIONS

Book Inventory   Value of the inventory that should be on hand as shown by the accounting records.

Estimated Physical Inventory   Value of inventory that is determined by subtracting estimated shortage from book inventory.

Estimated Shortage   The amount of shortage that probably has occurred based on past experience.

Overage   Difference between book inventory and physical inventory when book inventory is smaller.

Perpetual Inventory System   A system of accounting whereby all transactions affecting the value of the inventory are posted to the records on a frequent basis, perhaps daily, providing a book inventory value.

Physical Inventory   Value of inventory determined by actually counting the merchandise.

Retail Method of Inventory (RIM)   A procedure whereby the approximate cost value of the ending inventory and, consequently, the cost value of merchandise sold are determined from the retail value of the closing inventory.

Return to Vendor (RTV)   Merchandise returned to the vendor, usually requires vendor's permission.

Shortage or Shrinkage   Difference between physical inventory and book inventory when book inventory is larger.

Chapter 7 • Summary Problems

1. Determine shortage or overage percent (specify which). Net sales for the hosiery department in May were $28,480. Book inventory at the end of the month showed that $97,831 should be on hand. Physical inventory showed $97,997.

$$\text{overage } \% = \frac{\$97,997 - 97,831}{\$28,480}$$

$$= \frac{\$166}{\$28,480}$$

$$= 0.58\%$$

2. Using the following figures, determine closing book inventory. (Not all information given may be needed.)

Opening inventory	+$62,980
Gross purchases	+ 43,620
RTV	− 860
Cash discounts	− 680
Markdowns	5,246
Markdown cancellations	318
Employee discounts	784
Gross sales	49,318
Customer returns	1,918

TMH = $105,740

RD = $53,112

CBI = $52,628

3. Calculate shortage or overage percent.

   GIVEN:

Opening inventory	$ 34,680
RTV	3,816
Gross purchases	175,424
Customer returns	15,768
Gross sales	171,083
Transfers in	12,219
Transfers out	9,769
Markdowns	13,352
Markdown cancellations	487
Employee discounts	1,906
Closing physical inventory	35,763

$TMH = \$208,738$

$RD = \$170,086$

$CBI = \$38,652$

$Shortage = \$2,889$

$Shortage \% = \dfrac{\$2,889}{\$155,315}$

$= 1.877\%$

1.86%

4. Calculate estimated physical inventory if shortage is estimated to have been 1.80%.

   GIVEN:

Net sales	$380,670
Closing book inventory	64,388

$\$380,670 \times .018 = \$6,852.06$

$EPI = \$64,388 - 6,852.06 = \$57,535.94$

$\$57,536$

5. Determine (a) cumulative markup percent, (b) gross cost of merchandise sold, and (c) maintained markup percent.

GIVEN:

	Cost	Retail
Opening inventory	$24,890	$42,914
Net purchases	9,116	18,709
Freight	98	
Net transfers out	− 394	− 816
Gross sales		20,368
Customer returns		1,933
Net markdowns		1,014
Employee discounts		461

Handwritten annotations:

$33,710 → $60,807

$18,435 → $19,910

CMU% = 44.56%

C% = 55.44%

CBI $22,673 $40,897

GCOMS $11,037

MMU% = $\frac{\$18,435 - 11,037}{\$18,435}$ = 40.13%

6. GIVEN:

	Cost	Retail
Opening inventory	$ 34,556	$ 60,836
Gross purchases	+128,091	+ 248,720
RTV	− 3,305	− 6,520
Freight	+ 998	
Net transfers in	+ 956	+ 1,824
Gross sales		249,384
Customer returns		15,560
Markdowns		+ 19,025
Markdown cancellations		− 645
Employee discounts		+ 1,742
Closing physical inventory		48,108
Cash discounts	4,676	
Alteration costs	638	

Handwritten annotations:

$161,296 $304,860

NS = $233,824

$135,842 $253,946

C% = 52.91%

CBI = $50,914

Shortage = $50,914 − 48,108 = $2,806

Shortage % = $2,806 ÷ 233,824 = 1.20%

TCOMS = $135,842 − 4,676 + 638 = $131,804

HMU% = $\frac{\$233,824 - 135,842}{233,824}$ = 41.90%

GM% = $\frac{\$233,824 - 131,804}{\$233,824}$ = 43.63%

FIND:

(a) Shortage percent *1.20%*

(b) Gross cost of merchandise sold *$135,842*

(c) Maintained markup percent *41.90%*

(d) Gross margin dollars and percent *43.63%*

7. Calculate (a) maintained markup percent and (b) gross margin percent.

	Cost	Retail
Opening inventory	$45,000	$ 82,000
Gross purchases	54,524	110,482
Freight	1,018	
Returns to vendors	1,838	3,528
Cash discounts	891	
Transfers out	947	1,864
Transfers in	825	1,649
Markdowns		16,285
Markdown cancellations		693
Additional markup		281
Gross sales		119,682
Employee discounts		1,418
Customer returns		10,284
Alteration costs	632	

Handwritten annotations:

$98,582 $189,??0 TMH   C% = 52.15%

$126,408

NS = $109,398

$32,652 $62,612

CAI =

GCOMS = $65,930

MMU% = $\dfrac{109,398 - 65,930}{109,398}$ = 39.73%

TCOMS = $65,930 + 632 - 891 = $65,671

GM% = $\dfrac{109,398 - 65,671}{109,398}$ = 39.97%

The Dollar Merchandise Plan

OBJECTIVES

- To complete the steps involved in planning sales, stocks, reductions, and purchases leading to the finalized merchandise plan.
- To determine the average inventory and stock turnover rate.
- To calculate beginning of month (BOM) stock according to the basic stock method, the weeks' supply method, and the stock-sales ratio method.

KEY POINTS

- The two major tools of merchandise planning are the dollar merchandise plan and the open-to-buy.
- The dollar merchandise plan serves as a guide for achieving desired sales and profit goals and provides a means for comparing and evaluating merchandising results.
- Merchandise planning begins with sales planning. It is important that the planned sales figure be as realistic as possible because this figure is the basis on which all other figures are planned.
- Stock turnover serves as a guide in determining the efficiency of money invested in a store's inventory.
- Methods used to plan the inventory needed to achieve planned sales include: (1) the basic stock method, (2) the weeks' supply method, and (3) the stock-sales ratio.

One of the most difficult tasks facing the retail merchandiser is determining what to carry. Careful planning is necessary if the retailer is to carry the "right" stock in the "right" quantities. Thus, planning is of great importance in merchandising goods to achieve a profit. To a great extent, the success or failure of the merchandising division is dependent on the degree and quality of the planning that takes place.

Merchandise planning involves establishing realistic goals to be achieved. Planning serves the following purposes:

1. Goals represent the objectives for which the retailer is striving.
2. Plans provide the map to be followed in reaching the established goals.
3. Plans provide a means by which effectiveness can be measured and permit a detailed analysis that should lead to improved results.

TOOLS OF MERCHANDISE PLANNING

The two major tools of merchandise planning are the dollar merchandise plan and the open-to-buy. The merchandise plan projects to the future, serving as a guide for the selling period that has not yet begun. The plan is reviewed and adjusted as the selling period progresses. The open-to-buy covers a shorter term and is a control device used to see that purchasing is done according to the merchandise plan.

The Dollar Merchandise Plan is the dollar control budget for the store. It projects in dollars the amount of merchandise needed to achieve planned sales. This plan balances stocks and sales by coordinating sales, stocks, purchases, and markdowns with initial markup, gross margin, and stock turnover goals. Some stores also include in their merchandise plans stock shortages, cash discounts, operating expenses, sales promotion expenses, and net profit.

The Open-to-Buy is the amount of merchandise that a store may order during the balance of a period. It is the amount of money remaining to be spent from an existing budget after some purchases have been made. Open-to-buy (OTB) can be expressed in dollars and in units. Calculation of OTB is explained in Chapter 9.

THE MERCHANDISE PLAN

The detail involved in the merchandise plan varies with store size and number of departments within the store. Even in the smallest operation some planning is important in order to spend the store's capital wisely. Proper planning for any size organization should lead to improved profit.

In a large retail store, a detailed merchandise plan is essential because of the involvement of many departments and numerous store personnel. In a large store, top management usually determines the profit requirements of the store based on projected sales volume, gross margin, and operating expenses. The overall plan for the store is then distributed to the various merchandise divisions, where detailed plans are formulated.

The general merchandise manager is responsible for interpreting top management's overall merchandise plan into detailed plans for each division and each store. The divisional merchandise manager works with the buyers in his/her division. The detailed plans are then consolidated and reviewed by the general merchandise manager before being finalized and approved by top management.

Although the period covered by a merchandise plan may vary from one month to one year, merchandise plans are normally made for a six-month period. Thus, two merchandise plans are compiled for the year, one for the spring season (February through July), and a second for fall (August through January). The six-month seasonal plan is subdivided into monthly or even weekly plans.

Development of the six-month plan begins several months in advance of the beginning date of the plan. Buyers and divisional merchandise managers usually play an active part in the development of these merchandise plans.

FORMAT FOR THE MERCHANDISE PLAN

The form used for the merchandise plan varies from store to store; however, all plans have certain common characteristics. Figure 8-1 is a typical form for a merchandise plan. Less formal and detailed plans may be used by small stores, whereas large-volume stores may use a plan with more detail.

The essential elements of a merchandise plan include sales, stocks, markdowns/reductions, markup, and purchases. A plan may also include stock turnover, cash discounts, alteration costs, selling costs, sales promotion expenses, and gross margin. Forms for the merchandise plan usually provide room for planned figures, last year's figures, and actual figures for the plan period. Last year's figures (LY) provide a guide in determining this year's figures (TY).

The dollar merchandise plan is similar to a personal budget. It shows income expected and expenditures anticipated for the period of the plan. The merchant

SIX-MONTH MERCHANDISE PLAN

Department Name

Department Number

Merchandise Manager

Buyer

Period

	Plan	Actual
% initial markup		
% reductions		
% maintained markup		
% alteration expense		
% cash discount		
% gross margin		
% operating expense		
% net profit		
season turnover		
average stock		
basic stock		

	SPRING FALL	February August	March September	April October	May November	June December	July January	SEASON TOTALS
SALES	Last Year							
	Plan							
	Planned % of Season							
	Revised Plan							
	Actual							
EOM STOCK	Last Year							
	Plan							
	Revised							
	Actual							
MARKDOWNS	Last Year							
	Plan							
	Revised							
	Actual							
	% of Plan MD							
BOM STOCK	Last Year							
	Plan							
	Revised							
	Actual							
PLANNED PURCHASES AT RETAIL	Last Year							
	Plan							
	Revised							
	Actual							
PLANNED PURCHASES AT COST	Last Year							
	Plan							
	Revised							
	Actual							

Figure 8-1. Form for six-month merchandise plan.

constantly checks the actual results against the plan and makes adjustments as the season progresses. Figures for the plan are based on the following sources:

1. Store sales figures, including last year's figures and the trend over several years.
2. The changing picture of competition.
3. Trade statistics.
4. Economic forecasts from various sources, including banks, government agencies, business schools, and trade associations.

In planning, emphasis should be placed on last year's operation, including merchandise carried, physical changes in the store, and store policies regarding buying, selling, and promotion. When the planned sales are consolidated, they are compared to the overall store plan to see whether the figures appear too high or too low. Planning sales on the basis of last year's sales trends saves time and confusion. Obviously revisions will be necessary as the plan period progresses in order to keep departments from becoming overbought or to permit more open-to-buy to meet increasing sales demand. It is important to realize that the planned figures become the objective toward which the store or department aims. These planned figures should always represent goals that are reasonably attainable.

PLANNING SALES

Actual planning begins with sales. The planned sales figure should be as accurate and realistic as possible, because this figure is the basis on which all other figures are planned. Sales are planned on a net basis (gross sales minus customer returns). Realistic sales planning is critical because sales are the key to profit.

Many factors influence sales. Some of these factors can be controlled by the store and some cannot. As planning is carried out, the retailer must take into account the major influences on sales. The retailer must be aware of factors affecting the customer's ability and motivation to buy. Shifts in customer demand occur for a variety of reasons. In addition, sales are influenced by such external factors as employment conditions, the state of the economy, inflation, population trends, and the changing competitive situation. Fashion is another external force that greatly influences sales. For example, when the accepted fashion for women is pants, the dress business suffers and sportswear flourishes. Changes in the supply of goods and new products on the market also require attention when planning sales.

Certain factors within the store also influence sales. However, the store has considerable control over these internal factors. The addition of new stores or physical changes within an existing store influence sales. Changes in store policies, such as an increased emphasis on sales promotion or a stronger emphasis on carrying designer fashions, may serve to stimulate or retard sales in certain departments within the store.

The successful merchant learns to study and evaluate all factors that may influence sales. These must be carefully considered in developing the merchandise plan. It should always be remembered that plans must be based on facts in order to be realistic.

In order to understand how to make a six-month merchandise plan, we begin by determining the sales goal for the store. Remember (1) all planning begins with sales, and (2) plans must be realistic. Begin by analyzing all sales figures by using the following steps:

1. Obtain sales from last year for each month of the plan.
2. Determine projected sales volume for each month in the plan.
   Note: Remember to consider factors influencing sales, including changes in promotional dates, competition, department size, or layout. Review past sales history and current trends.
3. Figure percent increase or decrease of planned sales over the last year's sales.

To determine percent increase or decrease in sales, divide the difference between this year's (TY) planned sales and last year's (LY) actual sales by last year's actual sales.

$$\% \text{ Sales Increase or Decrease} = \frac{\text{TY Planned Sales} - \text{LY Actual Sales}}{\text{LY Actual Sales}}$$

EXAMPLE 8-1

If last year's actual sales were $270,000 and planned sales for this year are $300,000, what is the planned percent increase in sales for this year?

Solution:

$$\% \text{ Sales Increase} = \frac{\text{TY Sales} - \text{LY Sales}}{\text{LY Sales}}$$

$$= \frac{\$300,000 - \$270,000}{\$270,000}$$

$$= \frac{\$30,000}{\$270,000}$$

$$= 0.1111 = 11.11\% \text{ increase}$$

A store does not always plan for an increase in sales. A decision may be made to reduce the volume of a department or classification because of reduced demand.

EXAMPLE 8-2

GIVEN: Current year planned sales $250,000
            Previous year actual sales $270,000

Solution:

$$\% \text{ Sales Decrease} = \frac{\text{LY Sales} - \text{TY Sales}}{\text{LY Sales}}$$

$$= \frac{\$250,000 - \$270,000}{\$270,000}$$

$$= \frac{\$20,000}{\$270,000}$$

$$= 0.07407 = 7.41\% \text{ decrease}$$

Although there is not a formula for planning sales, knowing the percent increase or decrease in sales during a several-month period provides one type of information that is crucial in projecting sales. The merchandiser evaluates all the information available to make decisions that will serve as the basis for the department's/store's future operation.

EXAMPLE 8-3

Given the following figures, plan the sales for the month of November.

Month	Sales Last Year	Sales This Year	% Increase
July	$268,000	$288,100	7.50%
August	292,500	316,193	8.10%
September	286,749	314,196	9.57%
October	281,119	306,376	8.98%
November	324,500		

Solution: The percent of sales increase has varied from 7.5% to 9.5%. For November, the merchandiser would plan a sales increase between 8.5% and 9.0%.

$$\text{Planned Sales for November} = \$324,500 + (\$324,500 \times 8.5\%)$$
$$= \$352,083$$

$$= \$324,500 + (\$324,500 \times 9.0\%)$$
$$= \$353,705$$

Note: November sales should be planned somewhere between $352,083 to $353,705. Other factors would need to be taken into consideration before a final decision is made.

In some instances, the season's total sales are planned and then sales are allocated to individual months depending on the percent of season's sales expected for each individual month. If the season's (6 months) total sales are planned to be $886,000 and it is estimated that 16% of the sales will occur in August, August's planned sales will be $141,760.

Practice Problems • Exercise 8.1

1. Planned sales for the month of August this year are $145,000. If the actual sales for the month last year were $130,000, what is this year's planned percent increase in sales?

$$\frac{145,000 - 130,000}{130,000} = 11.54\%$$

2. Actual sales in the stationery department last year totaled $518,000. If the department planned a 15% increase for this year, what is the dollar amount of sales planned?

$$\$518,000 \times 1.15 = \$595,700$$

3. Because of a reduction in the number of stores with a yard goods department, the buyer is planning a 20% reduction in sales for the department. If last year's sales were $218,000, what is this year's planned sales figure?

$$\$218,000 \times .80 = \$174,400$$

4. Sales for August of this year totaled $90,000, and for September, $96,000. If the planned seasonal sales distribution is as follows, figure the dollar sales for the remaining months of the period.

Total Sales = $600,000

August	15%	
September	16%	
October	14%	$84,000
November	19%	$114,000
December	24%	$144,000
January	12%	$72,000

645,833
620 000

5. Figure the percent increase in sales for each of the following months, and determine the probable sales for June in a department that had the following sales pattern:

Month	LY Actual	TY Planned	
March	24% $140,000	$155,000	10.71%
April	26% 155,000	170,000	9.68%
May	24%.145,000	160,000	10.34%
June	26% 152,000	166,500 ?	9.5%
		165,000	

6. Plan sales for the months of August through January, given:

Month	Sales LY	Sales TY
February	$ 64,819	$ 70,632
March	97,236	106,340
April	118,876	130,090
May	97,284	106,726
June	86,398	94,692
July	75,613	83,174
August	90,116	
September	96,261	
October	83,968	
November	119,407	
December	144,154	
January	71,993	

PLANNING STOCKS

After estimating sales, the next step in merchandise planning is to plan stocks. Stocks represent capital investments, and retailers are vitally interested in return on capital investment. Too much inventory at any one time can seriously inhibit the investment return for an entire season. Too much inventory causes an overbought condition with a resulting lack of new merchandise. Excessive merchandise results in increased markdowns.

The buyer determines the amount of stock needed at the beginning of each month (BOM) in order to meet planned sales figures. The student should remember that the end of the month (EOM) stock for one month is the same as the (BOM) stock for the following month. In other words, **the EOM stock for February would be the same as the BOM stock for March**.

Retailers use a variety of methods to plan stock in order to provide for a balanced inventory in relation to estimated sales. These methods include (1) the basic stock method, (2) the weeks' supply method, and (3) the stock-sales ratio method. Turnover is an important tool in evaluating efficient use of capital invested in inventory (stock). The basic stock method for planning inventory levels is based on a stock turnover goal.

Stock Turnover

Stock turnover (also referred to as stock turn or inventory turn) serves as a guide to the merchant in determining the efficiency of a store's operation. It can be used to evaluate planned stock. Stock turn may be figured based on retail, on cost figures, or on units of merchandise. As we have already seen, most retailers keep their records at retail; therefore, figuring stock turn at retail is the most common method. Unit stock turn is appropriate with certain types of merchandise. For example, with large or expensive items such as major appliances, furniture, diamonds, and automobiles, it is possible to use unit stock turn.

Stock turn is defined as the number of times the average stock is sold during a given period of time in relation to the sales for the same period. To determine stock turn at retail, both sales and stock figures must be expressed as retail values.

$$\text{Stock Turnover} = \text{Net Sales at Retail} \div \text{Average Stock at Retail}$$

Stock turnover may be figured for any period of time. Most commonly, stock turn is figured based on a year or six months; however, it may be determined for a week, a month, three months, or any period of time.

Figuring Stock Turnover at Retail. To determine stock turn at retail you must first calculate average stock. The amount of stock in a department varies from time to time. The objective is to determine an average that reflects the ups an downs of the inventory.

Average stock for any period is the stock at the beginning of that period, plus stock at the beginning of similar periods, plus the stock at the end of the period, divided by the total number of stock listings.

$$\text{Average Stock} = \frac{\text{BOM Stock for Each Month in the Period} + \text{EOM Stock for Last Month}}{\text{Number of Months in the Period} + 1}$$

For example:

$$\text{1-month Average Stock} = \frac{\text{BOM Stock} + \text{EOM Stock}}{2}$$

$$\text{6-month Average Stock} = \frac{\text{BOM Stock for Each Month} + \text{End of Period Stock}}{7}$$

$$\text{1-year Average Stock} = \frac{\text{BOM for Each Month} + \text{Last Month's EOM}}{13}$$

Some stores report inventory figures weekly. In such cases, average stock may be determined based on weekly stock. For a year's time, this results in 53 figures (52 weeks plus 1). Stock turnover can be figured using EOM figures but is not done by most retailers.

EXAMPLE 8-4

Figure the stock turn at retail for a period of one month when given:
$32,000 BOM stock at retail, $38,000 EOM stock at retail, and $14,000 net sales for the month.

Solution:

(a) $\text{Average Stock} = \dfrac{\text{BOM Stock} + \text{EOM Stock}}{2}$

$= \dfrac{\$32,000 + \$38,000}{2}$

$= \dfrac{\$70,000}{2}$

$= \$35,000$

(b) Stock Turn $= \text{Net Sales} \div \text{Average Stock}$

$= \$14,000 \div \$35,000$

$= 0.4$ for the month

EXAMPLE 8-5

Figure the stock turn at retail for a six-month period, February through July.

GIVEN: Net sales for six-month period were $88,000.

Month	BOM Stock
February	$39,000
March	38,000
April	35,000
May	35,000
June	34,000
July	26,000
August	33,000

Note: The BOM stock for a month is the EOM stock from the previous month. Therefore, the EOM stock for July (the last month in the six-month period) is $33,000, which is the BOM stock for August.

Solution:

(a) $\text{Average Stock} = \dfrac{\text{BOM Stock for Each Month} + \text{End of Period Stock}}{7}$

$$= \dfrac{\$39,000 + \$38,000 + \$35,000 + \$35,000 + \$34,000 + \$26,000 + \$33,000}{7}$$

$$= \dfrac{\$240,000}{7}$$

$$= \$34,286$$

(b) $\text{Stock Turn} = \text{Net Sales} \div \text{Average Stock}$

$$= \$88,000 \div \$34,286$$

$$= 2.57$$

If stock turnover equals net sales divided by average stock, it follows that average stock equals net sales divided by stock turnover.

$$\text{Average Stock} = \text{Net Sales} \div \text{Stock Turnover}$$

EXAMPLE 8-6

Figure average stock when net sales are $55,000 and the stock turn is 3.5.

Solution:

$$\text{Average Stock} = \text{Net Sales} \div \text{Stock Turnover}$$

$$= \$55,000 \div 3.5$$

$$= \$15,714$$

1. A store had a BOM stock of $300,000 at retail. Net sales for the month were $146,000. The EOM inventory was $350,000. What was the stock turnover for the month?

   Stock turn = NS ÷ Ave. stock

   Ave. stock = 300,000 + 350,000
   = $325,000

   Stock turnover = $146,000 ÷ 325,000 = .45

2. Junior dresses had an opening inventory of $36,000 at retail. Net sales for the period were $12,389. If the closing inventory were $37,000, what was the rate of stock turnover for the period?

   Ave. stock = $36,000 + 37,000 = $36,500

   Stock turnover = $12,389 ÷ 36,500
   = .34

3. Determine the average stock in a department with annual sales of $1,650,000 and an annual stock turn of 4.5.

   Ave. stock = $1,650,000 ÷ 4.5
   = $366,667

4. What is the six-month stock turnover based on the following figures and net sales of $450,000?

Month	BOM Stock
February	$60,000
March	63,000
April	75,000
May	72,000
June	68,000
July	65,000
August	75,000

   Ave. stock = $68,286

   Stock turnover = $450,000 ÷ 68,286
   = 6.59

5. Find the turnover for the six-month spring–summer season (February to July) from the following data:

Month	Sales	BOM Stock
February	$10,000	$21,000
March	18,000	18,000
April	16,000	25,000
May	12,000	26,000
June	14,000	29,000
July	10,000	24,000
August	6,000	18,800
September	12,000	26,000
October	11,000	25,000
November	14,000	29,500
December	19,000	35,000
January	13,000	24,000

6. Using the data in the previous problem, calculate turnover for the following:

(a) four-month period, February–May

(b) three-month period, October–December

(c) the month of June

Figuring Stock Turnover at Cost. Stock turnover may be figured based on cost. This is practical only when records are kept at cost. To figure stock turn at cost, both stock and sales figures must be cost values. The cost method of figuring stock turnover is seldom used because most retailers keep their merchandise records at retail.

Figuring Stock Turnover by Units. Stock turn may also be figured by units rather than by dollars. With categories of merchandise comprising of many small items, unit stock turn is impractical. With large or high-priced items, such as major appliances, fine jewelry, and furniture, unit stock turn becomes practical.

EXAMPLE 8-7

Calculate unit turnover for the month, given:

BOM stock of 100 units
EOM stock of 75 units
Units sold during the month 200 units

Solution:

(a) Average Stock $= \dfrac{\text{BOM Units} + \text{EOM Units}}{2}$

$= \dfrac{100 + 75}{2}$

$= \dfrac{175}{2}$

$= 87.5$

(b) Stock Turnover $=$ Net Sales in Units $\div$ Average Stock in Units
$= 200 \div 87.5$
$= 2.2857$ per month

Note: Remember that stock turn is based on the average amount of stock on hand in relation to sales for that same period.

Significance of Stock Turnover. Money, if put to work properly, will make money. In order to make money "work," it must be used over and over again within a relatively short period of time. In merchandising this means buying merchandise, selling it at a profit with reasonable promptness, and reinvesting the money in more stock, the same cycle continuing. Turnover measures this very factor of stock purchase, sale, and repurchase.

A good turnover rate depends on the type of merchandise and time period involved. Turnover may range from a low of less than 2 for some merchandise up to 20 or more turns for other merchandise. There is a wide variation in stock turn rate, depending on the kind of merchandise a store or department carries. See Table 8-1 for median stock turn rates for various departments in all department stores for 1997 as reported by the National Retail Federation (NRF).

To some extent, stock turns vary with the frequency of purchase by customers. Frequently purchased items such as gasoline or perishable food items have a high stock turn rate. Less frequently purchased items like furniture or fine jewelry have a much lower stock turn. The turnover is also reduced for items that must be carried in a wide assortment of styles, colors, sizes, and other selection factors.

Table 8-1
Median Stock Turn Rates for Department Stores in 1997

Type of Merchandise	Annual Stock Turn Rate
Food, candy, and beverages	3.8
Junior dresses	3.2
Misses' sportswear	2.8
Handbags	2.0
Men's and boys' sportswear	2.4
Costume jewelry	1.7
Men's and boys' clothing	1.3
China and glassware	1.1
Children's footwear	1.2
Silverware	1.2

Note: From *FOR/MOR, The Combined Financial, Merchandising, and Operating Results of Retail Stores in 1997* by Alexandra Moran (Ed.), 1998 (73rd ed.). Copyright 1998 by the National Retail Federation.

The buyer can influence the stock turn rate by the way merchandise is purchased. Buying in small amounts and replenishing the stock frequently will result in a higher stock turn. Selling from sample stock, which is sometimes done with furniture sales, will also increase the stock turn rate. If a store or department is close to being overbought, the buyer may need to make purchases more frequently, thus increasing stock turn.

A rapid rate of turnover has several advantages. By limiting its investment in merchandise, a store reduces expenses such as interest, taxes, storage for merchandise, and insurance on merchandise. A store may achieve larger sales with a smaller stock that is fresh and more appealing to the customer. Fewer markdowns will occur because of old or soiled merchandise, and return on investment may rise.

Stock turn, however, can be too high. Too rapid a turnover rate may lead to lost sales. Smaller and more frequent orders may increase transportation costs and expenses related to handling merchandise and keeping records. Quantity discounts may be lost because of buying in small quantities. The primary disadvantage with too high a stock turn is that sales may be lost from goods the customer wants to buy that are out of stock because the store is buying in small quantities. There is a need to strike a profitable stock turnover rate.

Basic Stock Method

This method of stock planning requires that the BOM stock be sufficient to cover the sales for that month and allow for a reserve of basic stock. **Basic stock is defined as the minimum stock that should be maintained at all times.**

It is a reserve that provides some assortment for customer selection and protects the department against stock contingencies. The basic stock method is recommended for use when the annual stock turnover is 6 turns or less per year. At higher stock turns, the basic stock method results in an unrealistic basic stock figure. The basic stock method is most appropriate for departments with a high proportion of nonfashion merchandise.

The basic stock method of stock planning is based on the assumption that there should always be a basic inventory on hand that remains constant regardless of the rate of sale. The stock to be carried at the beginning of the month is determined by adding the dollar value of the basic stock to the planned sales for that month.

BOM Stock = Sales for the Month + Basic Stock

The basic stock is equal to the average stock for the season minus the average monthly sales. Average stock is determined by dividing the sales for the season by the stock turnover for the season.

$$\text{Basic Stock} = \text{Average Stock} - \text{Average Monthly Sales}$$

$$\text{Average Stock for Season} = \frac{\text{Sales for the Season}}{\text{Stock Turnover for Season}}$$

EXAMPLE 8-8

A department has a planned stock turnover of 4 and planned sales of $160,000 for a six-month season. Plan the BOM stock for April if planned sales for April are $20,000.

Solution:

(a) Average Stock for Season $= \dfrac{\text{Sales for Season}}{\text{Stock Turnover for Season}}$

$= \dfrac{\$160,000}{4}$

$= \$40,000$

(b) Average Monthly Sales $= \dfrac{\text{Sales for Season}}{\text{Number of Months in Season}}$

$= \dfrac{\$160,000}{6}$

$= \$26,667$

(c) BOM Stock $= \text{Sales for Month} + \text{Basic Stock}$

$= \$20,000 + (\$40,000 - \$26,667)$

$= \$20,000 + \$13,333$

$= \$33,333$

Week's Supply Method

The weeks' supply method plans stock on a weekly basis by setting stocks equal to a predetermined number of weeks' sales. It is applicable to merchandise that does not fluctuate much in sales volume from week to week. Stores or departments that use this method of stock planning plan sales by weeks rather than on a monthly basis. With the weeks' supply method of stock planning, the number of weeks' supply that is to be kept on hand during a period is dependent on the rate of stock turnover required for the store or department.

EXAMPLE 8-9

If a stock turnover of 10 times a year is desired, how many weeks of supply should be on hand at all times?

Solution:

$$\text{Weeks' Supply} = 52 \text{ weeks} \div \text{Desired Stock Turnover}$$
$$= 52 \text{ weeks} \div 10$$
$$= 5.2 \text{ weeks' supply needed on hand every week}$$

Management must decide whether weeks' supply is to be calculated using exactly 5.2 or 5 weeks, for ease of calculation. Use of computers allows easy calculation of 5.2 weeks' supply once weekly sales have been planned. Table 8-2 shows planned inventory levels based on 5.2 weeks' supply.

Table 8-2
Inventory Needed to Provide 5.2 Weeks' Supply

Week	Planned Sales	Inventory Needed
1	$10,200	$55,050
2	10,400	56,050
3	10,700	56,630
4	10,600	56,750
5	10,900	56,750
6	11,250	56,890
7	11,000	56,880
8	10,900	57,300
9	10,500	57,780
10	11,000	58,120
11	11,200	57,700
12	11,400	57,000
13	11,500	56,060
14	10,900	54,920
15	10,600	
16	10,500	
17	10,500	
18	10,300	
19	10,600	
20	10,800	

Stock-Sales Ratio

A common method for planning how much stock should be on hand at a particular time is the stock-sales ratio. It relates the stock on hand at the beginning or sometimes the end of the month to the projected retail sales for that month. For fast-moving stocks, the stock-sales ratio may be figured weekly. If the buyer knows the stock-sales ratio for the period being planned, the amount of stock that should be on hand at the beginning of each month can be planned easily.

Median stock-sales ratio figures for the fiscal year ending January 1998 for all specialty stores, as reported by the National Retail Federation, are shown in Table 8-3. These median stock-sales ratios are for an entire store and are provided to emphasize that stock-sales ratios vary throughout the year. During periods of high sales, a store or department can operate with a lower stock-sales ratio than during periods of slow sales.

Table 8-3
Stock-Sales Ratios for Fiscal Year 1997 for Specialty Stores with Sales over $20 Million

Month	Stock-Sales Ratio	Month	Stock Sales Ratio
February	6.76	August	6.44
March	5.43	September	6.85
April	6.58	October	7.39
May	6.58	November	5.91
June	5.57	December	3.96
July	6.24	January	7.00

Note: From *FOR/MOR, The Combined Financial, Merchandising, and Operating Results of Retail Stores in 1997* by Alexandra Moran (Ed.), 1998 (73rd ed.). Copyright 1998 by the National Retail Federation.

Figuring Stock-Sales Ratio When Retail Stock and Sales for a Given Period Are Known. To determine the stock-sales ratio for a period of one month, the BOM stock at retail is divided by the retail sales for that month.

$$\text{Stock-Sales Ratio} = \text{BOM Retail Stock} \div \text{Sales for the Month}$$

EXAMPLE 8-10

Determine the stock-sales ratio when BOM stock at retail is $50,000 and retail sales for the month are $35,000.

Solution:

$$\begin{aligned}
\text{Stock-Sales Ratio} &= \text{BOM Stock at Retail} \div \text{Net Sales for Month} \\
&= \$50,000 \div \$35,000 \\
&= 1.4286
\end{aligned}$$

Note: The inventory needs to be 1.43 times sales for the month, or in other words, the store must have $143 of merchandise to sell $100.

Figuring BOM Stock When Planned Sales and Stock-Sales Ratio Are Known. Conversely, the amount of BOM stock that is needed can be determined if planned sales and the desired stock-sales ratio are known.

$$\text{BOM Stock} = \text{Planned Monthly Sales} \times \text{Stock-Sales Ratio}$$

EXAMPLE 8-11

The girls' department had planned sales of $60,000 for the month of April. Past records indicate a stock-sales ratio of 5.4. What should be the planned BOM stock for April?

Solution:

$$\begin{aligned}
\text{BOM Stock} &= \text{Planned Monthly Sales} \times \text{Stock-Sales Ratio} \\
&= \$60,000 \times 5.4 \\
&= \$324,000
\end{aligned}$$

Comparison of Stock-Sales Ratio and Stock Turnover. Both stock-sales ratio and stock turnover provide a measure of the relationship between sales and stocks. However, stock-sales ratio differs from stock turnover in the following ways:

1. The period covered for stock-sales ratio usually involves a shorter time period than that for stock turnover. Stock-sales ratio is figured for a single month, whereas stock turnover is based on average stock.
2. Stock-sales ratio is based on stock on hand at a specific time, usually the beginning of the month, whereas stock turnover is based on average stock.
3. The numerators and denominators are reversed in the two calculations. When determining stock-sales ratio, stock is divided by net sales; whereas when determining stock turnover, net sales are divided by average stock.

1. At the beginning of September, sleepwear and robes had a retail stock of $65,000. Sales for the month were $18,200. What was the stock-sales ratio for September?

   $65,000 ÷ 18,200 =
   3.57

2. Planned sales in the lingerie department for August are $32,000, and the planned stock-sales ratio is 3.8. On August 1, how much stock should be on hand?

   $32,000 × 3.8 = $121,600

3. If planned sales for the month are $18,000, and the stock-sales ratio is planned at 1.5, what BOM stock is needed to realize this ratio?

   $18,000 × 1.5 = $27,000

4. Planned sales in the costume jewelry department for May are $130,000, and the planned stock-sales ratio is 3.4. On May 1, how much stock is needed?

   $130,000 × 3.4 = $442,000

5. What is the planned stock-sales ratio when BOM stock is planned at $64,500 and planned sales are $29,000?

   $64,500 ÷ 29,000 = 2.22

6. During a six-month period, a department had planned sales of $180,000 and planned turnover of 3.2. Using the basic stock method, determine the BOM stock for March if planned sales for March are $28,000.

   ave. stock = $180,000 ÷ 3.2 = $56,250
   ave. sales = $180,000 ÷ 6 = $30,000
   Basic stock = $56,250 − 30,000 = $26,250
   BOM stock = $26,250 + 28,000
           = $54,250

7. A department has a planned stock turnover of 4.2 and planned sales of $252,000 for a six-month period. August sales are estimated at $38,000 and September sales at $45,000. Using the basic stock method, determine the BOM stock for August and the BOM stock for September.

Avl. stock = $252,000 ÷ 4.2 = $60,000

ave sales = $252,000 ÷ 6 = $42,000

Basic stock = $60,000 − 42,000 = $18,000

BOM stock$_{aug}$ = $18,000 + 38,000 = $56,000   BOM stock$_{sept.}$ = $18,000 + 45,000 = $63,000

8. Calculate BOM inventory values for February through July based on the information given.

Month	Planned Sales		Stock-Sales Ratio	
February	$ 96,000	X	3.6	= $345,600
March	112,000	X	3.2	= $358,400
April	144,000	X	2.9	= $417,600
May	144,000	X	2.9	= $417,600
June	176,000	X	2.7	= $475,200
July	128,000	X	3.4	= $435,200

PLANNING REDUCTIONS

The next step in merchandise planning is to plan retail reductions. **Reductions reduce the retail value of the inventory and include markdowns, discounts to employees and customers, and stock shortages.** Each must be anticipated, estimated, and included in the planning process.

In establishing the merchandise plan, reduction percents are estimated based on past experiences and current factors that may increase or decrease these percents. The merchandise planner must determine reductions as realistically as possible. Reductions, such as markdowns, are expressed as a percent of net sales. As discussed in Chapter 6, the markdown percent is calculated by dividing the dollar amount of net markdown by net sales. Because markdowns are the largest component of reductions, many firms plan only markdowns rather than total reductions.

> Markdown % = $ Amount of Markdown ÷ Net Sales

Conversely, planned dollar markdowns can be determined by multiplying the net sales by the planned markdown percent.

> Planned $ Markdowns = Planned Sales × Planned Markdown %

PLANNING PURCHASES

A primary objective of merchandise planning is to assist the buyer in timing the purchase of goods in order to maintain a balance between stock and sales throughout the season. Planned purchases are the amount of merchandise that is **planned for delivery** to the store or department during a given period without exceeding the planned closing stock for that period. Planned purchases for a month must be adequate to cover the sales and reductions to be made during that month, as well as provide an ending inventory that will allow the following month's sales to be made. Purchases must be based on planned sales, stock, and markdown figures. To plan monthly purchases, use the following formula:

> Planned Purchases at Retail = Sales + EOM Stock + Markdowns − BOM Stock

---

EXAMPLE 8-12

Determine planned purchases for the month of September given:

Sales for September	$190,000
Stock for September 1	318,200
Markdowns	16,500
Stock for October 1	304,800

Solution:

Planned Purchases at Retail = Sales + EOM Stock + Markdowns − BOM Stock
= $190,000 + $304,800 + $16,500 − $318,200
= $193,100

EXAMPLE 8-13

Determine planned purchases for the months of June, July, and August, given the following information:

Month	Planned Sales	Planned BOM Stock	Planned Markdowns
June	$12,500	$42,000	$1,900
July	17,400	39,000	2,800
August	19,000	43,000	2,200
September	20,500	44,000	1,600

Solution:

Planned Purchases at Retail = Sales + EOM Stock + Markdowns − BOM Stock

	June	July	August
Planned Sales	$12,500	$17,400	$19,000
+ Planned EOM Stock	39,000	43,000	44,000
+ Planned Markdowns	1,900	2,800	2,200
− Planned BOM Stock	− 42,000	− 39,000	− 43,000
Planned Purchases	$11,400	$24,200	$22,200

CONVERTING RETAIL VALUE TO COST VALUE

Planned purchases are determined at retail and must be converted to cost if cost value is desired. This is done by using the following formula:

Planned Purchases at Cost = Planned Purchases at Retail × (100% − Planned Markup %)

EXAMPLE 8-14

If planned retail purchases for the month were $208,000 and the planned markup was 45%, determine planned purchases at cost.

Solution:

Planned Purchases at Cost = Planned Purchases at Retail × (100% − Planned Markup %)
= $208,000 × (100% − 45%)
= $208,000 × 55%
= $114,400

Practice Problems • Exercise 8.4

1. Calculate planned June purchases at cost:

June Sales	$175,000
Reductions	+ 20,000
BOM Stock for June	− 250,000
BOM Stock for July	+ 150,000
Markup	48%

$95,000 X .52 = $49,400

C% = .52

2. Determine planned purchases (a) at retail and (b) at cost for a month with the following planned figures:

Sales	$ 40,000
Markdowns	+ 2,000
BOM Stock	− 98,000
EOM Stock	+ 101,000
Markup	46%

C% = .54

(a.) $45,000

(b.) $45,000 X .54 = $24,300

3. If markdowns in the shoe department were $7,680 and net sales were $48,000, what was the markdown percent for the month?

MD% = $7,680 ÷ 48,000

= 16.00%

4. Determine the planned purchases for September (a) at retail and (b) at cost for the children's department when the seasonal merchandise plan indicates the following planned figures:

Sales	$75,000
Markdowns	+ 9% = 6,750
BOM Stock	− $68,000
EOM Stock	+ $54,000
Markup	48%

C% = .52

(a.) $67,750

(b.) $67,750 X .52 = $35,230

PREPARATION OF THE MERCHANDISE PLAN

Although merchandise plans often display many factors, the minimal factors shown on a merchandise plan/budget are sales, stock, reductions, purchases, and initial markup percent. Prior to planning for the next season, last year's actual monthly figures would be entered on the form. Showing last year's figures on the merchandise plan provides an easy comparison. On Figure 8-2, last year's figures have been omitted to avoid confusion. Season turnover and percents for expenses, reductions, profit goal, cash discounts, and gross margin have been planned and entered on the form.

When working through Example 8-15, refer to Figure 8-2 along with the discussion of each step required to complete the merchandise plan. Example 8-15 utilizes the basic stock planning method for planning inventories. Remember that this is only one of several methods for planning inventory levels. The steps for developing a merchandise plan are the same regardless of the inventory planning method. The steps to complete the merchandise plan are:

1. If given, enter the planned percents for initial markup, maintained markup, alteration costs, cash discounts, gross margin, operating expenses, net profit, and season turnover. (You may want to review Chapter 5).

2. Determine the total planned sales for the season and distribute for each month.

SIX-MONTH MERCHANDISE PLAN

	Plan	Actual
% initial markup	57.02%	
% reductions	14.00%	
% maintained markup		
% alteration expense		
% cash discount	1.30%	
% gross margin	52.30%	
% operating expense	44.90%	
% net profit	7.40%	
season turnover	2.9	
average stock		
basic stock	$ 49,885	

Department Name _____

Department Number _____

Merchandise Manager _____

Buyer _____

Period _____

	SPRING / FALL	February August	March September	April October	May November	June December	July January	SEASON TOTALS
SALES	Last Year							
	Plan	$ 44,800	$ 47,600	$ 36,400	$ 50,400	$ 61,600	$ 39,200	$ 280,000
	Planned % of Season	16%	17%	13%	18%	22%	14%	
	Revised Plan							
	Actual							
EOM STOCK	Last Year							
	Plan	97,485	86,285	100,285	111,485	89,085	96,552	
	Revised							
	Actual							
REDUCTIONS	Last Year							
	Plan	7,448	7,840	8,624	6,664	3,920	4,704	39,200
	Revised							
	Actual							
	% of Plan MD	19%	20%	22%	17%	10%	12%	
BOM STOCK	Last Year							
	Plan	94,685	97,485	86,285	100,285	111,485	89,085	
	Revised							
	Actual							
PLANNED PURCHASES AT RETAIL	Last Year							
	Plan	55,048	44,240	59,024	68,264	43,120	51,371	321,067
	Revised							
	Actual							
PLANNED PURCHASES AT COST	Last Year							
	Plan	23,660	19,014	25,369	29,332	18,533	22,079	137,987
	Revised							
	Actual							

Figure 8-2. Completed merchandise plan for Example 8-15.

3. Determine BOM stock figures.

4. Determine EOM stock levels. **Remember**: The EOM stock for any month is the same as the BOM stock for the next month. When using the basic stock method, the average inventory value can be used as the last month's EOM inventory.

5. Determine reductions or markdowns planned for each month. Reductions include markdowns, shortages, and discounts to employees and special customers.

6. Determine monthly planned purchases at retail.

7. Convert monthly planned purchases at retail to cost. (Some forms do not have a place to show monthly planned purchases at cost.)

EXAMPLE 8-15

Complete the seasonal merchandise plan based on the following data:

		Month	% Season's Sales	% Season's Reductions
Planned net sales	$280,000	August	16	19
Operating expenses	44.9%	September	17	20
Planned profit	7.4%	October	13	22
Cash discounts	1.3%	November	18	17
Reductions	14.0%	December	22	10
Stock turnover	2.9%	January	14	12

Solution:

Step 1. Calculate initial markup %.

$$\text{Initial Markup \%} = \frac{\text{Expenses} + \text{Profit} + \text{Reductions} - \text{Cash Discounts}}{\text{Sales} + \text{Reductions}}$$

$$= \frac{44.9\% + 7.4\% + 14\% - 1.3\%}{100\% + 14\%}$$

$$= \frac{65\%}{114\%}$$

$$= 57.02\%$$

Calculate gross margin %.

$$\text{Gross Margin \%} = \text{Expenses} + \text{Profit}$$
$$= 44.9\% + 7.4\%$$
$$= 52.3\%$$

Step 2. Distribute monthly planned sales.

Monthly Planned Sales = % of Season's Sales × Net Sales

= August	16% × $280,000 =	$ 44,800
= September	17% × 280,000 =	47,600
= October	13% × 280,000 =	36,400
= November	18% × 280,000 =	50,400
= December	22% × 280,000 =	61,600
= January	14% × 280,000 =	39,200
Total	100%	= $280,000

Step 3. Determine BOM stock figures.

(a) Basic Stock = Average Inventory – Average Monthly Sales

$$= \frac{\$280,000}{2.9} - \frac{\$280,000}{6}$$

$$= \$96,552 - \$46,667$$

$$= \$49,885$$

(b) BOM Stock = Planned Monthly Sales + Basic Stock

August	=	$44,800	+	$49,885	=	$ 94,685
September	=	47,600	+	49,885	=	97,485
October	=	36,400	+	49,885	=	86,285
November	=	50,400	+	49,885	=	100,285
December	=	61,600	+	49,885	=	111,485
January	=	39,200	+	49,885	=	89,085

Step 4. Determine EOM stock figures. (When the basic stock method is used, plan the last month's EOM inventory equal to the average inventory).

August	=	$ 97,485
September	=	86,285
October	=	100,285
November	=	111,485
December	=	89,085
January	=	96,552

Step 5. Determine total $ reductions and distribute for each month.

(a) Find total planned reductions = $280,000 × 14%
= $39,200

(b) Distribute monthly planned reductions

August	19% ×	$39,200 =	$ 7,448
September	20% ×	39,200 =	7,840
October	22% ×	39,200 =	8,624
November	17% ×	39,200 =	6,664
December	10% ×	39,200 =	3,920
January	12% ×	39,200 =	4,704
Total	100%		$39,200

Step 6. Determine monthly planned purchases at retail.

August	$44,800 + $ 97,485 + $7,448 – $ 94,685 =	$55,048
September	47,600 + 86,285 + 7,840 – 97,485 =	44,240
October	36,400 + 100,285 + 8,624 – 86,285 =	59,024
November	50,400 + 111,485 + 6,664 – 100,285 =	68,264
December	61,600 + 89,085 + 3,920 – 111,485 =	43,120
January	39,200 + 96,552 + 4,704 – 89,085 =	51,371

Step 7. Convert monthly planned purchases at retail to cost.

August	$55,048 ×	42.98% =	$23,660
September	44,240 ×	42.98% =	19,014
October	59,025 ×	42.98% =	25,369
November	68,246 ×	42.98% =	29,332
December	43,120 ×	42.98% =	18,533
January	51,371 ×	42.98% =	22,079

Practice Problems • Exercise 8.5

1. Develop a merchandise plan based on the following information. Sales for the six-month spring/summer season have been planned to total $650,000. Reductions for the total season are to be 22% of planned sales, and season's turnover should be 1.9. BOM inventory values are to be planned using the basic stock method. In this problem, ending inventory will be the same as the average inventory. (Merchandise plan forms are provided at the end of this chapter.)

Month	% of Season's Sales	% of Season's Reductions
February	15.5	15
March	17.5	12
April	19.0	19
May	18.0	16
June	15.5	18
July	14.5	20

(a) Total sales for the season are $650,000. Determine sales for each month.

(b) Calculate total $ reductions and allocate reductions to each month based on percents given above.

(c) Using the basic stock method, calculate BOM inventory values for each month.

(d) Enter the EOM inventory values on the form. July's ending inventory has been given as the average inventory.

(e) Calculate planned purchases at retail.

(f) Calculate initial markup percent needed, given:

Reductions	22.0%
Operating expenses	34.0%
Profit desired	7.5%
Alteration costs	0.5%
Cash discounts	1.6%

2. Using the merchandise plan completed in problem #1, calculate stock-sales ratios for each month.

3. The sport dress classification of a specialty store was given the following figures to use in developing a merchandise plan for the spring/summer season. Develop a merchandise plan using the form provided.

Month	% of Season's Sales	BOM Stock-Sales Ratio	Reductions % of Monthly Sales
February	14.0	3.8	6.6
March	16.0	4.2	4.9
April	20.0	3.5	4.3
May	17.5	3.6	4.8
June	16.5	3.7	5.4
July	16.0	3.9	7.5

(a) Distribute total season's sales of $222,600 for each month.

(b) Calculate monthly dollar reductions and total season dollar reductions.
    Note: reductions are a percent of the *monthly* planned sales.

(c) Plan BOM stock values.

(d) Enter EOM values. Use $124,359 for the July EOM.

(e) Calculate monthly planned purchases at retail.

(f) Calculate turnover for the season.

DEFINITIONS

Average Stock   Sum of the stock at the beginning of a period, stock at the beginning of similar periods, and the stock at the end of the period, divided by the total number of stock listings.

Basic Stock   The assortment of merchandise that should be maintained at all times. This merchandise consists of staples that have a highly predictable sales rate because customer demand remains relatively consistent.

Dollar or Seasonal Merchandise Plan/Six-Month Plan   A projection of the sales goals of a department, a classification, or an entire store for each month of a six-month period. It indicates the rate at which money should be used for purchases in order to maintain the desired balance between stock and sales.

Planned Purchases   The dollar amount of merchandise that should arrive in the store during a month in order to make planned sales and maintain appropriate stock level.

Open-To-Buy   The balance of the amount of merchandise that a buyer may order during a given period, usually one month. Open-to-buy may be calculated in dollars or units of merchandise.

Stock-Sales Ratio   The ratio that exists between the stock on hand at the beginning of the month (or sometimes the end of the month) and the retail sales projected for that same month. It is one method used to determine the proper amount of stock to be kept in inventory.

Stock or Inventory Turnover/Stock Turn Rate   The number of times during a given period that the average inventory on hand is sold and replaced. It is a ratio commonly calculated for one year or a six-month season. Stock turnover is determined by dividing net sales by average inventory at retail.

Weeks' Supply   A method of planning stock whereby the needed inventory is equal to the sales for a specific number of weeks.

Chapter 8 • Summary Problems

1. Planned sales for June this year are $120,000. Last year the actual sales for June were $110,000. Determine the planned percent increase in sales for the month.

$$\frac{\$120,000 - 110,000}{110,000} = \frac{\$10,000}{\$110,000} = 9.09\%$$

2. The rug department is planning a 15% reduction in sales this year. If last year's sales were $525,000, what is this year's planned sales figure?

$$\$525,000 \times .85 = \$446,250$$

3. The planned sales for a department are $38,000, and the stock-sales ratio is planned at 1.8. Find the BOM stock that is needed to realize this ratio.

$$\$38,000 \times 1.8 = \$68,400$$

4. During a six-month period, a department had planned sales of $250,000 and planned turnover of 3.2. The planned sales for May are $38,000. Using the basic stock method, determine the BOM stock for May.

$$\text{Ave. stock} = \$250,000 \div 3.2 = \$78,125$$
$$\text{ave. sales} = \$250,000 \div 6 = \$41,666.67$$
$$\text{Basic stock} = \$78,125 - 41,666.67 = \$36,458.33$$
$$\text{BOM stock May} = \$38,000 + 36,458.33 = \$74,458.33$$

5. During February, junior dresses had BOM stock of $200,000 and net sales for the month were $151,250. The EOM inventory was $275,000. What was the stock turnover for the month?

$$\text{Stock turn} = \frac{\$NS}{\text{ave. stock}}$$
$$\text{Ave. stock} = \frac{\$200,000 + 275,000}{2} = \$237,500$$
$$\text{stock turn} = \$151,250 \div 237,500 = .64$$

6. Determine the dollar sales for April, May, June, and July, given the following seasonal sales distribution: (You must first determine total sales for the season.)

Month	% of Season's Sales	Monthly Sales
February	12%	$ 96,000
March	14	112,000
April	18	144,000
May	22	176,000
June	20	160,000
July	14	112,000

$Sales = $96,000 ÷ .12
= $800,000

7. Calculate the average stock in a department with annual sales of $1,840,000 and an annual stock turnover of 5.4.

$1,840,000 ÷ 5.4 = $340,741

8. Determine the stock turnover for a six-month period (February to July) from the following information:

Month	Sales	BOM Stock
February	$20,000	$32,000
March	28,000	38,000
April	27,000	35,000
May	24,000	36,000
June	18,000	29,000
July	23,000	34,000
August	25,000	36,000
September	29,000	38,000
October	23,000	32,000
November	26,000	35,000
December	32,000	42,000
January	28,000	36,000

ave. stock = $34,285.71
NS = $140,000
stock turnover = 4.08

9. Determine the stock-sales ratio when the planned sales for August are $36,000 and the retail stock for August 1 is $120,000.

$120,000 ÷ 36,000 = 3.33

10. Find the planned April purchases (a) at retail and (b) at cost with the following figures:

Sales	$220,000
BOM Stock for April	− $380,000
BOM Stock for May	+ $240,000
Markup	51% C%= .49
Markdowns	$5,060 2.3%

(a.) $85,060
(b.) $41,679.40

11. The linen department has planned sales of $375,000 for the spring/summer season. Turnover goal for the season is 1.8. Develop a six-month merchandise plan (using the form provided) based on the following information:

Reductions ↗ $37,500	10%
Operating expenses	40%
Profit	5.5%
Cash discounts	0.9%

$$\frac{54.6}{110} = 49.647\%$$

ave. stock = $375,000 ÷ 1.8 = $208,333
ave. sales = $375,000 ÷ 6 = $62,500
Basic stock = $208,333 − 62,500 = $145,833

Month	% of Season's Sales		% of Season's Reductions		BOM stock	EOM stock	Planned Purch.
February	$60,000	16	$5,625	15	$205,833	202,083	61,875
March	56,250	15	6,750	18	202,083	205,833	66,750
April	60,000	16	5,625	15	205,833	209,583	69,375
May	63,750	17	7,500	20	209,583	217,083	78,750
June	71,250	19	6,000	16	217,083	209,083	69,250
July	63,750	17	6,000	16	209,583	208,333	68,500

(a) Calculate initial markup %. 49.647%
(b) Distribute monthly planned sales.
(c) Determine monthly dollar markdowns. TMD = $375,000 × .10 = $37,500
(d) Determine BOM stock figures.
(e) Find monthly planned purchases at retail.

12. Calculate monthly planned purchases for the men's clothing department when the planned total fall/winter season's sales are $860,000. (Use the merchandise plan form provided.) Total markdowns for the season are planned at 14.6% of the season's sales. January's EOM inventory is planned at $510,000.

Month	Sales	% of Season's Sales	BOM Stock	Stock-Sales Ratio		% of Season's Markdowns	EOM Stock	Planned Purch. Retail
August	120,400	14%	505,680	4.2	22,601	18%	550,400	187,721
September	137,600	16	550,400	4.0	18,834	15	528,900	134,934
October	129,000	15	523,900	4.1	18,834	15	526,320	145,254
November	146,200	17	526,320	3.6	15,067	12	632,960	267,907
December	197,800	23	632,960	3.2	16,323	13	528,900	110,063
January	129,000	15	528,900	4.1	33,901	27	510,000	144,001

125,560

SIX-MONTH MERCHANDISE PLAN

Department Name _____

Department Number _____

Merchandise Manager _____

Buyer _____

Period _____

	Plan	Actual
% initial markup		
% reductions		
% maintained markup		
% alteration expense		
% cash discount		
% gross margin		
% operating expense		
% net profit		
season turnover		
average stock		
basic stock		

SPRING / FALL	February / August	March / September	April / October	May / November	June / December	July / January	SEASON TOTALS
SALES Last Year							
Plan							
Planned % of Season							
Revised Plan							
Actual							
% of LY Sales							
EOM STOCK Last Year							
Plan							
Revised							
Actual							
MARKDOWNS Last Year							
Plan							
Revised							
Actual							
% of Plan MD							
BOM STOCK Last Year							
Plan							
Revised							
Actual							
Plan Stock-Sales Ratio							
PLANNED PURCHASES AT RETAIL Last Year							
Plan							
Revised							
Actual							
PLANNED PURCHASES AT COST Last Year							
Plan							
Revised							
Actual							

Figure 8-3. Additional merchandise plan forms for student use.

SIX-MONTH MERCHANDISE PLAN

	Plan	Actual
Department Name		
Department Number		
Merchandise Manager		
Buyer		
Period		

	Plan	Actual
% initial markup		
% reductions		
% maintained markup		
% alteration expense		
% cash discount		
% gross margin		
% operating expense		
% net profit		
season turnover		
average stock		
basic stock		

		SPRING FALL	February August	March September	April October	May November	June December	July January	SEASON TOTALS
SALES		Last Year							
		Plan							
		Planned % of Season							
		Revised Plan							
		Actual							
		% of LY Sales							
EOM STOCK		Last Year							
		Plan							
		Revised							
		Actual							
MARKDOWNS		Last Year							
		Plan							
		Revised							
		Actual							
		% of Plan MD							
BOM STOCK		Last Year							
		Plan							
		Revised							
		Actual							
		Plan Stock-Sales Ratio							
PLANNED PURCHASES AT RETAIL		Last Year							
		Plan							
		Revised							
		Actual							
PLANNED PURCHASES AT COST		Last Year							
		Plan							
		Revised							
		Actual							

Figure 8-3. Additional merchandise plan forms for student use.

SIX-MONTH MERCHANDISE PLAN

Department Name _____

Department Number _____

Merchandise Manager _____

Buyer _____

Period _____

	Plan	Actual
% initial markup		
% reductions		
% maintained markup		
% alteration expense		
% cash discount		
% gross margin		
% operating expense		
% net profit		
season turnover		
average stock		
basic stock		

	SPRING FALL	February August	March September	April October	May November	June December	July January	SEASON TOTALS
SALES	Last Year							
	Plan							
	Planned % of Season							
	Revised Plan							
	Actual							
	% of LY Sales							
EOM STOCK	Last Year							
	Plan							
	Revised							
	Actual							
MARKDOWNS	Last Year							
	Plan							
	Revised							
	Actual							
	% of Plan MD							
BOM STOCK	Last Year							
	Plan							
	Revised							
	Actual							
	Plan Stock-Sales Ratio							
PLANNED PURCHASES AT RETAIL	Last Year							
	Plan							
	Revised							
	Actual							
PLANNED PURCHASES AT COST	Last Year							
	Plan							
	Revised							
	Actual							

Figure 8-3. Additional merchandise plan forms for student use.

SIX-MONTH MERCHANDISE PLAN

Department Name _____

Department Number _____

Merchandise Manager _____

Buyer _____

Period _____

		Plan	Actual
% initial markup			
% reductions			
% maintained markup			
% alteration expense			
% cash discount			
% gross margin			
% operating expense			
% net profit			
season turnover			
average stock			
basic stock			

SPRING FALL		February August	March September	April October	May November	June December	July January	SEASON TOTALS
SALES	Last Year							
	Plan							
	Planned % of Season							
	Revised Plan							
	Actual							
	% of LY Sales							
EOM STOCK	Last Year							
	Plan							
	Revised							
	Actual							
MARKDOWNS	Last Year							
	Plan							
	Revised							
	Actual							
	% of Plan MD							
BOM STOCK	Last Year							
	Plan							
	Revised							
	Actual							
	Plan Stock-Sales Ratio							
PLANNED PURCHASES AT RETAIL	Last Year							
	Plan							
	Revised							
	Actual							
PLANNED PURCHASES AT COST	Last Year							
	Plan							
	Revised							
	Actual							

Figure 8-3. Additional merchandise plan forms for student use.

CHAPTER 9

Dollar Open-To-Buy

OBJECTIVES

- To calculate dollar and unit open-to-buy.
- To understand the difference between a basic stock list and a model stock plan.

KEY POINTS

- Open-to-buy (OTB) is used as a control device to see that purchasing is done according to the merchandise plan. The OTB enables the buyer to determine the balance of purchases remaining in dollars or in units for any given time period.
- OTB cannot be determined unless the amount of stock on hand is known. This may be either obtained by a physical inventory count or calculated through the retail method of inventory (RIM).
- Although dollar planning is the most basic type of planning, unit planning is another tool used in balancing the merchandise assortment with customer demand.
- Assortment plans may be developed in two ways: (1) basic stock list and (2) model stock plan. A basic stock list is used for basic items that remain consistent in demand, whereas a model stock plan is used for fashion merchandise.

As stated in the previous chapter, the two major tools of merchandise planning are the dollar merchandise plan and the open-to-buy (OTB). The merchandise plan projects to the future and serves as a guide for a selling period that has not yet begun. **The open-to-buy, also known as open-to-receive, serves as a control device to see that purchasing is carried out according to the figures outlined in the six-month merchandise plan.** Through the open-to-buy, store management controls the purchasing activity of the buyers so that only the merchandise needed to fulfill the plan is procured and excessive purchasing of inventory is avoided.

The seasonal merchandise plan indicates the dollar amount of purchases planned for each month of a season. These planned purchase figures represent the amount of stock the buyer may plan to receive into stock during the month and determine the purchase limit for the month.

The open-to-buy (OTB) is used as a control device to see that purchasing is done according to the merchandise plan. Usually, a retailer does not purchase all of the inventory at the beginning of the month, but rather at various times during the month. Also, at the first of the month, the buyer may have outstanding orders, which will reduce the amount of additional purchases allowed for the month. The OTB enables the buyer to determine, as of any specific date during the month, the amount of merchandise to be purchased for delivery to the store for the balance of the month without exceeding the planned closing stock level. The retail value of these purchases is the OTB.

Formally defined, **open-to-buy is a calculation made at frequent intervals throughout a given period to find the amount of merchandise that may be received into stock during the period without exceeding the planned closing stock level at the end of the period.** OTB may be calculated in dollars or in units of merchandise. Dollar OTB is always calculated at retail unless otherwise stated.

In its simplest form, OTB is calculated by subtracting the merchandise available from the merchandise needed to meet the plan.

$$\text{OTB} = \text{Merchandise Needed} - \text{Merchandise Available}$$

Merchandise available to the buyer includes merchandise on hand, merchandise received, merchandise in transit, and outstanding orders. The merchandise that the buyer needs consists of planned sales, planned markdowns or reductions, and EOM inventory.

$$\text{OTB} = \text{Planned Sales} + \text{Planned EOM Stock} + \text{Markdowns}$$
$$- \text{Inventory on Hand} - \text{Merchandise on Order}$$

If need is greater than merchandise available, the buyer is OTB. If the reverse is true and the buyer has more merchandise available than needed, the buyer has overbought and does not have any OTB.

It is important for buyers to hold back some of their OTB dollars for several reasons. (1) New lines or items may appear that the buyer wishes to purchase. (2) Special promotions from vendors may become available. (3) Reorders may need to be placed to fill in staple stock or replace fast-selling items.

Successful buyers know that some OTB should always be kept available to allow them to take advantage of good buying opportunities and to react to changing consumer demand.

INCREASING OPEN-TO-BUY

Sometimes a buyer is overbought or does not have sufficient open-to-buy to make a desired purchase. Increasing the merchandise needed and/or decreasing the merchandise available will increase the funds available to purchase additional stock. To increase an inadequate OTB or to correct an overbought situation, the buyer may consider the following actions:

1. **Increase the planned sales.**   This should be done only when conditions truly indicate that increased sales will occur. If the planned sales increase is not met, the buyer will have excess inventory at the end of the period. Thus, the overbought problem is not resolved.

2. **Increase planned markdowns.**   Markdowns should be taken only if they are needed to move the goods to increase sales. Taking unnecessary markdowns is a costly way to increase OTB.

3. **Reduce the stock on hand.**   This can be done by returning goods to vendors or transferring goods to another store or department. Returning goods to the vendor is often unethical; however, the buyer can check to see whether goods are in stock that may be legally returned to the vendor. Sometimes agreements are made with vendors allowing the return of merchandise that has not been sold by a specified date. Additionally, it may be possible to transfer goods to another department or store, such as to the company's outlet store.

4. **Postpone outstanding orders to a later month.**   If an outstanding order has not yet been received, it may be possible to postpone delivery until a future month. This would reduce the outstanding orders for the current month and make it possible to place new orders for current delivery. A vendor that is having difficulty meeting a delivery date may be willing to postpone the delivery date.

5. **Cancel outstanding orders.**   This is a legitimate practice if orders are overdue; otherwise, it is unethical. If an order has not been received by the due date specified on the order form, the buyer may cancel the order because the vendor has failed to meet the purchase contract. This will reduce the figure for on-order merchandise and thereby increase OTB.

6. **Increase planned closing stock.**   This procedure is justified if the original stock plan was inaccurate or if the sales for the following month are likely to be more than originally estimated.

FIGURING OPEN-TO-BUY

The following examples illustrate how to figure OTB at the beginning of the month and during the month. You can determine OTB when the stock on hand is known and when the value of the on-hand stock is unknown. Example 9-1 illustrates how to find OTB at the beginning of a month when the value of the inventory is known.

EXAMPLE 9-1

A buyer had an inventory of $30,000 on May 1 and planned EOM stock of $34,000 for May 31. Planned sales for the department were $26,000 and planned markdowns for the month were $2,500. As of May 1, the buyer had merchandise on order of $8,000 at retail to be delivered during the month. Planned initial markup was 45%. Calculate the buyer's OTB at retail and at cost as of May 1.

Solution:

OTB = Planned Sales + Planned EOM + Markdowns − Inventory on Hand − Stock on Order

Merchandise needed:

Planned sales	$26,000	
Planned markdowns	2,500	
Planned EOM stock	34,000	
		$62,500

Merchandise available:

Actual BOM stock	$30,000	
Stock on order	8,000	
		− 38,000
OTB at retail		$24,500

$$
\begin{aligned}
\text{OTB at Cost} &= \text{OTB at Retail} \times (100 - \text{Initial Markup \%}) \\
&= \$24,500 \quad \times (100 - 45\%) \\
&= \$24,500 \quad \times 55\% \\
&= \$13,475
\end{aligned}
$$

The buyer often needs to know OTB during the month. Variances in actual figures from the plan require the buyer to make adjustments in order to maintain the balance between stock and sales. **Actual on-hand and on-order stock amounts are used when available.** Example 9-2 demonstrates how OTB is figured during the month when the value of the stock on hand is known.

EXAMPLE 9-2

Determine the OTB as of June 15 given the following information (sales and markdowns for the **remainder of the month** are the differences between plan and actual for first 15 days):

Merchandise on hand, June 15	$36,000
Planned sales, June 1 to 30	26,000
Actual sales, June 1 to 15	14,000
Planned markdowns for June	2,000
Actual markdowns, June 1 to 15	900
Planned stock at retail, July 1	30,000
Stock on order, June 15	3,000

Solution:

Merchandise needed, June 15 to 30:

Planned EOM stock, June 30		$30,000	
Planned sales, June 1 to 30	$26,000		
Actual sales, June 1 to 15	– 14,000		
Balance of planned sales, June 15 to 30		12,000	
Planned markdowns, June 1 to 30	2,000		
Actual markdowns, June 1 to 15	– 900		
Balance of planned markdowns, June 15 to 30		1,100	
Total merchandise needed, June 15 to 30			$43,100
Merchandise available as of June 15:			
Stock on hand, June 15	$36,000		
Stock on order, June 15	3,000		
Total merchandise available, June 15			– 39,000
OTB, June 15			$ 4,100

The buyer can easily determine OTB when the amount of stock on hand is given. Sometimes this information is not readily available and must be calculated in order to find OTB. This may be either obtained by a physical inventory or calculated through the retail method of inventory (RIM). Example 9-3 shows how to determine OTB during the month when the value of stock on hand is unknown.

EXAMPLE 9-3

Calculate the buyer's OTB as of March 11, based on the following information:

BOM stock, March 1	$42,000
Purchases received, March 1 to 11	10,000
Merchandise on order, March 11	5,000
Planned sales for March	18,000
Actual sales, March 1 to 11	5,500
Planned markdowns	2,000
Actual markdowns, March 1 to 11	800
Planned EOM stock, March 31	40,000

Solution:

Merchandise needed, March 11 to 31:

Planned EOM stock, March 31		$40,000	
Planned sales for Month	$18,000		
Actual sales, March 1 to 11	− 5,500		
Balance planned sales, March 11 to 31		12,500	
Planned markdowns for Month	$ 2,000		
Actual markdowns, March 1 to 11	− 800		
Balance planned markdowns, March 11 to 31		+ 1,200	
Total merchandise needed			$53,700
Merchandise available as of March 11:			
BOM stock, March 1	$42,000		
Purchases received, March 1 to 11	+ 10,000		
Total merchandise handled		52,000	
Actual sales, March 1 to 11	5,500		
Actual markdowns, March 1 to 11	+ 800		
Total deductions in inventory		− 6,300	
Merchandise on hand,* March 11		45,700	
Merchandise on order, March 11		+ 5,000	
Total merchandise available, March 11			− 50,700
OTB, March 11			$ 3,000

*Note: When stock on hand is not known, it is determined by subtracting the total deductions in inventory (sales and markdowns) from the total merchandise handled (BOM stock + purchases received).

Practice Problems • Exercise 9.1

1. On the basis of past sales and current business conditions, a buyer estimates that October sales will be $7,500. The stock at retail on October 1 is $20,000 and $6,000 stock at retail is on order for the month. Markdowns are planned at $700 for the month, and the planned EOM stock is $19,000. What is the buyer's OTB on October 1?

2. Given the following data, determine the OTB as of May 10:

Stock on hand at retail, May 10	$16,500	
Stock on order, May 10	3,100	
Planned BOM stock, June 1	17,800	
Planned sales for May	3,500	
Actual sales as of May 10	1,200	
Planned markdowns for May		3%
Actual markdowns as of May 10	75	

3. March figures for the misses' dress department are as follows:

Planned sales	$84,000	
Planned markdowns	2,400	
Planned BOM stock	187,000	
Outstanding orders	64,000	
Planned EOM stock	168,000	
Planned markup %		49.5%

Calculate the OTB at retail and at cost.

4. Determine the buyer's OTB as of November 15 using the following information:

Planned sales for November	$80,000
Actual sales, November 1 to 15	65,000
Stock on hand, November 15	100,000
Planned stock, December 1	100,000
Planned markdowns	6,000
Actual markdowns, November 1 to 15	2,800
Stock on order, November 15	20,000

5. A buyer had an inventory on June 1 of $50,000 and a planned EOM stock of $60,000. As of June 1, the buyer had merchandise on order of $25,000 at retail to be delivered during the month. Planned markdowns for the month were $3,800 and planned sales were $40,000. The planned initial markup was 52%. Find the buyer's OTB for the month at retail and at cost.

6. Determine the buyer's OTB as of September 10 based on the following information: (Use RIM to work problem.)

Planned sales for September	$ 54,000
Actual sales, September 1 to 10	18,000
Planned markdowns	4,500
Actual markdowns, September 1 to 10	1,500
BOM stock, September 1	126,000
Planned EOM stock	120,000
Purchases received, September 1 to 10	25,000
Stock on order, September 1 to 10	10,000

UNIT PLANNING AND OPEN-TO-BUY

Another tool used in balancing the merchandise assortment with customer demand is unit planning. Although the most basic type of planning is dollar planning, in some merchandise classifications it is desirable to supplement dollar planning with unit planning.

Frequently the inventory gets out of balance with the customer demand. For example, slow-selling sizes and/or colors may accumulate, creating a situation where the dollar inventory appears adequate, but sales are lost because of lack of inventory in desired sizes. The first step in developing an assortment plan is to identify the selection factors (also called parameters) that are most important to the customer. For clothing, size is an important selection factor. Color, price, brand, fabric, detailing, and so forth, may be important selection factors depending on the individual item or classification. Selection factors are characteristics that differentiate one item from another and consequently provide the basis for the customer's selecting or requesting the item.

An assortment plan allocates the dollars and/or units to selection factors considered most important. Assortment plans may be developed in two ways: (1) **basic stock list** and (2) **model stock plan**.

A basic stock list consists of the items and number of units that are to be continuously maintained in stock.

A model stock plan is used by buyers of fashion goods and provides an assortment of stock broken down according to identifiable selection factors, such as fabric, color, size, and classification at a specific point in time.

When working with assortment plans, it is important to recognize the differences between basic and fashion merchandise. Fashion merchandise is accepted by the customer over a shorter period of time than is basic merchandise. Some retailers make a distinction between staple basics and fashion basics.

Basics are items continually desired by customers that should be maintained in stock at all times.
Staple basics rarely change and are maintained in stock for several seasons.
Fashion basics are items that sell throughout the entire planning period. With perhaps a change in color, fashion basics may sell for more than one planning period.

Basic merchandise does not provide excitement for a department; however, it should always be maintained in stock. It is the bread and butter for a department. Customers expect to be able to buy basic merchandise when needed. Customer loyalty is quickly lost by the store that does not maintain a stock of basic items.

PERIODIC REORDER QUANTITIES

The buyer must make a decision as to the most appropriate technique for maintaining an adequate stock of basic items. One technique is to have the merchandise on hand counted and reordered at regularly scheduled, periodic intervals. This allows the store to guide the flow of merchandise, balancing customer purchases with reorders.

When basics are to be counted regularly, a periodic inventory sheet facilitates maintaining the system. Periodic count sheets may be set up in several ways. A few

PERIODIC REORDER FORM

Department:	General cosmetics	Line:	Soft as silk
Department No:	# 23	ITEM:	Beauty care items
Buyer:	E. L. Jones	Prices:	$2.98 to 7.98

Item/ Color	Reserve quantity	Size	Maximum quantity	Date				Date				Date				Date			
				OH	O	R*	S	OH	O	R*	S	OH	O	R*	S	OH	O	R*	S
Hand	36	10 oz.	144	71	73	72*	61	82	62	72*	89	65	79	84*				*	
lotion	24	16 oz.	124			*				*				*				*	
	15	24 oz.	72			*				*				*				*	

* Check packaging considerations.

Note:
OH   On hand
O   Quantity ordered (needed in order to reach maximum)
R*   Quantity received
S   Sales

Figure 9-1. Form used for periodic reorders.

manufacturers (cosmetic firms, for example) supply their retail accounts with forms especially designed for control of their merchandise. However, most retailers design their own periodic count sheets. See Figure 9-1 for an example.

Unit OTB (reorder quantity) can be calculated at any time using the following information:

Reorder period (RP) refers to the period of time, in weeks, between planned stock counts. A reorder will be placed after each stock count.

Delivery period (DP) refers to the period of time, in weeks, between the count and the date the reordered merchandise is on the selling floor.

Lead time (LT) is the sum of the reorder and delivery period.

Rate of sale (RS) is the average number of units sold per week.

Reserve (R) is a quantity of merchandise to be maintained on hand to cover increase in sales and/or delay of reorders.

Merchandise on hand (OH) is the amount of stock available in units.

Merchandise on order (OO) is the number of units of merchandise ordered but not yet received.

Maximum (also called **provision**) **quantity (M)** is the order-up-to quantity. It is the quantity to be made available—on hand plus on order—at any reorder point. The maximum quantity is never on hand at any one time.

The formula for calculating maximum quantity is:

Maximum = Rate of Sale (Reorder Period + Delivery Period) + Reserve

Because reorder period + delivery period = lead time, the formula can also be written:

$$\text{Maximum} = \text{Rate of Sale (Lead Time)} + \text{Reserve}$$

Let's review:

RP is the number of weeks in a reorder period.
DP is the number of weeks in a delivery period.
LT is the number of weeks included in lead time.
RS is the average number of units sold per week.
R is the number of units to be maintained for reserve.
OH is merchandise on hand.
OO is merchandise on order.
M is the maximum amount of stock needed to be available at any given time.

EXAMPLE 9-4

The notions buyer inventories hair care items every four weeks. A local wholesaler provides one-week delivery service. Brand X hair spray sells at an average rate of 30 cans per week. The reserve has been set at 48. Calculate the maximum (order-up-to quantity).

Solution:

$$
\begin{aligned}
\text{Maximum} &= \text{Rate of Sale (Reorder Period + Delivery Period)} + \text{Reserve} \\
&= 30 \, (4 + 1) + 48 \\
&= 30 \, (5) + 48 \\
&= 150 + 48 \\
&= 198
\end{aligned}
$$

The quantity that should be reordered (OTB) can be calculated by subtracting the amounts on hand and on order from the maximum quantity.

$$\text{OTB} = \text{Maximum} - (\text{Merchandise on Hand} + \text{Merchandise on Order})$$

EXAMPLE 9-5

Using the previous example, if there were 75 cans of hair spray on hand, 123 should be reordered.

Solution:

$$
\begin{aligned}
\text{OTB} &= \text{Maximum} - (\text{Merchandise on Hand} + \text{Merchandise on Order}) \\
&= 198 - (75 + 0) \\
&= 123
\end{aligned}
$$

In most instances a reorder will have been received prior to the next inventory so that the quantity on order (OO) will be zero; however, if merchandise is on order, it is important to allow for that quantity.

EXAMPLE 9-6

The buyer for bedding has determined that beige, cotton/polyester, queen size sheets sell at an average rate of 5 per week. The buyer plans to reorder every six weeks, and delivery takes two weeks. The reserve quantity has been set at 16. If there are 23 on hand and none on order, how many should be reordered?

Solution:

$$\text{Maximum} = \text{Rate of Sale (Reorder Period + Delivery Period) + Reserve}$$
$$= 5\,(6 + 2) + 16$$
$$= 40 + 16$$
$$= 56$$

$$\text{OTB} = \text{Maximum} - (\text{Merchandise on Hand + Merchandise on Order})$$
$$= 56 - (23 + 0)$$
$$= 33$$

The reorder period (RP) and rate of sale (RS) can be calculated from information shown on the periodic count form. The reorder period is the time between counts.

EXAMPLE 9-7

If an item were inventoried on October 1 and again on October 29, find the reorder period.

Solution:

Reorder Period = Number of Days Between Stock Counts ÷ Number of Days in a Week

$$= 28 \text{ days} \div 7 \text{ days a week}$$
$$= 4 \text{ weeks}$$

The following formula can be used to calculate the weekly rate of sale (RS).

$$\text{Rate of Sale} = \frac{\text{Beginning Inventory + Receipts - Ending Inventory}}{\text{Reorder Period}}$$

EXAMPLE 9-8

On October 1, an inventory showed 68 pairs of medium knee-hi hose in suntan on hand. At that time 36 were reordered; the reorder was received and put in stock. Now, on October 29, there are 56 on hand. What was the rate of sale during this time?

(*Hint: Refer to previous example for reorder period*)

Solution:

$$\text{Rate of Sale} = \frac{\text{Beginning Inventory} + \text{Receipts} - \text{Ending Inventory}}{\text{Reorder Period}}$$

$$= \frac{68 + 36 - 56}{4}$$

$$= 12 \text{ units sold on average per week}$$

EXAMPLE 9-9

On November 2, there were 98 bottles of hand lotion on hand. At that time, 48 were reordered; the reorder has been received. Now, on November 23 there are 83 bottles on hand. Delivery requires two weeks. If reserve has been set at 36, how many should be reordered?

(*Hint: Break the problem into steps. Because the reorder period and rate of sale are not given, calculate both from the information given.*)

Solution:

Step 1. Determine reorder period (RP). The first count was on November 2; the next count was November 23, or 21 days later.

$$RP = \frac{21 \text{ days}}{7 \text{ days per week}} = 3 \text{ weeks}$$

Step 2. Determine rate of sale (RS).

$$\text{Rate of Sale} = \frac{\text{Beginning Inventory} + \text{Receipts} - \text{Ending Inventory}}{\text{Reorder Period}}$$

$$= \frac{98 + 48 - 83}{3} = 21 \text{ units sold on average per week}$$

Step 3. Calculate maximum (M).

$$\text{Maximum} = \text{Rate of Sale (Reorder Period} + \text{Delivery Period)} + \text{Reserve}$$
$$= 21 \, (3 + 2) + 36 = 141$$

Step 4. Calculate reorder quantity (OTB).

$$\text{OTB} = \text{Maximum} - (\text{On Hand} + \text{On Order})$$
$$= 141 - (83 + 0) = 58*$$

*Note: Small items such as hand lotion will be prepackaged with a specific quantity per carton. If this item is packaged with $2\frac{1}{2}$ dozen (30 bottles) per carton, 2 cartons or 60 units will be ordered.

EXAMPLE 9-10

A buyer estimates that a reserve of 40 sweaters in the $30 price line is needed. He plans to reorder stock every two weeks. It takes one week for delivery after an order has been placed. There are 50 sweaters in stock and 12 on order. Sales are estimated at 20 per week. Calculate the unit OTB, average stock, and unit turnover/year.

Solution:

Step 1. Calculate provision (P). This is also called maximum quantity.

$$\text{Provision} = \text{Rate of Sale (Delivery Period + Reorder Period) + Reserve}$$
$$= 20\,(1 + 2) + 40 = 100$$

Step 2. Determine OTB.

$$\text{OTB} = \text{Provision} - \text{(Merchandise on Hand + Merchandise on Order)}$$
$$= 100 - (50 + 12) = 38$$

Step 3. Calculate average stock.

$$\text{Average Stock} = \text{Reserve} + \tfrac{1}{2}\,\text{(Rate of Sale} \times \text{Reorder Period)}$$
$$= 40 + \tfrac{1}{2}\,(20 \times 2)$$
$$= 40 + 20 = 60$$

Step 4. Calculate turnover. (Unless otherwise specified, turnover is calculated for a year.)

$$\text{Net Sales} = \text{Rate of Sale} \times \text{52 Weeks per Year}$$
$$= 20 \times 52 \text{ weeks} = 1{,}040 \text{ units}$$

$$\text{Turnover} = \text{Net Sales (in units)} \div \text{Average Stock}$$
$$= 1{,}040 \div 60 = 17.33$$

Some stores use this periodic fill-in technique for maintaining their assortment or groups of merchandise. Items that are similar may be considered as a basic unit. A general type of sport shirt, such as plaid, short sleeve, or cotton/polyester blend, could be treated as one unit and merchandise ordered from more than one vendor. Another example of merchandise that might be handled as a staple unit is white linen dinner napkins.

The size of the reserve quantity will depend on the degree of protection desired against the possibility of running out of stock. Formulas can be used to calculate reserve quantities; however, most buyers estimate reserve quantities based on experience or refer to tables.

Practice Problems • Exercise 9.2

1. On December 1, an inventory showed 50 pairs of white knee socks in stock and 30 pairs on order. The reorder was received and put in stock. On December 29, 40 pairs were on hand. Determine the rate of sale during the period.

2. The buyer for linens has 35 beige beach towels in stock. A reserve of 12 is maintained. Stock is reordered every five weeks, and delivery requires one week. Sales average 10 per week. Determine the quantity that should be reordered.

3. The rate of sale of leather chairs is estimated at 4 per week. The buyer places orders every five weeks, and delivery takes six weeks. A reserve equal to two-weeks' estimated sales is maintained. There are 20 leather chairs on hand and 15 on order. Calculate (a) the unit OTB and (b) the unit annual stock turnover.

4. A buyer has 125 blouses in her $40 price line in stock and 60 on order. Sales are estimated at 20 per week. A reserve of 70 blouses is considered adequate. Stock is reordered every three weeks. It takes four weeks for delivery after an order has been placed. Calculate (a) the unit OTB, (b) average stock, and (c) unit annual stock turnover.

DEFINITIONS

Assortment Plan   A projection of the variety and quantity of merchandise to be carried in a department or store to meet customer demand. Amounts may be stated in terms of dollars or in units. Assortment plans may be developed either through the basic stock list method or the model stock plan.

Basic Stock   The assortment of merchandise that should be maintained at all times. This merchandise consists of staples that have a highly predictable sales rate because customer demand remains relatively consistent.

Basic Stock List   A method for developing an assortment plan used for staple items. Included on the basic stock list are the name of the item, brand, physical description, cost and retail price, and other information that precisely identifies the merchandise. A basic stock list is more specific than a model stock plan.

Fashion Basics   Items that sell throughout the entire planning period.

Fashion Merchandise   Distinctive goods possessing considerable current customer appeal. Such goods have a short product life span and unpredictable level of sales.

Maximum Quantity   The quantity of goods to be made available (on hand plus on order) at any reorder point. Also called **provision**.

Model Stock Plan   A method for developing the assortment plan used in planning fashion merchandise. Although the model stock plan breaks down the composition of the stock according to identifiable selection factors such as fabric, color, size, and classification, it is less specific than the basic stock plan.

Open-to-Buy (OTB)   Also called **open-to-receive**, this is the amount of merchandise that a buyer may order during the balance of a given period, usually one month. OTB may be calculated in dollars or units of merchandise.

Rate of Sale   The average number of units of merchandise sold per week.

Reorder   A buyer's request for additional merchandise from a vendor to replenish depleted stocks of merchandise.

Reserve   The quantity of merchandise to be kept on hand to protect against stock-outs due to unexpected increases in sales and/or delivery time.

Selection Factors   Qualities inherent in merchandise that differentiate one item from another and provide the basis for the customer's buying behavior.

Staple Basic Stock   Items that rarely change and are maintained in the assortment for several seasons.

Staple Stock List   A list of all items to be carried regularly in the merchandise assortment.

Unit Control   The control of stock in terms of individual merchandise units rather than dollar value.

1. A buyer had an inventory of $45,000 on June 1 and a planned EOM stock of $51,000. Planned sales for the department were $39,000 and planned markdowns for the month were $3,200. As of June 1, the buyer had merchandise on order of $10,000 at retail to be delivered during the month. Planned initial markup was 48%. Calculate the buyer's OTB at retail and at cost as of June 1.

2. Given the following figures, determine the OTB as of October 10.

Retail stock on hand, October 10	$22,000
Merchandise on order	6,200
Planned BOM stock, November 1	24,000
Planned sales for October	9,500
Actual sales as of October 10	3,500
Planned markdowns for October	380
Actual markdowns as of October 10	200

3. The children's department had the following figures for October:

Planned sales	$500,000
Planned reductions	5,000
Planned stock, October 1	850,000
Planned stock, November 1	630,000
Outstanding orders	200,000
Planned markup	48.2%

   (a) Determine the planned October purchases at retail for the children's department.
   (b) What is the October OTB at cost?

4. On the basis of past sales, a buyer estimates that her sales will be $60,000 in July. The retail stock on July 1 is $47,000. The stock on July 31 is planned at $40,000, with markdowns estimated to be 3.2%. The buyer had merchandise on order of $30,000 at retail to be delivered during the month. Planned initial markup was 53%. Determine the buyer's OTB at retail and at cost as of July 1.

5. Calculate the OTB as of April 10 given the following:

Planned sales, April 1 to 30	$57,000
Actual sales, April 1 to 10	25,000
Merchandise on hand, April 10	75,000
Planned stock, May 1	64,000
Planned markdowns	3,500
Actual markdowns, April 1 to 10	1,500
Merchandise on order, April 10	12,000

6. A buyer maintains a reserve of 35 toasters. She has 30 toasters in stock and 24 on order. She plans to reorder every two weeks and delivery takes one week. Sales average 20 per week. Calculate the unit OTB.

7. On the first of the month, an inventory showed 30 pairs of men's black executive length socks in stock and 48 pairs on order. The reorder was received and put in stock. On the 29th day of the month, 26 pairs were on hand. Determine the rate of sale during this period.

8. The rate of sale for a patio furniture set is estimated at 5 per week. The buyer places orders every four weeks, and delivery takes six weeks. A reserve equal to two-weeks' sales is maintained. If there are 15 sets on hand and 15 on order, what is the unit open-to-buy?

9. On June 1, there were 54 bottles of hand lotion on hand. At that time, 48 were reordered. The order has been received. Now on June 22, there are 51 bottles on hand. Delivery requires two weeks. If reserve is 36, how many should be reordered?

10. A buyer has 90 pairs of jeans in his $25 price line in stock and 24 on order. Sales are estimated at 30 per week. A reserve of 60 is maintained, and stock is reordered every three weeks. It takes four weeks for delivery. Calculate (a) the unit OTB and (b) stock turnover.

CHAPTER 10

Performance Measures

OBJECTIVES

- To recognize and calculate productivity or efficiency measures, including sales percentages, sales per square foot, sales per linear foot of shelf space, sales per transaction, sales per employee hour, and sales per full-time employee equivalent.
- To calculate gross margin return on inventory.
- To understand the use of sales curves as a retailing tool.

KEY POINTS

- Both retailers and manufacturers use sales figures to measure productivity.
- Sales per square foot data are used to monitor the productivity of a department, a store, a merchandise category, a vendor, or an entire shopping center and may be used in planning sales and determining the space needed for a merchandise category.
- Supermarkets, drug stores, and discount stores use sales per linear foot of shelf space to determine a product's allotment of space.
- A common measure of productivity is sales per full-time employee equivalent because retail firms use a large number of part-time employees.
- A sales curve shows the relative importance of sales from one month to another by illustrating the peaks and valleys in customer demand for a particular item or category of merchandise and assists the buyer in knowing how many of an item to buy and when to buy it.

This chapter introduces concepts that measure productivity and financial performance. Productivity is the output produced compared with input expended. As a rule, the more output produced per employee hour or dollar investment, the more profitable a company is. Retailers continually strive to improve the productivity of their three principal assets—inventory, space, and human resources.

The most common measure of space productivity is sales per square foot of selling space. Productivity of human resources can be measured in a number of ways, including sales per employee, sales per full-time employee equivalent, and salespeople's salaries as a percent of sales.

Inventory productivity can be measure by stock turnover, which is defined as the total net sales divided by average inventory valued at retail prices. This ratio shows how rapidly inventory is sold on an annual basis. Another measure of inventory profitability is gross margin return on inventory (GMROI). GMROI indicates whether an adequate gross margin is being earned compared to the investment in inventory required to generate the margin dollars.

Calculations based on sales are used to measure productivity and financial performance of retail firms. Sales results presented in this chapter include sales percentages, sales per square foot, sales per linear foot of shelf space, sales per transaction, sales per employee hour, and sales per full-time employee equivalent. Also discussed are sales curves as a retailing tool—how they are generated and how they are used in the merchandising process to maximize sales and profit.

Remember that although it is extremely important to analyze financial information in dollars and cents, it is essential that percents and ratios be used if data are to be compared with past performance or industry standards.

SALES PERCENTAGES

Both retailers and manufacturers use sales figures to measure productivity or performance. Sales results are used to compare departments, stores, merchandise classifications, and vendors. For example, retailers calculate the percentage that each store unit or department's net sales are of the total store's net sales. If the women's shoe department had net sales for the past six-month season of $200,000 and total store sales were $4,000,000 for the same time, the shoe department's percentage of total net sales would be 5.00%. **To determine the department's percentage of total store sales, divide the department's total net sales by the total net sales for the entire store** (see Chapter 2 for a review of percents).

> Department's % of Total Store Sales = Department's Total Net Sales
> ÷ Store's Total Net Sales

EXAMPLE 10-1

If a department's sales were $200,000, and total store sales were $4,000,000, what was the department's percent of sales?

Solution:

Department's % of Total Sales = Department's Total Net Sales ÷ Store's Total Net Sales
= $200,000 ÷ $4,000,000
= 5.0%

COMPARISON OF THIS YEAR'S SALES TO LAST YEAR'S SALES

As you have seen in earlier chapters, retailers often compare this year's sales with last year's sales. The percent increase or decrease in sales is calculated in order to evaluate performance of the total company, individual stores, merchandise classifications, or vendors. As seen in Chapter 8, the seasonal merchandise plan includes both the planned figures for this year and last year's actual figures. Once this year's actual figures are known, retailers calculate the percent change in net sales over the previous year. The percent change is determined by dividing the difference between the figures for the two years by last year's sales. Remember, the previous year is always used as the base figure when determining the percentage increase or decrease.

When comparing sales growth, it is important to look at comparable or same store sales. Sales figures that include sales from new stores that have been opened since the previous year can be misleading.

> % Change in Net Sales = Difference Between Sales Figures ÷ LY Sales

SALES PER SQUARE FOOT

Sales per square foot data are used to monitor the productivity of a department or store and may be used in planning sales and determining the space needed for a merchandise category. If a unit is operating below company or industry standards, efforts may be taken to try to increase the sales volume or to consider reducing the amount of space. Sales per square foot are a rough measure of return on investment as the investment in a retail store is a function of the amount of space. Construction costs are usually measured as so many dollars per square foot, and rent for retail space is often charged as so many dollars per square foot. Although a given sales per square foot cannot be directly translated into a certain return on investment, it is true that a healthy sales per square foot figure is generally associated with a healthy return on investment.

Sales Per Square Foot as a Productivity Measure

Sales per square foot is the most common measure of space productivity in retailing. It is usually calculated for a total store and for individual departments but also may be calculated for a merchandise category, a vendor, or even for an entire shopping center. Although usually calculated on an annual basis, sales per square foot is sometimes calculated on a weekly basis. Supermarkets, for example, calculate weekly sales per square foot whereas department stores and apparel specialty stores use an annual figure. Sales per square foot may be based on gross space or selling space. Gross space includes all of the square footage in the store including nonselling areas. Selling space excludes all nonselling areas in the computation of sales per square foot.

Selling space is usually defined as the total floor space devoted to selling activities, including aisles, fitting rooms, and stockrooms immediately adjacent to the selling department. Space next to stairways, elevators, escalators, and store entrances is excluded from the departmental selling area. In addition, workrooms and remote stockrooms are not considered part of the selling area.

Sales per square foot is determined by dividing net sales by the appropriate square feet of space figure. Sales per square foot of gross space is based on total space and sales per square foot of selling space is based on selling space.

Sales per Square Foot of Gross Space = Net Sales ÷ Square Feet of Space in Store

---

Sales per Square Foot of Selling Space = Net Sales ÷ Square Feet of Selling Space

---

EXAMPLE 10-2

A family department store had sales last year of $23,994,000. If it has 86,000 square feet of selling space, what were the store's sales per square foot for last year?

Solution:

Sales per Square Foot = Net Sales ÷ Square Feet of Selling Space
= $23,994,000 ÷ 86,000
= $279

It is important to remember that an increase in sales per square foot from year to year does not mean that real productivity has increased. Inflation will cause sales per square foot to rise artificially. To measure true space productivity changes, inventory price indexes must be considered in evaluating increases in sales per square foot.

Sales Per Square Foot as a Planning Measure

An important use of sales per square foot data is in determining space requirements and planning sales. A store planner can estimate the amount of space needed to support a planned sales volume by using available sales per square foot data. When opening a new store, sales figures can be projected for the total store or a department using the experience of other stores in the chain operating in similar locations. **To estimate the amount of space needed to support a planned sales volume, divide the planned sales volume by the expected sales per square foot.**

Amount of Space = Sales Volume ÷ Sales per Square Foot

EXAMPLE 10-3

If the sales per square foot in the handbag department in a single unit of a chain store average $280 annually and the annual sales for a new store are planned at $252,000, what amount of space should be allocated to the new department?

Solution:

$$\text{Amount of Space} = \text{Sales Volume} \div \text{Sales per Square Foot}$$
$$= \$252,000 \div 280$$
$$= 900 \text{ square feet}$$

A store planner can also use sales per square foot data to estimate sales for a store or department. If the square footage allocated for a new department is known and the average sales per square feet for this department in other units of the store are known, sales for the new location can be estimated by multiplying the amount of space by the expected sales per square foot. It must be remembered that such estimates are only rough approximations that are based on the assumption that the new store is similar to other company sites. Store planners must consider factors such as the demographics of potential customers, geographical location, and competition. Estimates based on sales per square foot, however, can provide merchants useful data for further analysis. **Estimated sales are calculated by multiplying amount of space in the store and the sales per square foot.**

$$\text{Estimated Sales} = \text{Amount of Space} \times \text{Sales per Square Foot}$$

EXAMPLE 10-4

If 900 square feet in a new store have been allocated to the handbag department and the average sales per square foot for this department in other units of the store are $280, what annual sales volume would be expected?

Solution:

$$\text{Estimated Sales} = \text{Amount of Space} \times \text{Sales per Square Foot}$$
$$= 900 \times \$280$$
$$= \$252,000$$

SALES PER LINEAR FOOT OF SHELF SPACE

A productivity or efficiency measure similar to sales per square foot is sales per linear foot of shelf space. This measure relates sales to the number of linear feet of shelf space used by a department, merchandise category, or brand. Supermarkets, drug stores, and discount stores use sales per linear foot of shelf space to determine a product's allotment of space. In analyzing sales of different brands, a retailer may decide to increase the shelf space for a brand that has a higher sales per linear foot figure.

To determine sales per linear foot divide sales by the linear feet of shelving devoted to the product.

Sales per Linear Foot = $ Sales ÷ Linear Feet of Shelving

EXAMPLE 10-5

A store devotes 30 linear feet of shelving to hair spray. If sales per week for hair spray total $1,246, what are the sales per linear foot of shelving?

Solution:

Sales per Linear Foot = $ Sales ÷ Linear Feet of Shelving
= $1,246 ÷ 30
= $41.53

Practice Problems • Exercise 10.1

1. A large department store chain is planning sales of $450 million for this year. If sales for the previous year totaled $294 million, what is the planned percent increase for the current year?

2. A chain store had sales in 2000 of $102 million. If sales in 2001 totaled $194 million, what was the percent increase?

3. A designer's bridal collection contributed $2.5 million to his firm's annual wholesale volume of $12 million. What percent of sales did the bridal collection contribute to the total firm?

4. The designer firm of Christian Dior reported that annual sales for 2000 leaped 35% to $277.4 million. What did sales total the previous year?

5. If a company's net income increased 15% to $786.8 million, what was the net income for the previous year?

6. A discount department store reported that sales decreased from $12.3 billion the previous year to $10.9 this year. What was the percent decrease?

7. An exclusive, upscale shopping mall reported annual sales of $672 million. If the mall had 500,000 square feet of selling space, what were its sales per square foot?

8. A moderate-priced 86,000 square foot department store had annual sales per square foot of $279. Determine the store's total sales.

9. A branch department store has a total of 220,000 square feet of space. Twelve percent of the total space is considered nonselling. If last year's net sales were $59,000,000, determine the store's sales per square foot of selling space.

10. The deli department in a supermarket had sales last week of $13,500. If the department occupies 300 square feet of space, what were the department's sales per square foot?

11. A specialty store averages sales of $589 per square foot. How many square feet of selling space would be needed to produce total annual sales of $1,196,000?

12. A leathergoods store was planning a new store. The research department estimated that a new store could achieve annual sales of $2,500,000. If the chain averaged annual sales per square foot of $820 in its newer stores, approximately how much selling space should be planned for the new store?

SALES PER TRANSACTION

Other measures used to evaluate productivity are the number of transactions processed in a store or department and the average dollar sale per transaction. A sales transaction is the processing of one sale. When a customer buys a sofa in a furniture store and a salesperson charges the sale, this is one transaction. When a customer buys several items and the cashier rings all the items on the sales register, this is one transaction.

The number of transactions is important in evaluating the performance of salespeople. The dollar amount of sales made by individual salespeople does not tell the whole story. The salesperson with the highest dollar sales for a day might have had one high dollar transaction, whereas a salesperson with lower total sales may have had many transactions of smaller dollar amounts.

The average dollar sale per transaction is an important measure of productivity. When this dollar amount increases, it is apparent that stores are doing a better job of selling to the customer. In 1997, the National Retail Federation reported an average transaction size of $54.65 for department stores and $54.27 for specialty stores. As the 1992–1994 numbers for department stores were in the $36 to $41 range, this indicated that department stores were "capturing more of each customer's shopping basket."[1]

Sales per transaction relate total gross sales to the number of transactions processed. This is the same as the average sale. **To determine the average sale per transaction, divide the gross sales by the number of transactions.**

$$\text{\$ Sales per Transaction} = \text{Gross Sales} \div \text{Number of Transactions}$$

EXAMPLE 10-6

If gross sales totaled $25,400 on 112 transactions, determine the average sale per transaction.

Solution:

$$\text{\$ Sales per Transaction} = \text{Gross Sales} \div \text{Number of Transactions}$$
$$= \$25,400 \div 112$$
$$= \$226.79$$

SALES PER EMPLOYEE HOUR

Another measure of productivity used by some retailers relates sales for a period to the number of hours employees have worked during that period. Referred to as sales per employee hour, this measure of productivity is commonly used in food retailing. **It is determined by dividing net sales by the total number of hours worked by employees during the time period.**

$$\text{Sales per Employee Hour} = \text{Net Sales} \div \text{Number of Employee Work Hours}$$

---

[1]Moran, A. (Ed.). (1998). *FOR/MOR, The Combined Financial, Merchandising, and Operating Results of Retail Stores in 1997*, 73rd edition. New York: National Retail Federation.

EXAMPLE 10-7

During the past week, sales at one store totaled $359,000. During the week, employees worked 3,890 hours. What were the sales per employee hour for the week?

Solution:

$$\text{Sales per Employee Hour} = \text{Net sales} \div \text{Number of Employee Work Hours}$$
$$= \$359,000 \div 3,890$$
$$= \$92.29$$

SALES PER FULL-TIME EMPLOYEE EQUIVALENT

A common measure of productivity used by retailers is sales per full-time employee. Because many retail firms use a large number of part-time employees, this measure is calculated based on the number of full-time equivalent employees. Part-time hours worked are converted into the number of equivalent full-time employees. To determine the number of full-time equivalents the retailer totals the number of hours worked by part-time employees and divides by the number of hours considered to be a full-time week. A full-time week may range from 35 to 40 hours. The National Retail Federation uses 40 hours as a full-time week. Therefore, if part-time employees worked a total of 4,000 hours, the number of full-time equivalents for this part-time work would be 4,000 hours divided by 40 hours resulting in 100 full-time equivalent hours. **To determine sales per full-time equivalent, first find the number of full-time equivalent hours worked by part-timers, and add this number to the number of full-time employees. The number is then divided into the net sales.**

$$\text{Sales per Full-time Equivalent} = \text{Net Sales} \div \text{Number of Full-time Equivalent Employees}$$

EXAMPLE 10-8

A department had weekly sales of $35,600. Two full-time employees worked 35 hours each and 8 part-timers worked a total of 210 hours. If the store considers full-time 35 hours, determine the sales per full-time equivalent.

Solution:

Step 1: Determine the number of full-time equivalent employees by dividing the number of hours worked by part-time employees by the number of hours the store considers a full-time work week. Add this number to the number of full-time employees.

$$\text{Number of Full-time Equivalents} = 210 \div 35 = 6 + 2 = 8$$

Step 2: Divide total net sales for the department by the number of full-time equivalent employees.

$$\text{Sales per Full-time Equivalent} = \text{Net Sales} \div \text{Number of Full-time Equivalents}$$
$$= \$35,600 \div 8 = \$4,450$$

Other ways of measuring the productivity of salespeople include sales per salesperson and salespeople's salaries as a percent of sales. Although sales per salesperson is a good measure of selling effectiveness, it can be distorted by inflation. An advantage of using salespeople's salaries as a percent of sales is that this measurement is not distorted by inflation.

1. A specialty store had total gross sales last week of $100,890 with 620 transactions. What was the average sale per transaction?

2. The average sale in a department store was $25.76 during a month when the store processed 50,568 customers. What were the store's total sales for the month?

3. According to payroll records, during the past week, 45 employees worked. Of these employees, 21 were full-timers who worked a regular 40-hour week. Part-time employees worked a total of 480 hours, and sales for the week were $68,000. What were the sales per full-time employee equivalent?

4. If a store uses a 35-hour work week, determine the sales per full-time employee equivalent based on the following information: 5 full-time employees, 10 part-time employees working an average of 22 hours each, total sales of $28,900.

5. If sales for the week were $12,489 and employees worked 180 hours, determine the sales per employee hour.

GROSS MARGIN RETURN ON INVENTORY (GMROI)

A good measure of inventory profitability is gross margin return on inventory (GMROI). **GMROI is a ratio that measures the efficiency of the investment in inventory.** It is calculated by dividing the dollar gross margin by average inventory at cost. The average cost of inventory is calculated by adding the BOM cost inventory for each month in the period plus the EOM cost inventory for the last month in the period and dividing by 7 for a season or 13 for a year. GMROI indicates whether an adequate gross margin is being earned compared to the investment in inventory required to generate those margin dollars. Although GMROI can be used at the total company level, it is more useful when applied to individual product categories. This ratio is stated in terms of the number of times gross margin is earned on inventory. Many department and specialty store retailers use GMROI to measure the relative performance of departments or merchandise categories.

GMROI = Gross Margin $ ÷ Average Inventory at Cost

EXAMPLE 10-9

Calculate GMROI for a six-month season from the following data:

Gross margin
Inventory at Cost:	$365,945
BOM stock August	75,400
BOM stock September	80,200
BOM stock October	82,000
BOM stock November	95,000
BOM stock December	92,000
BOM stock January	72,000
EOM stock January	68,000

Solution: Step 1. Find the average inventory cost.

$$\frac{\$75,400 + \$80,200 + \$82,000 + \$95,000 + \$92,000 + \$72,000 + \$68,000}{7}$$

$$= \$564,600 \div 7 = \$80,657$$

Step 2. Divide gross margin by the average cost of inventory.

GMROI = Gross Margin ÷ Average Inventory at Cost
$$= \$365,945 \div \$80,657$$
$$= 4.54$$

SALES CURVES

A sales curve is a retailing tool used to express the variance in the rate of sale of a store unit, an item, or merchandise category over a period of time, usually six months or a year. A sales curve indicates the relative importance of sales from one month to another by showing the peaks and valleys in customer demand for a particular item or category of merchandise. Sales curves are used to maximize both sales and profit. They assist the buyer in performing the buying process by serving as a guide in determining how many of an item to buy and when to buy it. Sales curves also assist those who distribute merchandise to store units within a chain. For many types of merchandise, the curve remains relatively constant from one year to the next. For example, because of back-to-school, August is an important month for children's apparel. A store may sell 1,250 pairs of jeans in August but only 700 in July. Thus, the sales curve is higher in August than in July.

A sales curve can be expressed in several ways. The same sales curve can be expressed in units of sale, in dollars, as a percent, and as a ratio.

1. **As a Unit of Sale:** The number of units sold is recorded monthly, or sometimes weekly, for comparison. It can easily be seen what months have the highest sales. For example, the most candy is sold in October prior to Halloween. The second highest candy sales occur before Easter.

2. **As a Dollar Figure:** The dollar amount of sales is recorded weekly or monthly for comparison.

3. **As a Percent:** Each month is expressed as a percent of the total for the six month season or the year. Both units of sale and dollar sales may be expressed as a percent.

4. **As a Ratio:** In determining a ratio, the lowest sales month is used as the base month. If February is the lowest month, it is assigned a value of 1; so the ratio is 1:1. If March sales represent three times as many sales as February, the ratio is 3:1. If sales in April are five times as high as February, the ratio is 5:1

An example of each of these types of sales curves follows (Figures 10-1 and 10-2).

EXAMPLE 10-10

Unit Sales Curve

Month	Units	Percent
August	60	6
September	180	18
October	260	26
November	220	22
December	160	16
January	120	12
Total	1,000	100

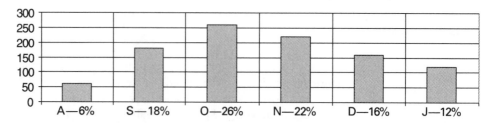

Figure 10-1. Unit sales curve.

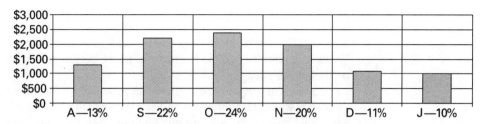

Figure 10-2. Dollar sales curve.

EXAMPLE 10-11

Dollar Sales Curve

Month	Dollars	Percent
August	$ 1,300	13
September	$ 2,200	22
October	$ 2,400	24
November	$ 2,000	20
December	$ 1,100	11
January	$ 1,000	10
Total	$10,000	100

The information in Examples 10-10 and 10-11 can also be presented as ratios. **To convert a sales curve to a ratio, use the month with the lowest percent as the base, and divide the percent of sales for each month by this figure.**

EXAMPLE 10-12

Sales Curves as a Ratio

Here is how the unit and dollar ratios in Examples 10-10 and 10-11 would look:

	Aug.	Sept.	Oct.	Nov.	Dec.	Jan.
Units	1:1	3:1	4.3:1	3.6:1	2.7:1	2:1
$	1.3:1	2.2:1	2.4:1	2:1	1.1:1	1:1

Determining Sales Curves

In order to establish sales curves, the retailer must have accurate sales estimates. As you have seen in previous chapters, sales estimates are based on accurate interpretation of sales records. A retail firm uses its own sales records from last year in each store to develop sales curves. In addition, national sales curve data are available that will provide a comparison. Most important, however, are a store's own records. It must be recognized that local climate, the type and age of customers, their income level, and many other factors make sales curves different from one store to the next. The buyer must ask many questions before making buying decisions. It is important to talk to store managers and sales personnel to see what they have to say about their merchandise offerings and customer preferences. It is essential for the buyer to look at merchandise presentation and advertising to determine what effect each has had on the rate of sale. Was the merchandise attractively displayed in the stores and was it advertised? Merchandise presentation and promotion influence the rate of sale. Weather conditions and the fluctuations of the economy also are important influences on the rate of sale.

Sales curves will vary greatly depending on the geographical location of a store. For example, swimwear will sell throughout the year in Miami, Florida, but in Michigan. swimwear sales are limited to the spring/summer season.

In Florida, women's swimwear would be carried throughout the year, and sales would be somewhat consistent because of the weather and vacationing tourists. The annual sales curve for women's swimwear in Florida might look like this:

February	5%	August	8%
March	9%	September	6%
April	9%	October	6%
May	14%	November	5%
June	12%	December	9%
July	9%	January	8%

In Michigan, the annual sales curve for women's swimwear is very different, and swimwear is not stocked during the winter months.

February	0%	August	10%
March	12%	September	0%
April	13%	October	0%
May	22%	November	0%
June	25%	December	0%
July	18%	January	0%

Another example would be misses' winter coats. In Louisiana, the six-month sales curve might look like this:

August	5%
September	5%
October	20%
November	35%
December	25%
January	10%

Whereas in New York, where it gets cold much earlier and stays cold much longer, the six-month sales curve might be distributed as follows:

August	20%
September	20%
October	25%
November	15%
December	10%
January	10%

It is important to research past sales history and review sales curves when completing buying plans. If you missed sales because you were out of stock, you would have to estimate how much business you missed and add it to the actual sales in order to adjust your sales curve.

EXAMPLE 10-13

Last year's records show that your dollar sales for swimwear for the six-month period February through July totaled $13,500. Monthly sales were as follows: February $1,000; March $2,000, April $2,000, May $2,500, June $4,500, July $1,500. You ran out of stock on some sizes on April 5, and you did not receive replacement stock until the end of April. You estimated that you could have sold an additional 20 swimsuits in April at an average retail of $35.00. Establish the actual percentage sales curve for the department, and adjust this sales curve to reflect true customer demand. By adding estimated sales that were lost because of being out of stock, a more accurate sales curve is obtained for the buyer to use in planning this year's sales.

	LY Sales	Lost Sales	New Estimate	New Curve
Feb	$1,000	—	$1,000	7.0%
Mar	2,000	—	2,000	14.1
April	2,000	$700	2,700	19.0
May	2,500	—	2,500	17.6
June	4,500	—	4,500	31.7
July	1,500	—	1,500	10.6
Total	$13,500	$700	$14,200	100.0%

Category Sales Curves

It is also important to develop sales curves for specific divisions within a merchandise category. For example, the sales curves for women's swimwear may differ by style. One-piece swimsuits may sell at a different rate than two-piece suits or bikinis. Two-piece suits may reach their peak sales earlier in the season. One reason for this could be that most bikinis are purchased by younger women who buy their swimsuits earlier in the year than older women do.

The buyer must apply judgment to adjusting sales curves. Fashion changes influence what styles will sell best. The buyer must be aware of fashion forecasts and changing customer preferences.

Some merchandise has a relatively flat sales curve. In other words, it sells at a relatively constant level throughout the year. Such merchandise is considered basic. Basic merchandise is defined as merchandise that is in continual demand and is kept in stock at all times. It has a highly predictable sales curve, with customer demand being stable over an extended period. Some examples are men's underwear, women's hosiery, cosmetics, and work clothes. As you saw in Chapter 9, when figuring open-to-buy, it is easier to control this type of merchandise. A rate of sale may be determined for each item and a reorder point established.

Some basic merchandise has a relatively flat curve all year long, except for one or two peaks. For example, more men's underwear is sold at back-to-school and at Christmas. It is important to know what percent of the annual sales volume these peaks represent so that additional merchandise can be purchased to meet the increased demand.

Retailers use sales curves to maximize sales, turnover, and profit. Sales curves are one tool the buyer uses to determine how many of an item to buy and when to buy it. By studying sales curves, the buyer is able to project estimated sales and adjust buying plans, thereby having the merchandise customers want when they want it. The buyer is able to maintain a lower inventory level and at the same time have the items the customer wants to purchase. This ensures a higher turnover, which generates more profit. Because the retailer will have fewer out-of-stocks when the customer wants the merchandise, sales volume will increase. Increased sales volume generates more gross profit. Additionally, because the buyer will not be overstocked with merchandise the customer does not want, markdowns should be lower, resulting in more gross profit.

1. From the following data, determine the GMROI: average inventory value at cost, $72,450; and gross margin, $245,400.

2. Find the GMROI given net sales of $340,000, gross margin of 38%, and average inventory at cost of $60,000.

3. Calculate GMROI from the following data: net sales, $235,000; beginning inventory at cost, $44,000; closing inventory at cost, $46,000; and gross margin, 39%.

4. Based on the unit sales curve data for one misses' swimwear style, figure the sales curve percents by month. February, 10 units; March, 22 units; April, 32 units; May, 48 units; June, 66 units; July, 22 units.

5. You are planning the sales of the same style swimsuit in problem #4 for the coming plan period. You estimate that this year you will sell 260 of the suits. Based on the percentage sales curve you figured in problem #4, calculate planned unit sales by month so purchases can be made for this year.

DEFINITIONS

Full-time Employee   A worker who is employed on a year-round basis and who works a full work week, generally 35 to 40 hours per week.

Full-time Equivalent Employees   The number of hours worked by part-time employees divided by the number of hours considered to be a full-time work week.

Gross Margin Return on Inventory (GMROI)   A measure of inventory profitability that relates a store's gross margin to the cost of the merchandise inventory needed to generate the profit.

Sales Curve   A retailing tool that is used to express the variance in the rate of sale of an item or group of items (category) over a period of time, usually six months or a year.

Sales per Employee Hour   The relationship between sales for a period of time and the number of hours employees have worked during that period.

Sales per Full-time Employee Equivalent   The relationship between sales for a period of time and the number of full-time equivalent employees.

Sales per Linear Foot of Shelf Space   The relationship between sales and the number of linear feet of shelf space used by a department, merchandise category, or brand.

Sales per Square Foot of Selling Space   A ratio that reflects the sales volume productivity of a retailer's selling space. Found by dividing net sales by square feet of selling space in store.

Sales Productivity Method of Space Allocation   The space to be allocated to a department or merchandise category is based on sales the product has achieved in the past on a square foot basis.

Sales Transaction   The processing of one sale.

Selling Space   The total floor space devoted to selling activities, including aisles, fitting rooms, and stockrooms adjacent to the selling department.

Chapter 10 • Summary Problems

1. The men's shoe department of a department store had net sales for the fall season of $102,680. If total fall sales for the store were $2,246,000, what percent of total net sales were in the men's shoe department?

2. Reflecting the closure of 25 stores in the year, an off-price specialty store chain reported that sales dropped to $338.4 million from $374.7 million. What was the percent decrease?

3. Neiman-Marcus Direct reported sales for fiscal year 2000 of $363.8 million, an increase of 13.1% over the previous year. What did the sales total in fiscal 1999?

4. Determine the average sale per transaction if gross sales for the month were $38,600 on 205 transactions.

5. The average sale in a discount department store was $23.45 during a week when the store processed 29,200 customers. What were the store's total sales for the week?

6. Eight employees worked during the past week in the gift department. Three worked a full-time, 36-hour week; five worked part-time, averaging 22 hours each. If departmental sales for the week were $35,000, what were the sales per full-time employee equivalent?

7. A large apparel chain posted sales of $13.7 billion for the year on 13.8 million square feet of retail space. What were the chain's sales per square foot?

8. A branch department store has a total of 200,000 square feet of space. If 10% of the total space is considered nonselling, what were the store's sales per square foot of selling space if total sales last year were $36,900,000?

9. The floral department in a supermarket had sales last week of $3,500. If the department occupies 200 square feet of selling space, what were the department's sales per square foot for the week?

10. A men's specialty store has annual sales of $650 per square foot. How many square feet of selling space would be needed to produce total annual sales of $14 million?

11. An apparel specialty store announced the opening of a four-level 22,000-square-foot flagship store in New York City. The store's first year volume was projected at $14 million. What sales per square feet were planned?

12. The women's hosiery department occupied 1,000 square feet and had sales of $129,000 last year. If sales stayed the same, what reduction in space would bring the store's sales per square foot in line with the industry average of $159 per square foot?

13. The manager of a specialty chain store was concerned that the store's sales per square foot of $219 was below the company average of $245. If the store had 3,600 square feet of space, what percent increase in sales would be needed to bring sales up to the company average?

14. Establish a six-month percentage sales curve for dress shirts, given the following sales information: February, $1,560; March, $2,040; April, $2,160; May, $2,160; June, $2,280; July, $1,800.

15. Express the sales curve in problem 14 as ratios.

16. In planning for the next year, the buyer in problem 14 noted that she ran out of white shirts on June 12 and did not receive more in stock until the end of the month. She estimated that she could have sold an additional 12 of them in June at an average retail of $30.00. Revise the percentage sales curve to reflect these lost sales.

17. Calculate GMROI from the following data: sales, $535,217; average inventory at cost, $66,176; and gross margin, 38%.

APPENDIX A

Review of Fractions

Fractions are values less than 1. The fraction $\frac{1}{4}$ means one of four parts. For example, $\frac{1}{4}$ of \$1.00 is \$.25. The fraction $\frac{3}{4}$ means three parts each of which is equal to $\frac{1}{4}$. The number on top is called the **numerator** and the number on the bottom is called the **denominator**.

$$\frac{3}{4} = \frac{\text{numerator}}{\text{denominator}}$$

Fractions are closely related to decimals and percents. Decimals are similar to fractions because they represent part of a whole quantity. Working with percents is another method of working with fractional parts; percents are fractions with a denominator of 100.

COMMON DENOMINATORS

Working some fraction problems requires finding a **common denominator**. Finding a common denominator simply means changing all the fractions in the problem to fractions with the same denominator. To do this, find a number (common denominator) that is divisible by all the denominators in the problem. Sometimes it is easier to multiply several of the denominators by each other to find a common denominator. For example, the fractions $\frac{2}{5}$ and $\frac{3}{4}$ can be converted to fractions with a common denominator of 20 (5×4).

Converting fractions into different yet equivalent fractions that have a common denominator is simply a matter of multiplying both the numerator and denominator by the same number. For example, to transform $\frac{2}{5}$ into a fraction with a denominator of 20, divide the denominator 5 into the desired denominator 20 ($20 \div 5 = 4$). Then use 4 as the multiplier for both the numerator and denominator. The numerator becomes 8 (4×2) and the denominator 20 ($5 \times 4 = 20$) to result with the fraction $^8/_{20}$. The two fractions $^2/_5$ and $^8/_{20}$ are equivalent.

Similarly, $^3/_4$ can be converted by dividing 4, the existing denominator, into the desired denominator 20 ($20 \div 4 = 5$). Use 5 to multiply by the numerator to finish the conversion ($5 \times 3 = 15$). The new fraction is $^{15}/_{20}$. Now the fractions of $^2/_5$ and $^3/_4$ can be added or subtracted by using the new converted forms of $^8/_{20}$ and $^{15}/_{20}$.

EXAMPLE 1

Convert the fractions $^1/_4$, $^1/_3$, and $^1/_6$ into fractions with a common denominator.

Solution: Multiply denominators together until a number is found that is evenly divisible by all three denominators. Multiply two denominators ($4 \times 3 = 12$). Twelve is evenly divisible by all three denominators, so it can become our common denominator. Divide each denominator into 12 to arrive at a new value that will be used as a multiplier for both the numerator and denominator. Convert the three fractions into equivalent fractions with a common denominator of 12.

$12 \div 4 = 3$ Use 3 as the multiplier: $^1/_4 \times ^3/_3 = ^3/_{12}$
$12 \div 3 = 4$ Use 4 as the multiplier: $^1/_3 \times ^4/_4 = ^4/_{12}$
$12 \div 6 = 2$ Use 2 as the multiplier: $^1/_6 \times ^2/_2 = ^2/_{12}$

Now the three fractions have a common denominator of 12:

$$^3/_{12}, ^4/_{12}, \text{ and } ^2/_{12}$$

REDUCING TO LOWEST TERMS

Reducing a fraction into its lowest terms means that both the numerator and the denominator cannot be further divided by a whole number.

For example, $^{15}/_{20}$ can be reduced by dividing the numerator and the denominator by the same number. That is, $^{15}/_{20} \div ^5/_5 = ^3/_4$. This does not change the value of the fraction.

$$\frac{5 \text{ into } 15 = 3}{5 \text{ into } 20 = 4} \text{ (5 goes into each)}$$

$$\frac{15}{20} \text{ reduces to } \frac{3}{4}$$

Sometimes the answer will be an **improper fraction**, a fraction with the numerator larger than the denominator. An improper fraction is reduced to lowest terms by dividing the denominator into the numerator.

EXAMPLE 2

$^{23}/_{20}$ is an improper fraction

$$20\overline{)23} \\ \underline{-20} \\ 3$$

(with quotient 1)

$^{23}/_{20}$ is reduced to $1^3/_{20}$

ADDING FRACTIONS

When adding fractions, change the fractions so that each contains a common denominator, and then add the numerators and reduce to lowest terms. You may find it easier to add fractions vertically instead of horizontally.

EXAMPLE 3

$$\frac{1}{3} + \frac{2}{5} + \frac{1}{15} =$$

$$\frac{5}{15} + \frac{6}{15} + \frac{1}{15} =$$

or

$$\frac{1}{3} = \frac{5}{15}$$

$$\frac{2}{5} = \frac{6}{15}$$

$$+ \frac{1}{15} = \frac{1}{15}$$

$$\frac{12}{15} = \frac{4}{5}$$

$$\frac{12}{15} = \frac{4}{5}$$

A mixed number is the combination of a whole number and a fraction, such as $4\frac{1}{2}$. Mixed numbers may be added by first adding the whole numbers and then adding the fractions.

EXAMPLE 4

Add the mixed numbers $4\frac{1}{2} + 2\frac{1}{2}$.

Step 1. Add the whole numbers: $4 + 2 = 6$

Step 2. Add the fractions: $\frac{1}{2} + \frac{1}{2} = \frac{2}{2} = 1$

$$4\frac{1}{2} + 2\frac{1}{2} = 6 + 1 = 7$$

Another way to add mixed numbers is to convert the numbers into improper fractions and then add.

EXAMPLE 5

$$4\frac{1}{2} + 2\frac{1}{2} =$$

$$\frac{9}{2} + \frac{5}{2} = \frac{14}{2} =$$

or

$$4\frac{1}{2} = \frac{9}{2}$$

$$+ 2\frac{1}{2} = \frac{5}{2}$$

$$\frac{14}{2} = 7$$

$$= 7$$

SUBTRACTING FRACTIONS

Subtracting fractions is very similar to adding them. First you must find a common denominator, then subtract the numerators and reduce to the lowest terms.

EXAMPLE 6

$$\frac{3}{4} - \frac{1}{2} = \qquad\qquad\qquad \frac{3}{4} = \frac{6}{8}$$

$$\frac{6}{8} - \frac{4}{8} = \frac{2}{8} \qquad \text{or} \qquad -\frac{1}{2} = \frac{4}{8}$$

$$\frac{2}{8} \text{ reduces to } \frac{1}{4} \qquad\qquad\qquad \frac{2}{8} = \frac{1}{4}$$

Mixed numbers can be subtracted by first subtracting the whole numbers and then subtracting the fractions. Another method is to change the mixed numbers into fractions and then subtract.

EXAMPLE 7

$$2\frac{1}{4} - 1\frac{1}{4} =$$

$$\frac{9}{4} - \frac{5}{4} = \frac{4}{4} = 1$$

MULTIPLYING FRACTIONS

To multiply fractions, multiply the numerator of one fraction by the numerator of the other fraction(s) and the denominator of one fraction by the denominator of the other fraction(s). Cancellation can be used in some problems to simplify the multiplication, saving time and minimizing errors. This means that both numbers have common factors that can be equally reduced or canceled. After multiplying, reduce answers to lowest terms.

EXAMPLE 8

$$\frac{3}{5} \times \frac{1}{2} = \frac{3}{10}$$

EXAMPLE 9

$$\frac{2}{5} \times \frac{1}{10} =$$

$$\frac{\overset{1}{2}}{5} \times \frac{1}{\underset{5}{10}} =$$

$$\frac{1}{5} \times \frac{1}{5} = \frac{1}{25}$$

EXAMPLE 10

To multiply mixed numbers, change the mixed numbers into improper fractions and then proceed as explained in Example 9.

$$2\tfrac{1}{2} \times \tfrac{1}{3} = \tfrac{5}{2} \times \tfrac{1}{3} = \tfrac{5}{6}$$

To multiply a fraction by a whole number, change the whole number to a fraction by placing it over one (1). For instance, 4 is the same as $\tfrac{4}{1}$. Thus, $4 \times \tfrac{3}{4} = \tfrac{4}{1} \times \tfrac{3}{4} = \tfrac{12}{4} = 3$.

EXAMPLE 11

Multiply the whole number 10 by $\tfrac{1}{3}$.

$$\tfrac{10}{1} \times \tfrac{1}{3} = \tfrac{10}{3} \text{ reduces to } 3\tfrac{1}{3}$$

DIVIDING FRACTIONS

To divide fractions, invert the divisor and then proceed as in multiplication of fractions. To invert a fraction means to interchange the places of the numerator and the denominator, for example, $\tfrac{3}{4}$ is inverted to $\tfrac{4}{3}$.

To invert a whole number, be sure to change it to a fraction first by placing it over one (1). For example, 6 is the same as $\tfrac{6}{1}$, which can be inverted to $\tfrac{1}{6}$.

EXAMPLE 12

$$\frac{7}{8} \div \frac{1}{8} = \frac{7}{8} \times \frac{8}{1} = \frac{7}{8} \times \frac{\overset{1}{8}}{\underset{1}{1}} = \frac{7}{1} = 7$$

$$\frac{3}{4} \div 2 = \frac{3}{4} \div \frac{2}{1} = \frac{3}{4} \times \frac{1}{2} = \frac{3}{8}$$

EXAMPLE 13

$$15\tfrac{1}{3} \div 1\tfrac{1}{6} = \tfrac{46}{3} \div \tfrac{7}{6} = \frac{46}{\underset{1}{8}} \times \frac{\overset{2}{1}\overset{6}{}}{7} = \tfrac{92}{7} = 13\tfrac{1}{7}$$

FRACTIONAL PARTS

Sometimes a fractional amount of an item is purchased, such as $\tfrac{3}{4}$ of a yard or $\tfrac{1}{4}$ of a dozen. To find the amount of the purchase, multiply the fraction or mixed number by the price.

EXAMPLE 14

$\frac{3}{4}$ yard of fabric at \$4.98 a yard.

$\frac{3}{4} \times 4.98 = \dfrac{14.94}{4} = 3.735$ rounded to \$3.74

Before starting to solve a problem, think about (a) the degree of accuracy needed, and (b) whether it is easier to solve using fractions or decimals.

EXAMPLE 15

$2\frac{1}{3}$ yards of fabric at \$6.00 a yard.

Using fractions: or   Using decimals:

$2\frac{1}{3} \times \$6 = \frac{7}{3}_1 \times \frac{^2 6}{1} = \frac{14}{1} = \$14.00$ $2.33 \times \$6.00 = \$13.98$ (incorrect)

$2.333 \times \$6.00 = \$14.00$

Calculating the cost of merchandise requires a high degree of accuracy. The cost in the above example should be \$14.00. If the problem is going to be solved using decimals rather than fractions, it is important to use the decimal as 2.333 (correct to three decimal places).

APPENDIX B

Selected Formulas

Average Stock =

(a) $\dfrac{\text{Net Sales for the Period}}{\text{Stock Turn for the Period}}$

also

(b) $\dfrac{\text{BOM Stock for Each Month (in the period) + End of Period Stock}}{\text{Number of Months in Period + 1}}$

Average Stock for the Season $= \dfrac{\text{Sales for the Season}}{\text{Stock Turnover for the Season}}$

Basic Stock = Average Inventory – Average Monthly Sales

BOM Stock = (a) Planned Sales for Month × Planned Stock-Sales Ratio

also

(b) Planned Sales for Month + Basic Stock

Book Inventory = Total Merchandise Handled – Total Retail Deductions

Contribution = Gross Margin – Direct Expenses

Cumulative Markup % =
$\dfrac{\text{Total Merchandise Handled at Retail – Total Merchandise Handled at Cost}}{\text{Total Merchandise Handled at Retail}}$

$$\text{Customer Return \%} = \frac{\text{Customer Returns}}{\text{Gross Sales}}$$

Estimated Shortage = Net Sales × Shortage % Estimated to have Occurred

Estimated Physical Inventory = Closing Book Inventory – Estimated Shortage

Gross Cost of Merchandise Sold = Cost of Total Merchandise Handled – Cost Value of Closing Inventory

Gross Margin \$ = (a) Net Sales – Total Cost of Merchandise Sold

also

(b) Profit + Expenses

also

(c) Maintained Markup + Cash Discounts – Alteration Costs

$$\text{Gross Margin \%} = \frac{\text{Net Sales – Total Cost of Merchandise Sold}}{\text{Net Sales}}$$

$$\text{GMROI} = \frac{\text{Gross Margin \$}}{\text{Average Inventory at Cost}}$$

$$\text{Initial Markup \%} = \frac{\text{Initial Retail Value of Merchandise – Cost Value of Merchandise}}{\text{Initial Retail Value of Merchandise}}$$

$$\text{Initial Markup \% Needed} = \frac{\text{Expenses + Profit + Reductions + Alteration/Workroom Costs – Cash Discounts}}{\text{Net Sales + Reductions}}$$

$$\text{Loaded Cost} = \frac{\text{Net Cost}}{\text{Complement of the Desired Cash Discount}}$$

$$\text{Maintained Markup \%} = \frac{\text{Net Sales – Gross Cost of Merchandise Sold}}{\text{Net Sales}}$$

$$\text{Markdown \% for a Period} = \frac{\text{Net Markdowns for the Period}}{\text{Net Sales for the Period}}$$

Markup = Retail – Cost

$$\text{Markup \% Based on Retail} = \frac{\text{\$ Markup}}{\text{\$ Retail}}$$

Maximum/Provision Quantity = Rate of Sales × (Reorder Period + Deliver Period) + Reserve Quantity

Net Markdown = Total \$ Markdown – Markdown Cancellation

OTB = (a) Planned Sales + Planned EOM Stock + Markdowns – Inventory on Hand – Merchandise on Order

also

(b) Planned Purchases – (Merchandise on Hand + Merchandise on Order)

also

(c) Maximum – (On Hand + On Order)

Planned Purchases at Retail = Planned Sales + EOM Stock + Reductions – BOM Stock

Profit/Loss = Gross Margin – Expenses

$$\textbf{Rate of Sale (per week)} = \frac{\text{Beginning Inventory} + \text{Receipts} - \text{Ending Inventory}}{\text{Reorder Period}}$$

$$\textbf{Sales per Square Foot of Selling Space} = \frac{\text{Net Sales for Year}}{\text{Square Feet of Selling Space}}$$

$$\textbf{Selling Cost \%} = \frac{\text{Gross Wages for Selling Staff}}{\text{Net Sales}}$$

$$\textbf{Shortage/Overage \%} = \frac{\text{Closing Book Inventory} - \text{Closing Physical Inventory}}{\text{Net Sales for Period}}$$

$$\textbf{Stock-Sales Ratio} = \frac{\text{BOM Retail Stock}}{\text{Net Sales for Month}}$$

$$\textbf{Stock Turnover} = \frac{\text{Net Sales at Retail for a Period}}{\text{Average Stock at Retail for a Period}}$$

Total Cost of Merchandise Sold = Gross Cost of Merchandise Sold – Cash Discounts + Alteration Costs

Unit Average Inventory = Reserve + $\frac{1}{2}$ (Rate of Sale × Reorder Period)

APPENDIX C

Answers to Practice Problems

CHAPTER 2

Exercise 2.1

1. (a) 132.81
   (b) 171.903
   (c) 875.515
   (d) $702.80

2. (a) 524.267
   (b) 0.74505
   (c) 55.421
   (d) $85.65

3. (a) $57
   (b) $175.88
   (c) $4.91
   (d) 0.7836

4. (a) $1,938.59
   (b) $98,956.56
   (c) 195,938.35
   (d) 813.33

5. (a) 7.10
   (b) 13.73727 = 13.74
   (c) 623.937 = 623.94
   (d) 26.597744 = 26.60

6. (a) $3,888.97
   (b) 1,024.549 = 1,024.55
   (c) $18,808.96
   (d) $5,846.15

7. (a) 405.33
   (b) 21.36
   (c) $21,544.90
   (d) 42,896.56
   (e) 0.10
   (f) 50.00
   (g) 1.0
   (h) 597.90
   (i) 10.37
   (j) 534.01

Exercise 2.2

1. 225

2. 445

3. 60,144

4. 30 dozen; 360 units

5. 13

6. 33

7. **(a)** 63
   (b) 28
   (c) 122
   (d) 262
   (e) 44
   (f) 21
   (g) 90
   (h) 140
   (i) 219
   (j) 273

Exercise 2.3

1. **(a)** $\frac{1}{4}$
   (b) $\frac{1}{400}$
   (c) $\frac{1}{500}$
   (d) $\frac{91}{200}$
   (e) $\frac{1}{200}$
   (f) $\frac{143}{400}$
   (g) $\frac{1}{125}$
   (h) $\frac{17}{20}$
   (i) $\frac{19}{20}$
   (j) $1\frac{11}{16}$

2. **(a)** 0.125
   (b) 2.0
   (c) 0.6
   (d) 0.8825
   (e) 1.548
   (f) 0.08
   (g) 1.45
   (h) 1.0
   (i) 0.05
   (j) 0.0058

3. **(a)** 2%
   (b) 12.5%
   (c) 50%
   (d) 150%
   (e) 1,086%
   (f) 125%
   (g) 33.50%
   (h) 265%
   (i) 4%
   (j) 179.65%

4. **(a)** 25%
   (b) 120%
   (c) 40%
   (d) 262.5%
   (e) 75%
   (f) 66.67%
   (g) 62.5%
   (h) 10%

Exercise 2.4

1. **(a)** $3.58
   (b) $411.95
   (c) 36.15
   (d) $4.97
   (e) 5.05

2. 23

3. $382.50

4. 21

5. 4

6. $61.60

Exercise 2.5

1. **(a)** 5.5
   (b) 55
   (c) 22.75
   (d) 55.2
   (e) 20

2. 6.25%

3. 68%

4. 60%

5. 35.6%

6. 67.21%

7. 45.57%

8. 2.86%

Exercise 2.6

1. (a) $292   **2.** $12,500   **3.** $62,500   **4.** $6,736
   (b) $576
   (c) 95
   (d) $1,502.40
   (e) 15.99

5. $6,800   **6.** 200   **7.** $27,500   **8.** 168

Exercise 2.7

1. 58.44%   **2.** 64%   **3.** 22.22%   **4.** 8.33%   **5.** 34.73%

6. 80.95%   **7.** 8.79%   **8.** 5.51%   **9.** 30.77%   **10.** 6.06%

CHAPTER 3

On operating statements, round dollar figures to nearest dollar but show all percents correct to two decimal places.

Exercise 3.1

1.
Net sales	$14,000	100.00%
Cost of merchandise sold	− 7,200	− 51.43
Gross margin	6,800	48.57
Expenses	− 5,900	− 42.14
Profit	900	6.43

2.
Net sales	$187,000	100.00%
Cost of merchandise sold	− 109,000	− 58.29
Gross margin	78,000	41.71
Expenses	− 71,995	− 38.50
Profit	6,005	3.21

3.
Net sales	$242,000	100.00%
Cost of merchandise sold	− 134,600	− 55.62
Gross margin	107,400	44.38
Expenses	− 91,960	− 38.00
Profit	15,440	6.38

4.
Net sales	$687,520	100.00%
Cost of merchandise sold	− 385,836	− 56.12
Gross margin	301,684	43.88
Expenses	− 273,633	− 39.80
Profit	28,051	4.08

5.
Net sales	$79,800	100.00%
Cost of merchandise sold	− 44,209	− 55.40
Gross margin	35,591	44.60
Expenses	− 35,910	− 45.00
Loss	(319)	(0.40)

6. Net sales | $300,000 | 100.00%
Cost of merchandise sold | – 153,000 | – 51.00
Gross margin | 147,000 | 49.00
Expenses | – 150,000 | – 50.00
Loss | (3,000) | (1.00)

7. Net sales | $168,750 | 100.00%
Cost of merchandise sold | – 120,950 | – 71.67
Gross margin | 47,800 | 28.33
Expenses | – 49,150 | – 29.13
Loss | (1,350) | (0.80)

8. Net sales | $150,000 | 100.00%
Cost of merchandise sold | – 81,100 | – 54.07
Gross margin | 68,900 | 45.93
Expenses | – 69,500 | – 46.33
Loss | (600) | (0.40)

9. 48.00%

10. 55.00%

Exercise 3.2

1. $93,920.51   **2.** 4.58%

3. 5.19%   **4.** 11.35%

5. (a) Alice 7.56%
Brandon 6.92
Carrie 10.49
David 6.27

(b) Department 7.82%

6. $501,049.14

7. Gross sales | $680,366 |
Customer returns | – 66,676 | 9.80%
Net sales | 613,690 | 100.00%
Cost of merchandise sold | – 342,439 | – 55.80
Gross margin | 271,251 | 44.20
Expenses | – 255,909 | – 41.70
Profit | 15,342 | 2.50

8. Gross sales | $86,536 |
Customer returns | – 9,214 | 10.65%
Net sales | $77,322 | 100.00%
Cost of merchandise sold | – 43,409 | – 56.14
Gross margin | 33,913 | 43.86
Expenses | – 35,289 | – 45.64
Loss | (1,376) | (1.78)

9. Gross sales $120,000
  Customer returns   – 18,562   15.47%
    Net sales   101,438   100.00%
    Cost of merchandise sold   – 56,218   – 55.42
    Gross margin   45,220   44.58
    Expenses   – 41,220   – 40.64
    Profit   4,000   3.94

10. (a) Christopher   4.69%
      Jonathan   15.80
      Jay   5.07
      Suzanne   4.72
      Zachary   4.31

  (b) Department   7.75%

Exercise 3.3

1. (a) 24.50%   **2. (a)** 25.00%   **3. (a)** 21.25%
  (b) 4.50%   **(b)** 3.60%   **(b)** 3.85%

4. (a) 32.10%   **5. (a)** 32.76%   **6. (a)** $290,040
  (b) 12.73%   **(b)** 4.18%   **(b)** 1.61%

7. Net sales $147,800   100.00%
  Cost of merchandise sold   78,630   53.20
  Gross margin   69,170   46.80
  Direct expenses   40,349   27.30
  Contribution margin   28,822   19.50
  Indirect expenses   25,600   17.32
  Profit/(loss)   3,222   2.18

Exercise 3.4

1. 10.90%   **2.** $1,176.47   **3.** 15.61%   **4.** 16.11%

5. 153.75 hours   **6.** 23.67 hours   **7.** 6.11%

8. (a) Frank   5.01%
      Gwen   5.15
      Heather   4.74
      Jason   6.77
      Kathy   6.32
      Lacey   5.91

  (b) Department   5.51%

9. 76.47 hours

CHAPTER 4

Exercise 4.1

1. $963.65   **2.** $14,510.44 or $14,510.45   **3.** $1,544.76   **4.** $536.73

5. $1,922.25   **6.** 53.20%   **7.** $28.00

8. (a) buyer 30%, 15%, and 5%
(b) manufacturer 25%, 15%, and 10%

9. Sears $299.25   **10.** $3,336.61
Kiki's $475

Exercise 4.2

(a) Cash discount due by	(b) Amount due ($)
a. February 16	485
b. September 8	485
c. August 10	460
d. November 24	470
e. May 10	460
f. September 13	470
g. December 13	495
h. October 10	485
i. July 10	460
j. October 11	470
k. June 10	485
l. December 11	495
m. November 11	470
n. August 17	485
o. February 3	470

Exercise 4.3

1. $937.63   **2.** $854.87   **3.** $787.07   **4.** $587.97

5. $1,587.22   **6.** $1,157.16   **7.** $2,410.50

Exercise 4.4

1. $51.66   **2.** $1,601.07   **3.** $1,475.90

4. $1,415.60   **5.** $2,389.77   **6.** $5,974.99

Exercise 4.5

1. Retailer   **2.** $969   **3.** $2,163.10   **4.** $1,183.56

5. $9,475.20   **6.** $980.18   **7.** $128,481

8. Option (a) is best for the buyer.
Cost for option (a) $2,716; option (b) $2,882

CHAPTER 5

Exercise 5.1

1. Cost $48.80; Cost 32.75%

2. Markup 49%; Cost 51%

3. Retail $91.96; Cost 50%

4. Cost $110; Cost 25%

5. Markup 33.33% or $33\frac{1}{3}$%; Cost 66.67% or $66\frac{2}{3}$

6. Retail $231.88; Cost 34.5%

7. Cost $1.15/unit; Cost 46%

8. Cost $13.21; Cost 57.5%

9. Retail $230.77; Cost 52%

10. Markup 46%; Cost 54%

11. Retail $178.57; Cost 56%

12. Cost $1.82; Cost 47.8%

13. Retail $21 unit; Cost 40%

14. Markup 42.31%; Cost 57.69%

15. Cost $40.11; Cost 42%

16. $28.57 unit retail or $342.86 per dozen

17. $83.25

18. $5,925.38

19. 59.09%

20. $29.32

21. $432

22. **(a)** Cost 46.15%
    (b) Markup 53.85%

23. **(a)** Cost 59.5%
    (b) Cost $10.71

24. 50%

25. **(a)** Markup based on retail 43.33%
    (b) Markup based on cost 76.47%

Exercise 5.2

1. 49.26%	**2.** 52.48%	**3.** 46.57%
4. 49.04%	**5.** 48.72%	**6.** 56.30%

Exercise 5.3

1. $2,609.58	**2.** $69.00	**3.** 66.84%	**4.** $243.35	**5.** 69.78%
6. $18.29	**7.** $28.67	**8.** $128.39	**9.** 62.96%	**10.** $15
11. $147.95	**12.** 55.47%	**13.** 43.67%	**14.** 59.00%	**15.** $86.75

Exercise 5.4

1. 47.55%	**2.** 47.30%	**3.** 48.37%
4. 47.46%	**5.** 50.34%	

Exercise 5.5

1. 43.83%   2. 48.25%   3. 56.61%

4. 54.51%   5. 52.57%

Exercise 5.6

1. (a) Maintained markup   48.75%
   (b) Gross margin   49.75%

2. (a) Maintained markup   52.81%
   (b) Gross margin   53.20%

3. 38.13%

4. 38.36%

5. (a) Maintained markup   47.50%
   (b) Gross margin   48.53%

CHAPTER 6

Exercise 6.1

1. 16%   2. 15.25%   3. $256,700

4. $545,000   5. 18.5%

Exercise 6.2

1. (a) $72   2. $90   3. (a) $30   4. $301   5. 14.45%
   (b) $168   (b) $1,020

6. (a) $540   7. $960   8. 10.02%   9. $3,354   10. $480
   (b) $810

Exercise 6.3

1. (a) $62.25   2. $551.32   3. $918.59   4. $107.87   5. $1,056.86
   (b) $201.69

CHAPTER 7

Exercise 7.1

1. $269,664   2. (a) $244,550   3. (a) $122,432   4. $108,505
                   (b) $55,576   (b) $31,462

Exercise 7.2

1. 1.90 % shortage   2. 0.81% overage   3. 1.16% overage

Exercise 7.3

1. (a) $32,484
   (b) 1.02%

2. (a) $28,185
   (b) $28,027

3. (a) $17,022
   (b) 1.02% overage
   (c) $16,770

Exercise 7.4

1. (a) $89,340
   (b) $46,680
   (c) $64,440

2. (a) $30,340
   (b) 2.03%
   (c) $12,880

3. See completed form for answers to Exercise 7.4 #3 (Figure C-1). These answers were calculated using cost % of 52.5445%.
   (a) gross cost of merchandise sold $88,182
   (b) total cost of merchandise sold $86,067
   (c) gross margin percent 44.72%

Merchandise Handled:	------------Cost ------------			------------Retail ------------		
Opening inventory		$31,680			$58,426	
Gross purchases	$86,780			$168,342		
Returns to vendors (minus)	2,320			4,127	164,215	
Net purchases		84,460				
Transfers out	2,324			4,470		
Transfers in	1,550			2,980		
Net transfers out (minus)		−774			−1,490	
Freight		1,018				
Additional markup					345	
Total merchandise handled			$116,384			$221,496
Cost % of total mdse. handled	52.5445%					
Deductions:						
Gross sales				168,050		
Customer returns				12,378		
Net sales					155,672	
Markdowns				11,136		
Markdown cancellations				476		
Net markdowns					10,660	
Employee discounts					480	
Total deductions						166,812
Closing book inventory						$54,684
Closing physical inventory*			28,202			53,672
Shortage						$1,012
Gross Cost of Merchandise Sold			$88,182			
Cash discounts (minus)			2,957			
Net cost of merchandise sold			$85,225			
Alteration costs (plus)			832			
Total Cost of Merchandise Sold			$86,057			
Gross Margin $	$69,615					
(Net sales – Total cost of mdse. sold)						
Gross Margin %	44.72%					
(Gross margin $ ÷ Net sales)						

* Cost value will be $28,199 if 52.54% is used.

Figure C-1. Solution to Practice Problem (Exercise 7.4) #3.

4. See completed form for answers to Exercise 7.4 #4 (Figure C-2).
38.64%   gross margin percent 38.64%

Merchandise Handled:	------------Cost ------------			------------Retail ------------		
Opening inventory		$147,460			$289,130	
Gross purchases	$452,660			$1,005,780		
Returns to vendors (minus)	2,690			5,380	1,000,400	
Net purchases		449,970				
Freight		29,730				
Additional markup					540	
Total merchandise handled			$627,160			$1,290,070
Cost % of total mdse. handled	48.6144%					
Deductions:						
Gross sales				870,430		
Customer returns				81,760		
Net sales					788,670	
Markdowns				216,910		
Markdown cancellations				13,680		
Net markdowns					203,230	
Employee discounts					2,780	
Total deductions						994,680
Closing book inventory						$295,390
Closing physical inventory*			137,467			282,771
Shortage						$12,619
Gross Cost of Merchandise Sold			$489,693			
Cash discounts (minus)			6,470			
Net cost of merchandise sold			$483,223			
Alteration costs (plus)			720			
Total Cost of Merchandise Sold			$483,943			
Gross Margin $	$304,727					
(Net sales – Total cost of mdse. sold)						
Gross Margin %	38.64%					
(Gross margin $ ÷ Net sales)						

* If 48.61% is used, this cost value will be $137,455

Figure C-2. Solution to Practice Problem (Exercise 7.4) #4.

Exercise 7.5

1. (a) 47.75%   **2. (a)** 50.87%   **3. (a)** 47.46%   **4. (a)** 40.12%
  (b) 43.72%   **(b)** 45.47%   **(b)** 43.35%   **(b)** 40.85%

CHAPTER 8

Exercise 8.1

1. 11.54%   **2.** $595,700   **3.** $174,400

4. October $ 84,000
   November $114,000
   December $144,000
   January $ 72,000

5. March   10.71%
   April   9.68%
   May   10.34%
   June   Trend not clearly established, increase of 10% reasonable.

6. Increase between 9.5% and 10.0%
   August $98,677 to $99,128
   September $105,406 to $105,887
   October $91,945 to $92,365
   November $130,751 to $131,348
   December $157,849 to $158,569
   January $78,832 to $79,192

Exercise 8.2

1. 0.45   **2.** 0.34   **3.** $366,667

4. 6.59   **5.** 3.46   **6. (a)** 2.35
                                    (b) 1.55
                                    (c) 0.53

Exercise 8.3

1. 3.57   **2.** $121,600   **3.** $27,000

4. $442,000   **5.** 2.22   **6.** $54,250

7. August $56,000   **8.** February $345,600
   September $63,000   March $358,400
                                  April $417,600
                                  May $417,600
                                  June $475,200
                                  July $435,200

Exercise 8.4

1. $49,400   **2. (a)** $45,000   **3.** 16%   **4. (a)** $67,750
                      (b) $24,300   **(b)** $35,230

Exercise 8.5

1. See completed six-month merchandise plan (Figure C-3) for answers for #1.

	(a) Sales	EOM (d) Stock	(b) Reductions	BOM (c) Stock	Planned (e) Purchases
February	$100,750	$347,522	$21,450	$334,522	$135,200
March	113,750	357,272	17,160	347,522	140,660
April	123,500	350,772	27,170	357,272	144,170
May	117,000	334,522	22,880	350,772	123,630
June	100,750	328,022	25,740	334,522	119,990
July	94,250	342,105*	28,600	328,022	136,933

(f) Initial markup needed = 51.15%

*Note: EOM for July is average inventory (Sales ÷ Turnover = $650,000 ÷ 1.9 = $342,105).

SIX-MONTH MERCHANDISE PLAN

	Plan	Actual
% Initial Markup	51.15%	
% Reductions	22.00%	
% Operating expenses	34.00%	
% Net profit	7.50%	
% Cash discount	1.60%	
% Alteration costs	0.50%	
Turnover	1.9	
Average stock	$342,105	
Basic stock	$233,772	

	SPRING FALL	February August	March September	April October	May November	June December	July January	SEASON TOTALS
SALES	Last Year							
	Plan	$100,750	$113,750	$123,500	$117,000	$100,750	$94,250	$650,000
	Planned % of Season	15.50%	17.50%	19.00%	18.00%	15.50%	14.50%	
	Revised Plan							
	Actual							
EOM STOCK	Last Year							
	Plan	347,522	357,272	350,772	334,522	328,022	342,105	
	Revised							
	Actual							
REDUCTIONS	Last Year							
	Plan	21,450	17,160	27,170	22,880	25,740	28,600	143,000
	Revised							
	Actual							
	% of Planned Red.	15.00%	12.00%	19.00%	16.00%	18.00%	20.00%	
BOM STOCK	Last Year							
	Plan	334,522	347,522	357,272	350,772	334,522	328,022	
	Revised							
	Actual							
PLANNED PURCHASES AT RETAIL	Last Year							
	Plan	135,200	140,660	144,170	123,630	119,990	136,933	800,583
	Revised							
	Actual							

Figure C-3. Completed merchandise plan for Practice Problem (Exercise 8.5) #1.

2. Stock-Sales Ratios

February	3.3
March	3.1
April	2.9
May	3.0
June	3.3
July	3.5

3. See completed six-month merchandise plan (Figure C-4) for answers to problem #3.

	(a) Sales	BOM (c) Stock	(b) Reductions	EOM (d) Stock	Planned (e) Purchases
February	$31,164	$118,423	$2,057	$149,587	$64,385
March	35,616	149,587	1,745	155,820	43,594
April	44,520	155,820	1,914	140,238	30,852
May	38,955	140,238	1,870	135,897	36,484
June	36,729	135,897	1,983	138,902	41,717
July	35,616	138,902	2,671	124,359	23,744

(f) Turnover for Season = 1.6

SIX-MONTH MERCHANDISE PLAN

	Plan	Actual
% Initial Markup		
% Reductions		
% Operating expenses		
% Net profit		
% Cash discount		
% Alteration costs		
Turnover	1.6	
Average stock	$137,604	
Basic stock		

	SPRING FALL	February August	March September	April October	May November	June December	July January	SEASON TOTALS
SALES	Last Year							
	Plan	$31,164	$35,616	$44,520	$38,955	$36,729	$35,616	$222,600
	Planned % of Season	14.00%	16.00%	20.00%	17.50%	16.50%	16.00%	
	Revised Plan							
	Actual							
EOM STOCK	Last Year							
	Plan	149,587	155,820	140,238	135,897	138,902	124,359	
	Revised							
	Actual							
REDUCTIONS	Last Year							
	Plan	2,057	1,745	1,914	1,870	1,983	2,671	
	Revised							
	Actual							
	% of Month's Sales	6.60%	4.90%	4.30%	4.80%	5.40%	7.50%	
BOM STOCK	Last Year							
	Plan	118,423	149,587	155,820	140,238	135,897	138,902	
	Stock-Sales Ratio	3.8	4.2	3.5	3.6	3.7	3.9	
	Revised							
	Actual							
PLANNED PURCHASES AT RETAIL	Last Year							
	Plan	64,385	43,594	30,852	36,484	41,717	23,744	240,777
	Revised							
	Actual							

Figure C-4. Completed merchandise plan for Practice Problem 8.5 #3.

CHAPTER 9

Exercise 9.1

1. $1,200

2. $530

3. Retail OTB $3,400
Cost OTB $1,717

4. Overbought $1,800

5. Retail OTB $28,800
Cost OTB $13,824

6. $17,500

Exercise 9.2

1. 10   **2.** 37   **3. (a)** OTB 17
(b) Turnover 11.56

4. (a) OTB 25
(b) Average stock 100
(c) Turnover 10.4

CHAPTER 10

Exercise 10.1

1. 53.06%   **2.** 90.2%   **3.** 20.83%

4. $205,481,480 or $205.48 million   **5.** $684,173,910 or $684.17 million

6. 11.38%   **7.** $1,344   **8.** $23,994,000   **9.** $304.75

10. $45   **11.** 2,031 sq. ft.   **12.** 3,049 sq. ft.

Exercise 10.2

1. $162.73   **2.** $1,302,631.60   **3.** $2,060.61

4. $2,559.79   **5.** $69.38

Exercise 10.3

1. 3.39   **2.** 2.15   **3.** 2.04

4. February   5%
   March   11%
   April   16%
   May   24%
   June   33%
   July   11%

5. February   13
   March   29
   April   42
   May   62
   June   86
   July   29

APPENDIX D

Answers to Pretest

1. (a) 795
   (b) $117.07
   (c) $2,418.51
   (d) 99.97

2. (a) $116.02

3. (a) $11.80
   (b) $129.56
   (c) $5,124.95

4. $767.00

5. (a) $138.29
   (b) $46,667.15

6. (a) 121.23
   (b) 599

7. $121.72

8. $77.50

9. (a) 50
   (b) 0.91
   (c) $25.00
   (d) 6.98

10. $76.49

11. $3,353.50

12. $48.01

13. $16.00

14. $780.00

Index